The Great Industrial War

The Great Industrial War

Framing Class Conflict
in the Media, 1865–1950

TROY RONDINONE

RUTGERS UNIVERSITY PRESS

NEW BRUNSWICK, NEW JERSEY, AND LONDON

First paperback printing, 2011

LIBRARY OF CONGRESS CATALOGING-IN-PUBLICATION DATA

Rondinone, Troy, 1973–
  The great industrial war : framing class conflict in the media, 1865–1950 /
Troy Rondinone.
    p. cm.
  Includes bibliographical references and index.
  ISBN 978–0–8135–4683–4 (hardcover : alk. paper)
  ISBN 978–0–8135–5188–3 (pbk. : alk. paper)
  1. Labor disputes—United States—History. 2. Social conflict—United States—
History. I. Title.
  HD5324.R65 2010
  305.50973′09041—dc22   2009008098

A British Cataloging-in-Publication record for this book is available from the
British Library.

This collection copyright © 2010 by Troy Rondinone

All rights reserved

No part of this book may be reproduced or utilized in any form or by any means,
electronic or mechanical, or by any information storage and retrieval system,
without written permission from the publisher. Please contact Rutgers University
Press, 100 Joyce Kilmer Avenue, Piscataway, NJ 08854–8099. The only exception to
this prohibition is "fair use" as defined by U.S. copyright law.

Visit our Web site: http://rutgerspress.rutgers.edu

Manufactured in the United States of America

For Kath

CONTENTS

ACKNOWLEDGMENTS

Since this project started to take shape, many people have helped to bring it to fruition. I would first like to thank John Laslett, Joyce Appleby, Alessandro Duranti, and Naomi Lamoreaux at UCLA. I cannot express deeply enough the gratitude I have toward them. I would also like to thank Joan Waugh, whose advice and insights helped me along as I worked.

I'd also like to thank the many fellow academics who read different parts of this book, in various forms, over the years. I apologize to those whose names I have left out. Hal Barron, Graham Cassano, Nancy Fitch, Jennifer Klein, Alan Lessoff, Nelson Lichtenstein, Christopher R. Martin, Anne C. Rose, Steven Ross, Robert Slayton, Frank Stricker, Josh Zeitz, and Leila Zenderland, along with readers at *American Quarterly* and *Journal of the Gilded Age and Progressive Era,* all provided excellent, helpful insights. Thanks as well to Leslie Mitchner and Rachel Friedman at Rutgers University Press for providing patient editorial oversight.

Thanks to the staffs of the UCLA and Yale libraries for their assistance in finding and gathering the many different sources used for this book.

Finally, I would like my friends and family, who have always provided a firm base of love and respect that has allowed me to devote so much of my time to my research. My parents, Jeff and Rochelle, my brother David, my extended family, Kerry Miller, Brenda Sullivan, and Alan and Marilyn Miller, and my friends Luis Rodriguez, Michael Carter, Ericka Carter, and Andrew Diaz all sustained me through the writing process. My beautiful children, Sophia and Catalina, provided a light that warmed me during the last three years of writing.

Lastly, I would like to thank my wife and life partner, Kathleen Rondinone. She has shared with me all of the pain and joy of writing this project, and indeed everything else. To her I lovingly dedicate this book.

The Great Industrial War

Introduction

A Question of the Age

Is Class Conflict Growing and Is It Inevitable?" This was the question posed in 1907 by the American Sociological Society to a select group of social scientists and reformers for an upcoming issue of its scholarly imprint, *American Journal of Sociology*.[1] At the bright dawn of the twentieth century, such a query might have seemed unduly negative. U.S. ports bustled with steamships pushing out finished goods to the rest of the world. The American presence abroad was strong and authoritative. The young country had recently become the wealthiest, most productive nation on the planet, producing more manufactures than its three nearest competitors combined.[2] In fact, if placed in comparative perspective, America appeared to be an unstoppable engine of democratic industry. In the inimitable words of tycoon Andrew Carnegie, "The old nations of the earth creep on at a snail's pace; the Republic thunders past with the rush of an express."[3]

And yet these were anxious times as well. With the passing of the agrarian America of wistful frontier myth, profound, troubling changes could be seen everywhere. Cities were crowded with "alien" non-English-speaking, non-Protestant immigrants from eastern and southern Europe. Massive factories dotted the countryside, belching out pillars of smoke and consuming immigrant labor and sooty coal. Distant, impersonal firms dominated the economy, with unseen corporate aristocrats pulling the levers of power. A serious bank panic burrowed into consumer confidence. Perhaps most alarmingly, if the newspapers were to be believed, the nation stood on the precipice of civil war.

By 1907, the American press had been continuously referring to an ongoing event known as the "industrial war" for four decades. This war did not concern slavery, geography, or political difference. It was a war of class, not region, an "irrepressible conflict" between the massive and opposing forces of capital and labor. In this struggle, each side had its own foot soldiers, lieutenants, and generals. Each developed strategies for conquest, with the ultimate objective of reshaping society in its own image. Both threatened to destroy the republic. When the American Sociological Society asked "Is Class Conflict Growing and Is It Inevitable?" it represented no foray into abstraction. It was a vital question of the age.

This book represents an inquiry into the ways in which the print media and a select group of influential public figures framed class conflict between the end of the Civil War and the beginning of the Cold War. While labor historians have long researched this critical era of industrial conflict, few have explored how the popular media presented strike events.[4] Understanding representation of class conflict is important. America has long been a nation of readers, and for the reading millions not direct witness to individual strikes at any given time, the heat of industrial unrest would typically be experienced textually. And as technology advanced—the advent of the Associated Press in the nineteenth century could place a single strike story into the homes of millions—Americans could not help but grow concerned with the fate of the republic. Such readers discussed, voted, and indirectly helped shape the federal response to a devastating cycle of strikes and unrest.

I ground my analysis in several interconnected theoretical traditions. From Marx I begin with the understanding that class conflict is a real, historical phenomenon, an aspect of capitalist accumulation. As Marx explains in *Capital,* volume I, "the nature of commodity exchange itself poses no limit to the working day, no limit to surplus labour." Capitalists necessarily seek to extend labor time and extract as much surplus labor as possible; workers seek to maximize their wage packages and reduce labor hours to a livable rate.[5] Historically, as workers come to face the alienating, overwhelming imperatives of wage labor and managerial cost-cutting (such as technological inroads on skill), a struggle arises on the shop floor and in the streets over how control is to be apportioned and exercised. Strikes, the object of this study, are direct evidence of the sharpest edge of this struggle, moments when workers close down operations and challenge capitalist authority at the level of operations. Covering this class conflict after 1865, the media employed a particular trope: unlimited war. To understand how the press did this, and its impact on the public and eventually on national labor policy, I turn to two other theoretical traditions—Antonio Gramsci's argument on the hegemonic importance of the print media and the insights of framing theory.

In *Further Selections from the Prison Notebooks,* Gramsci argues that for the state to exercise its power over the public, an ideologically friendly body of "printed matter" is necessary. He concludes, "The printed word is the most dynamic part of this ideological structure [of the 'dominant class']."[6] For Gramsci, the elite maintain and exert their power by maintaining cultural hegemony, fostering "the 'spontaneous' consent given by the great masses of the population to the general direction imposed on social life by the dominant fundamental group."[7] While the media played a crucial role in establishing and maintaining hegemony, the process was neither straightforward nor unchallenged in America. The story is more complex.

For starters, the press did not mechanistically toe the capitalist line. As I will illustrate in the pages to come, a straightforward "pro-capitalist" ideology is not necessarily evident in every piece of reportage about the major strikes. Indeed capitalism did shape the broadest contours of media's existence. As a privately controlled enterprise functioning in a market economy, the mainstream press followed certain imperatives—copies were sold for profit, advertisers were courted, efforts to curb costs never ceased, new technologies and labor regimes were adopted, and over time, a few large newspapers came to dominate their respective geographical markets.[8] Democracy and public service were never the top priority. As one Progressive Era sociologist explained, "As for the capitalist-owner, to exhort him to run his newspaper in the interest of truth and progress is about as reasonable as to exhort the mill-owner to work his property for the public good instead of for his private benefit."[9] Further, it is evident that direct ideological challenges to capitalist order were compromised by large media. The Associated Press, which enabled the transmission of a single story into newspapers across entire regions, and by the year 1900, across the country, was criticized by Upton Sinclair in 1920 as the "leading agency of capitalist repression." By diminishing and even excluding coverage of radicals in the early twentieth century, the AP certainly impressed on the greater reading public a pro-capitalist slant.[10] Further, newspaper management, as Warren Breed noted back in 1955, set "policy" guidelines that prevented reporters from deviating too far to the left.[11] Finally, on occasion, capitalist owners directly imprinted their own opinions in the pages of their periodicals. Yet one can also find plenty of evidence of empathy with the plight of the workers, or rage at the handling of the strike by the militia or police, or criticism of owners and managers, even in the largest media outlets.

To square how such pro-worker sentiment makes sense in an argument grounded in Gramsci's hegemony theory, I put forward two propositions. First, journalism *influenced* by capitalists did not translate to journalism *composed* by capitalists. As Joseph Pulitzer learned when he read a too-sympathetic editorial about Eugene Debs during the Pullman Strike, he could not force a retraction from his union card-carrying employee. Firing journalists has always been a rare event, and "policy" has not always been followed by them regardless. Further, as William Randolph Hearst and others recognized, with workers buying papers, it was not sound business to alienate them.[12] While the media did oftentimes portray unions as conspiracies and strikes as battles against the public, there frequently lurked devastating critiques of big business and even outright sympathy with the strikers. In the analysis to follow, I intend to show how both interpretations fit into the "master frame" of war. My second proposition is that the narrative of war and calamity itself, regardless of the individual journalist's slant, implied that certain strikes imperiled the nation. This absolutely served to facilitate capitalist hegemony. Ultimately, the frightening story of conflict overwhelmed even the most sympathetic pro-labor journalists.

The media, by and large, interpreted class conflict between 1865 and 1950 in a remarkably monolithic, unsubtle way. Big strikes were painted as wars. Strikers played the role of soldiers, often as enemy combatants battling the valiant forces of order, and almost always participating in a republic-threatening war act. When the state stepped in in the form of injunctions, soldiers, and police action, the hegemonic function of the press became clearer: the major press outlets would present a battle that could only be "won" by a return to a state of order, typically at the strikers' expense. Even if the capitalists found themselves equally blameworthy in the editorial pages for the strike violence, the war frame helped make the violence *itself* the story. The only positive outcome had to be a cessation of hostilities. The narrative of war trumped other possible narratives, and this terrifying plot line obscured any deeper criticism of the system that begat the violence in the first place.

This brings me to the mechanism with which the press articulated the sense of ongoing, catastrophic class warfare. Framing theorists argue that the media offers not a transparent window onto events, but rather creates narratives that compel certain interpretations by virtue of what *is* and *is not* included, and how characters and events are "cast." As one scholar explains, "when a topic is 'framed' its context is determined; its major tenets prescribed; individuals, groups, and organizations are assigned the roles of protagonist, antagonist, or spectator; and the legitimacy of varied strategies for action is defined."[13] The frame itself disciplines the range of interpretive options, "policing the boundaries of common sense," as Christopher Martin puts it.[14] By delivering a narrow range of "common sense" interpretive possibilities, the media can regulate public discourse.[15] In a democratic society, it is precisely at the level of popular discourse that legislation is articulated, supported, and justified. Framing the strikes as battles and the participants as soldiers influenced popular perceptions of the labor movement and thus fueled demands for direct federal intervention.

War, I argue, served as the "master frame" for class conflict during the period of this study. As explained by John A. Noakes, master frames tend to be "abstract or generic interpretive schema that render events or occurrences meaningful."[16] The abstraction of war permitted a variety of ideological value systems to enter the discussion of class conflict on speaking terms. Using war-coded language (from overt terms like "battle" and "armies" to more subtle signifiers such as "movement" and "rank"), multiple interpretations of industrial America could coexist in the media's public sphere. Ultimately, industrial war language did not serve the interests of organized labor since "war" was a state of affairs to be avoided and ultimately dealt with by a pro-capitalist state. Still, the shaping of public policy was not merely a cynical process of self-serving capitalists using war rhetoric to crush labor. Sometimes, within the master frame of total war, a struggle over the nature of state interference arose. Thus the influence of a man like John Commons, an academic concerned with making capitalism "good" and even counteracting the undue influence of corporations at the political level, cannot be written off as an act of owner-class domination. Rather, the master frame helped provide a flexible scaffolding of interpretive language that tended to hurt labor in a broad, Gramscian hegemonic sense rather than explicitly, purposely serving capitalist interests.[17]

To analyze how the media framed class conflict, I focus on a set of national strikes that captured the public's attention. By "national strike," I mean to separate particular mass (large-scale) strikes from others. Most strikes in American history were relatively contained in scale and scope and ended without causing too great a stir. Some of the largest ones earned the designation "mass" to call attention to their size and intensity. These strikes often involved thousands of workers and jeopardized the continuance of production of large segments of American industry. A close relative, the general strike, sometimes threatened to occur when mass strikes gained a degree of popular momentum. These strikes meant that the working people in several industries would simultaneously walk out within a given locality. When mass work stoppages (general or otherwise) attracted the attention of a wide variety of interest groups across the country and entered into the broadest public discourse, they became national strikes.

Sometimes, national strikes consisted of a single turn out that spread to many cities, such as in the Great Railroad Strike of 1877. Other times, a strike in a single region took on national importance, especially when it affected a core industry such as steel or coal. Additionally, the socio-economic climate of the country disposed the public to ascribe increased importance to certain mass strikes, such as some of those occurring during the hard years of the Great Depression or the anxious years following World War II. During every national strike a general sentiment prevailed that the work stoppage was making a powerful and extensive impact on America's society and economy.

Historically, the phenomenon of the national strike appeared on the American scene following the explosive growth in both communications and corporate enterprise in the closing decades of the nineteenth century. Working in tandem, these factors facilitated a national marketplace, a broad public dialogue, and a rapidly growing wage-labor force, the necessary ingredients for such a phenomenon.[18] The novelty and alarming unrest resulting from these strikes inspired debates concerning the nature and future of industrial America.

There are three reasons why I use these strikes to understand class conflict discourse. The first reason is that massive strikes offer unique moments when the reading public's attention is dramatically focused on industrial relations, with the print media offering extensive discussion and description of class conflict. The second reason is that, as moments when workers challenge capitalist imperatives, strikes serve as episodes when journalists and commentators have an opportunity to speculate on the deeper nature of class relations. Therefore, major strikes allow me to sample popular understandings of class as expressed by those whose careers entail interpreting the nature of society for the masses. The third reason is more pragmatic—this small sample of events permits me to cover a lot of time in a relatively efficient manner. The story told here, I believe, can only be understood along a deep time line that runs from the Early Republic to the dawn of the Cold War. The handful of major strikes discussed offer individual moments that tie together to form a rise and fall story of "industrial war" in the print media.

For each of these strike events, I have examined a set of major newspapers and print journals and closely analyzed the ways in which the writers "set the stage" for the event, exploring the network of keywords and narrative strategies used to convey meaning to the reader. I began by gathering a set of some of the widest circulating, most influential newspapers and journals during the time of each strike.[19] I have found both microfilm collections and databases such as the American Periodical Series to offer excellent sources of widely read media outlets. I then highlighted common terms such as "battle," "movements," "general," "volley," and so on, and analyzed how the writer connected them to the broader framework of meaning in the piece.[20] I also paid attention to the audience, the ideological bent of the writer (this often being difficult with the absence of by-lines), and the ideological cast of the editor where I could. However, the individual ideologies of the writers will be viewed as secondary to the impact of the periodicals themselves. The focus here is not on the author so much as on the power of the message.

The American Sociological Society's "Is Class Conflict Growing and Is It Inevitable?" roundtable article, though intended for a narrow audience and clearly not "strike coverage" per se, presents a useful example of how the print media framed class conflict in the period covered by this study. To begin with, the audience here must be considered. Although small, the readership of the *American Journal of Sociology* was arguably quite influential. At this point in history, academics and intellectuals who read such journals were playing very meaningful roles in the drafting of labor legislation. The rise of "professionalization" at the end of the nineteenth century meant newfound influence for activist scholars whose expertise was increasingly relied on to settle thorny social issues.[21]

The main author of this piece is also part of the equation. Labor economist John Commons, himself a product of professionalization, had served as facilitator of talks between federal and union representatives during a massive coal strike in 1902 and had drafted a landmark piece of legislation in his home state of Wisconsin that created commissions of experts to regulate public utility companies. The significance of this legislation was in Commons's provision that safety regulations be determined and updated by experts rather than by politicians. The 1907 law served as a model for Commons's Industrial Commission work in 1911 and would be copied by many other states in the years ahead.[22]

Next, the title. Often, this discloses the agenda of a piece's narrative frame, and the audience likely keeps the title in mind when making sense of the writing to follow. In this case, "Is Class Conflict Growing and Is It Inevitable?" implies that there is indeed class conflict, and that its increase is something worthy of the concern of the leading public thinkers who are posed the question. In his response, Commons recognizes immediately the "apparent antagonism of employing and wage-earning classes." He elaborates that class conflict could be seen most openly in the "strike," which represented the "incipient rebellion" of the "practically unpropertied class against propertied rights." Here keywords implying violence and social collapse help establish the idea that there exists a conflict between two groups—whose numbers he actually attempts to quantify. He further notes that the conflict *was* worsening, in part due to rapid changes in industry that saw the rise of massive trusts that would "alienate classes" far more intensely than previous corporate forms could. He observes that the very progress lauded by many, such as the "astounding reductions of cost, the unheard of efficiency of labor, the precise methods of scientific experiment and tests," is only one side of the coin. On the other, darker side, workers in their homes can be heard uttering "grumblings of class struggle." All of the oft-praised scientific efficiency of the day was in fact causing workers to see themselves differently, as a *class,* and this was dangerous. With this sobering sense of irony Commons concludes that the conflict between workers would only worsen until the "public" stepped in via remediative legislation.[23]

In a later public dispatch, Commons would offer an even bleaker synopsis. In his narrative in the United States Commission on Industrial Relations report delivered a few years later, he noted that labor struggles had "frequently resulted in civil war," and that the world of capital and labor had become an arena of "permanent struggle." Most alarmingly, he explained, "It is claimed by some that this contest is irrepressible."[24] Just as in his American Sociological Society piece, he was employing the framing technique of total war. As I will argue, this was no mere rhetorical flourish. Rather, it was part of a pervasive idiom of class war that had been a staple in the print media ever since America had faced the single most devastating event in its brief history—the Civil War.

The Fingerprints of a Total War

At the heart of this story is the argument that the American Civil War played a crucial role in shaping the popular representation of class conflict after 1865. This aspect of the evolution of American class language, which has yet to be fully explored by historians, is based on the premise that discourse evolves in relation to national experiences.[25] The American Revolution, for example, bequeathed a legacy of rights language and justifiable public protest, both of which contributed to popular discussion of work stoppages in the early nineteenth century (as will be discussed in chapter 1). The Civil War similarly played a stage-setting role for class language. Taking place at a moment of transition when the United States metamorphosed from agricultural backwater into industrial powerhouse, the war experience infused public discourse with martial metaphors and a narrative framework of battle that could be applied to the great strikes that tore through cities and along rail circuits.

The most significant national experience since the Revolution, the Civil War forced Americans to reconsider the nature of social order, imparting upon popular parlance a martial style that favored grand battle over less catastrophic, alternative means of explanation. Like the Revolution of 1848 for the Germans or the Chartist Revolts for the English, the American Civil War provided an idiom of combat for labor activists in the United States.[26] As a group of Boston laborers resolved in an 1865 meeting: "While the rebel aristocracy of the South has been crushed . . . we want it to be known that the workingmen of America will demand in the future a more equal share of the wealth their industry creates . . . and a more equal participation in the privileges and blessings of those free institutions defended by their manhood on many a bloody field of battle."[27] Perhaps more significantly, the war provided an essential, reducible metaphorical framework for understanding the complex period of modern class formation and industrial growth.[28] To flesh out this point, an historical overview is necessary.

During the antebellum period, newspapers represented labor conflicts as community affairs belonging to the world of street festivals and equal rights oratory. The American Revolution had proved a potent example of justifiable resistance to egregious conditions, and in the Early Republic laborers framed their disagreements with employers in terms of inherited rights and freedoms. Despite the compelling notion of righteous battle evident in early strike discourse, walkouts never attracted much national press and were rarely elevated to the status of national concern.

After the Civil War, strikes appeared to be much more threatening. Applying techniques developed to cover battles during the war, newspapers began treating strikes as episodes of organized combat. Featuring bold headlines, maps of strike zones, and lists of casualties, press coverage took on a distinctive, battlefield dispatch style. Martial framing appeared in other forms of public discourse as well, as war rhetoric suffused the speeches and writings of politicians, social scientists, and labor activists. The effects of this popular new trope would be significant. Labor organizers understood themselves to be involved in an epic battle with the forces of capital, rallying their constituencies with military-style organizations. Employers arranged themselves into defensive alliances (such as the railroads' General Managers' Association) designed explicitly to limit the capacity of unions to wage effective strikes. Politicians similarly employed war metaphors to assemble wider constituencies, form industrial commissions, and implement interventionary labor laws. As departments of labor studies took shape in universities, labor scholars voiced their self-appointed industrial "peacemaking" mission with language dependent upon recognition of the industrial war and the attendant possibilities of diplomacy. The idea of total war remained key to popular representations of the industrial scene through the opening decades of the twentieth century. It was replaced only gradually, as the "public" came to be configured as the central part of a new, tripartite social model. Once situated as an entity set apart from and with final power over the armies of capital and labor, the "public"—a concept I shall define more fully later on—became first the arbiter of the battle and finally the rhetorical shield behind which the state could intervene in industrial affairs. With the General Motors strike of 1945–1946 and the apparent "accord" signed between organized labor and big business in the years that followed, a new trope of "industrial pluralism" emerged. Brought to life, fittingly, by the diplomatic exigencies demanded by war framing, the new narrative model conferred upon strikes a far less frightening appearance. They became employee disputes with "management," events circumscribed by a publicly mandated federal policy and a new, bureaucratic idiom.

Outline of Argument

To understand this process, I begin my study in the early nineteenth century, before strikes summoned forth terrifying images of blood and battle. Chapter I explores the various meanings assigned to strikes in the press prior to the Civil War, focusing on the ways that revolutionary rights language intertwined with other themes of strike discourse, such as slavery, foreignness, millennial Christianity, and war. Evaluating the role of the press and its manipulation of these themes in shaping perceptions of labor struggles, this chapter sets a baseline of analysis from which I can examine the remarkable differences in representation occurring in the wake of the Civil War. Chapter 1 closes with a brief look at the largest antebellum strike, the Great Shoemakers' Strike of 1860, in which the early themes of strike analysis provided only a hint of the chaos of the war-ravaged era to come.

In chapter 2, I focus on the impact of the Civil War on popular perceptions of industrial conflicts. Looking at a variety of contemporary sources in the postbellum years, I argue that the war changed the whole landscape of rhetorical possibility by providing a martial frame through which Americans comprehended political and economic struggles. The railroads, which had grown to a remarkable size by this point, further helped set the new milieu by facilitating the national organization of regimented divisions of capital and labor. The Great Railroad Strike of 1877 would be the event in which the industrial armies would clash on a national scale for the first time. With a new style of battlefield reportage and an abundance of culturally mainstream combat terms, war discourse found fertile ground in 1877, helping to cast an antagonistic model of class relations that would be used for decades to come.

In chapter 3, I further develop the notion of the potency of war language by looking at the massive strikes in the decades following the Great Railroad Strike of 1877. Now represented as organized battles, strikes took their place as events along the path to social cataclysm. During the tumultuous years of the 1880s and 1890s, consolidating capital and labor faced off in major strikes along the rails, culminating in a nationwide walkout and battle in 1894. Importantly, the Civil War itself no longer mattered in directing understandings of labor strife. Having supplied a foundational framework of interpretation, the Civil War left the scene, its memory proceeding along its own path of cultural significance.

Chapter 4 foreshadows the process by which industrial war framing would be dismantled. The "public," situated as a third class in the previously bifurcated arrangement of capital versus labor, would come to the fore at the end of the nineteenth century as an intermediary body. Placed perilously between the battling forces of capital and labor, the public stood as both the victim of class war and the potential savior of a besieged republic. During the national Anthracite Coal Strike of 1902, appeals to the "public" grew intense, culminating in a presidential strike intervention carried out in its name.

Chapter 5 explores the connections, facilitated by print media, made between the state and the public that ultimately worked to undermine the

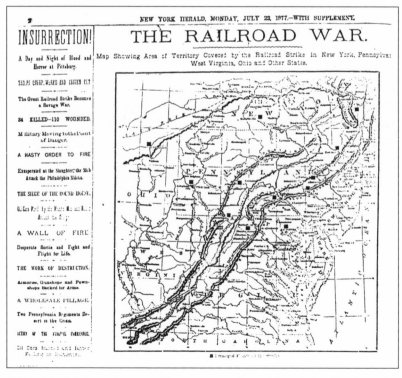

FIGURES 1 & 2 These two newspaper pages, one from 1862 and the other from 1877, show the transplantation of Civil War imagery and language onto a new experience.

Sources: *New York Times*, June 13, 1862; *New York Herald*, July 23, 1877.

cogency of the war metaphor. Once President Theodore Roosevelt had decisively cast the state in the role of industrial mediator during the Anthracite
Coal Strike of 1902, it would be up to the federal government to represent
the public's interest in industrial peace. With the Commission on Industrial
Relations of 1911–1915, the state took another tentative step in the direction
of becoming public guardian. It would be the First World War, however,
that would trigger the most remarkable shift in federal responsibility, as
the state compelled both capital and labor to work harmoniously. The First
Industrial Conference of 1919 and the steel strike of that same year illustrated the new role of the government in drafting an industrial peace for
the public interest.

In chapters 6 and 7, I chart the demise of industrial war framing in the
1930s and 1940s. Though the Great Depression created a climate in which
strikes and working-class agitation flourished, it also offered an unprecedented opportunity for the state to fully appropriate the role of public
guardian. With unmatched aplomb, the Franklin D. Roosevelt administration
captured the position of public caretaker by encouraging union organization
and giving the appearance of curtailing capital. Facilitated by a new rhetoric
of rights and citizenship, organized labor rushed into the public fold, situating itself as one interest group among many. The General Motors strike of
1945–1946 illustrates the distance traveled in the direction of social integration and pluralism.

The book ends with a conclusion, entitled "The End of Class Conflict?" in
which I discuss the ways that an interest-group-driven "industrial pluralism"
replaced the war frame in the 1950s. I argue that while class conflict never
ended, the pervasive belief in its existence in popular discourse did. This
entailed more than just wishful thinking on the part of optimistic observers.
It was part and parcel of the demise of "war" as the reigning mode of class
analysis. With the ascent of the pluralist model, the industrial war ceased to
hold resonance, and the sense of a looming labor cataclysm faded into the
shadows of history, forgotten.

1

With Colors Flying

Strikes in Antebellum America

In 1806 a group of Philadelphia shoemakers, or "cordwainers," found themselves on trial for conspiring to restrain trade. Responding to a recent wage reduction and lower pay scales than shoemakers received in other major cities, the journeymen cordwainers walked off the job in the winter of 1805–1806. The strike leaders were arrested immediately, and reports of the subsequent trial soon made their way into the local press. William Duane, editor of the radical-leaning newspaper *Aurora,* made sure that the public received a sympathetic account of the affair.[1]

In a piece entitled "The Price of Labor" published immediately after the arrest of the strike leaders, Duane warned his readers that this was much more than a strike. The hard-won spoils of the Revolution were in danger. Jailing men for "proposing to demand an augmentation of the reward for their manual labor" indicated a dangerous backslide to the conditions of servitude impressed on American shoulders by the king. The action of the court was an instance of the resurrection of English common law, brought forth because American workers were asking too much of their aristocratic employers. Freedom itself was in peril. Duane asked, "Is there any power that can lawfully and constitutionally determine the price of a man's labor to be less than what he chuses [*sic*] to accept voluntarily of his free choice?" Just as slavery was a "deplorable curse entailed upon us" by England, so this application of English common law was an attempt to close "the doors of industry" so that "a breed of *white slaves* may be nursed up in poverty to take the place of the *blacks* upon their emancipation."[2]

During the trial, the prosecution reflected on the power of the press in shaping opinions of the strike, noting that "the newspaper called the *Aurora,* has teemed with false representations and statements . . . with a view (if not with the declared intention), to poison the public mind." The prosecution was confident that the jury, upon hearing the "facts," would "not be biased by newspaper attempts, to delude and mislead you." Bringing in the "public" on several occasions, the prosecution noted that the strike was an assault "against the public welfare."[3] Carrying the danger to the extreme, they noted that such illegal "combinations" carried out by shoemakers, carpenters, butchers, bricklayers, and eventually "the whole community" would lead to the formation of "hostile confederacies" and eventually "bloodshed and civil war."[4]

For its part, the defense alternately argued that "every inconvenience sustained even by the public, is not an indictable offence" and that the master shoemakers (the striking journeymen shoemakers' employers) had falsely presented their position as "brought forward from public motives" rather than the "selfish" behavior at the heart of their case.[5] Back at the strike's outset in November 1805 Duane had published "Address of the Working Shoemakers" in the *Aurora,* in which the journeymen had connected their strike to the Constitution and the cause of liberty, claiming that the "master shoemakers, as they are called after the slavish style of Europe," had violated both "the laws of God and the laws of our country." They boldly charged the masters with the crime of tyranny, surely an accusation aimed at triggering the sensitivities of a public concerned with preserving the precious fruits of liberty.[6]

Just as both sides claimed to embody the public's interest, both sides claimed to be the true inheritors of the Revolution. The journeymen's defense strategy called for continued references to the Revolution, the Constitution, and "liberty." At one point, defense council Caesar Rodney argued that the loss of this case would symbolize the ascent of the hated English code of laws, and would in effect entail a "fatal reverse" of the hard-won gains of the Revolution. The prosecution similarly contended that their side represented "the spirit of '76." For the jurors, the prosecution presented the better case, and the journeymen received a small, symbolic fine.[7]

The journeymen shoemakers' strike and trial encapsulate a number of key elements of strike discourse in the Early Republic and antebellum years. For one thing, this strike had moved beyond the immediate sphere of these employers and employees and into the realm of public opinion. The transcript of the trial was published in 1806, and, combined with a few press reports, the reading public received a fairly detailed account of the strike to discuss and debate. The coverage tapped into a number of themes common to strike reportage that would endure for years to come. Both sides of the conflict appealed to the "public interest," consciously addressing the masses and claiming to be their true representative. Both employed colorful war metaphors (with the strikers claiming "defense" and the prosecution warning of impending "civil war"). Both warned of the dangerous "foreignness" of the other side. Biblical references framed key parts of the arguments of each. The strikers' side called forth the specter of slavery to buttress its points. Most importantly, both groups maintained that the spirit of the Revolution was in their provenance alone, and that their opponents worked to undermine basic constitutional liberties.

Examining the nature and meaning of early strikes and the ways in which the Revolution influenced pre–Civil War class discourse, this chapter aims to set the stage for the remarkable change in the media representation of class conflict after 1865. While the above-noted themes of public interest, war, foreignness, and religion would carry on in some form throughout the nineteenth century, in this period they were bound to a world very much different from the one to come. Strikes had yet to connote a fearful chasm of class against class. The battles were largely symbolic, the sides drawn with politics rather than armies in mind. This America was not yet riven by class discord on a massive scale. The industrial war had yet to begin.

Turn Outs in the Early Republic

Three years after the Philadelphia cordwainers' case, another group of shoemakers wound up in court in New York City facing similar charges. They too lost, receiving symbolic fines of one dollar each for taking part in what lawyers referred to as a "strike or turn out."[8] In the earlier 1806 Philadelphia case, the word "strike" was not used, but rather "turn out." The phrase "turn out," an expression synonymous with both "strike" and "parade" by 1809, offers a clue to the public reception of strikes in the Early Republic.

Not yet freighted with the connotation of conflict, turn outs were primarily public events that fit in better with the world of street festivals and oral political culture than with the industrial one in which they would later become notorious. Typically nonviolent and quite brief, the turn out was a relatively rare occurrence during which workers expressed dissatisfaction with their conditions. Turn outs took place in the community rather than the workplace, with participants taking to the streets to restore the balance of just wages and justifiable profits. They were democratic, social affairs; workers would often unfurl banners proclaiming their rights and deploy strike "cards" with lists of grievances printed on them. Employers would also appeal to the public, explaining in small newspaper ads that the unions were the *real* wrongdoers.[9]

Early nineteenth-century strikes received scant attention in the press. This undoubtedly reflected a broader perception that situated strikes somewhere between a workingmen's parade and a novel action alien to the

American scene. As late as 1831, Webster's *American Dictionary of the English Language* still considered strikes to be foreign affairs outside the realm of normal American social relations: "*To strike,* among *workmen in manufactories, in England* [italics in original], is to quit work in a body or by combination." Many periodicals continued to italicize the word or put it in quotations, as if to separate the term and its dismal industrial connotations from America's pastoral ideal.[10] Periodicals sympathetic to labor might reprint a paragraph explaining worker grievances, but typically only the occasional instance of violence would justify any extended treatment.

One chaotic turn out at the beginning of the nineteenth century provides a rare example of this limited coverage. The April 11, 1800, issue of the *Baltimore Federal Gazette* recounted an incident in New York a month earlier in which a "large mob" of sailors "turned out for higher wages" and were "parading the streets . . . in wild confusion." The strikers then attempted to board a vessel on which scabs were said to be working, "with drums and fife, and colours flying." Their efforts were unsuccessful. After being "repulsed" repeatedly by those on board, they abandoned their efforts and limped off with "broken heads and bloody noses." The report ended on a note of relief—no lives were lost.[11]

This unusual event discloses some suggestive things about popular representations of strikes in the early nineteenth century. The reporter clearly framed the incident as the act of a wild and witless bunch whose misguided efforts to assert their rights resulted in an unsuccessful maneuver to punish those who they felt betrayed them. The elaborate procession of workers recalled eighteenth-century maritime turn outs, although the march here could also have been meant to connect these men to the Revolution.[12] The condescending tone of the article also illuminates the uneven terrain workers strode upon when taking justice into their own hands. Strikers were depicted as members of a confused mob, carrying on a vain skirmish for retribution. The music and flags suggested that to the sailors this event constituted a real battle, although clearly symbol meant more than tactical efficiency—they apparently fought with no weapons. Recognized as a type of public spectacle, early strikes like this one carried the potential of justifiable rebellion, an action acceptable in the moral economy of the post-Revolutionary world of laboring men.

Reportage of another New York sailors' strike two years later similarly depicted use of "drums and colors" by the strikers to rally others to their cause. In this strike, an even more distressing phenomenon was also noted— "the black seamen in the port united in the combination." The strikers had proceeded to "take possession of a schooner just ready for sea, and with great coolness and order proceeded to dismantle her of her sails and rigging, which they carefully stowed away in the hold." The "evil" of their "riotous" actions was ended when public magistrates sided with the merchants and arrested the leaders.[13]

The aspect of war evident in both of the seamen's strikes helps to connect early labor unrest with the post–Civil War period. Never merely festive parades, these strikes raised concerns that workers were upsetting the natural order of things. The sailors had inverted the social order by taking possession of the masters' ships and forming their own military-style forces. In the case of the 1802 turn out, the strike leaders fashioned themselves "*commodores*" (with the African American leaders playing the role of "*black commodores*") and managed to prevent a number of vessels from leaving. The fear of social collapse seen in the newspaper accounts in 1800 and 1802 is mirrored in the cordwainer strike trial reports a few years later; the prosecutor of the 1809 conspiracy case explained that the strikers had disturbed the "tacit compact that all classes reciprocally enter into," and were in effect waging "war with public policy."[14] As public actions carried out by the lower orders of society that unsettled daily rhythms of the market, strikes such as these contained the seeds of disorder and chaos. In the wake of a carpenters' strike in 1810, for example, masters noted the "increasing evils and distressing tendency" of journeymen to defy them.[15] The word's primary deployment as an intransitive verb at this point suggests that the *strike* was understood to be an action carried out by a group whose concerted effort made it formidable and unified. Observers recognized the potential for violence thinly masked by the expression.

Yet strikes remained a marginal part of everyday news. There are several reasons for the scant and typically uninspired coverage accorded them. Strikes were rare, and those on strike would rhetorically connect their activities to homegrown themes of liberty and equal rights rather than to a more alarming antagonism of the system that placed them in such desperate straits. The largely agrarian and artisanal nature of the economy meant that strikes were localized and communal rather than national or even regional affairs. Wage labor and rigid layers of hierarchical management had yet to become the norm; face-to-face relations encouraged an alliance of interest.

Perhaps most importantly, newspapers at this time simply did not concern themselves with strike news. Dubbed "the dark ages of partisan journalism," this period featured a highly biased press that catered to an audience of political partisans and refined intellectuals.[16] Generally quite limited in circulation, newspapers typically contained a miscellany of market reports, extended advertising columns, much political propaganda, bits of useful information, and brief reports on European happenings. A strike made an appearance only as a paragraph of grievances printed in a labor-friendly periodical or a denunciatory report of strike-related mobbery.

All this started to change in the late 1820s. Characterized by its profoundly leveling democratic rhetoric and an upsurge in popular political participation, the Jacksonian era has been called the "first awakening" of American labor. A dramatic increase in unionization and labor militancy took shape as the wage-pressure of the maturing national economy cut older sources of labor autonomy adrift.[17] The transportation revolution had already begun—by mid-century freight rates were nearly cut in half along with the time required to move it—and this helped the national market to mature, facilitating capital accumulation and competition, spurring the rise of cities and the number of workers per business. By 1850, shops that formerly might have contained two or three workers now had an average of ten employees. Although workshops and manufacturers exhibited a remarkable diversity in terms of size and character, a growing impersonality in the workplace and the deskilling of a number of traditional artisanal crafts, such as carpentry and shoemaking, elicited poignant working-class complaints. Particularly in those areas most touched by the newly accelerated arteries of transportation, larger and more threatening worker upheavals became more commonplace.[18]

Following a depression that accompanied the Panic of 1819, the number of strikes spiked when the economy improved and workers demanded higher wages.[19] Within a few years the Northeastern states saw the development of a number of working-class political and labor organizations, such as the Workingmen's Party of New York and the General Trades' Union.[20] Stridently confident laborites and a new flock of social critics ushered in an unprecedented wave of pro-labor agitation. One issue that stirred up a good deal of the workingman's ire was the length of the workday. As pre-industrial rhythms of work fell away and work came to be measured increasingly in terms of units of time, laborers sought to gain control over their working lives in what labor leader John Ferral referred to as "our bloodless revolution."[21] In 1825, Boston carpenters struck on a wide scale for shorter hours, the first in a series of ten-hour struggles that culminated in a massive general strike in Philadelphia in 1835. Strikes over such things as higher wages and the closed shop also increased. Most significantly, for the first time, strikes drew press coverage and a wide audience.

Revolutionary Accents

Making sense of labor strife involved an imaginative refashioning of Revolutionary language to suit a changing economic landscape. That this should be the case is unsurprising; as the central event in the memory of the young nation, the American Revolution loomed large over all areas of American social life. In the broadest sense, the Revolution had politicized popular language and created a platform on which writers could comfortably express concern over the "aristocrats" who threatened their delicate republican system. Following a virtual deluge of words that flooded the colonies in the

1760s and 1770s with terms like "liberty" and "rights" (interspersed liberally with biblical-sounding diatribes against political opposition), the public grew accustomed to a popular writing style characterized by invectives hurled with abandon.

As evident in the above-mentioned cordwainers cases, public voices often depicted American workers as having been instrumental in carrying out the Revolution and shattering aristocratic privilege. The leveling undercurrent involved in throwing off elite authority seduced many. The *Pennsylvania Packet* went so far as to suggest back in 1776 that the Revolution would lead to a time when once again "all ranks and conditions would come in for their just share of the wealth."[22] The Revolution worked such an undermining of established hierarchy that a new bipartite social order emerged: the lazy, aristocratic minority and the hard-working, democratic majority.[23]

Slicing society into groups of "the Few and the Many," writers like William Manning in the 1790s asserted that the few "cannot bear to be on a level with their fellow creatures, or submit to the determination of a legislature where (as they say) the swinish multitude are fairly represented."[24] The political battles waged between the Jeffersonian Republicans and the Federalists established an archetypal formula for envisioning the world divided in absolute terms.[25] The wave of democratic rhetoric that followed Independence and crystallized during the Jeffersonian political revolution helped to legitimize social protest while simultaneously undermining the self-evidency of the authority of those in power.

Legitimizing the new social division required constant reference to the American Revolution. Despite a popular rhetoric of classlessness that decried those who used social division to advance their cause, the "workies" of the late 1820s employed Revolutionary language in persuasive ways. Leading the way in keeping "equal rights" talk relevant to working-class life, labor advocates connected current strikes with the struggles of their Revolutionary forefathers.[26] In a strike manifesto issued to the public by the Journeymen House-Carpenters in New York City in April 1809, for instance, the carpenters connected their demand for eleven shillings per day with "the unalienable rights of man," being "life, liberty, and the pursuit of happiness." Having tied the strike to the Declaration of Independence and the "social compact" between the classes, they proceeded to outline their expenses to demonstrate the "justice" of the raise.[27]

Workers understood that breaching public order required careful strategy. Securing popular support was essential. They proudly marched in public processions carrying ceremonial regalia of their professions, even working in mock workshops on rolling floats along parade routes. In a well-attended march celebrating the opening of the Erie Canal, combmakers even distributed free combs to cheering spectators.[28] Union activists also communicated regularly with other tradesmen in an effort to find unity in their experience and battle the moneyed parasites together. In a circular to promote a broad alliance of journeymen printers, the Cincinnati Typographical Association explained that "our association . . . is not to oppress others, but for self-defence [sic]." The Cincinnati printers told others in their craft that it was important to understand this self-defense as an effort in "maintaining our rights."[29]

Harking back to the generation of '76 for inspiration and legitimacy, workers called forth the Revolution as a glorious touchstone to justify taking to the streets with fifes, drums, and banners. Ten-hour advocates likened their struggle to that of those "toil-worn veterans of '76 *who nobly moistened the soil with their own blood* in defense of equal rights and equal privileges" [italics in original].[30] A "Ten-Hour Circular" issued during the strike years of the 1830s and published in periodicals such as *The Man* and the *National Trades' Union* declared, "We claim by the blood of our fathers, shed on our battle fields in the war of Revolution, the rights of American freemen, and no earthly powers shall resist our righteous claims with impunity."[31] In that vein, striking women textile workers in New Hampshire in 1834 publicly declared themselves "daughters of freemen." The same year, female laborers in Lowell, Massachusetts, put out a strike pledge asking for those "who imbibe the spirit of our patriotic ancestors" to join them. Twelve hundred women responded.[32]

The Revolutionary image had power, and while conservative publications could dismiss such talk as either ignorant or dangerous, the workingman's claim as heir to a righteous cause had an undeniable authority.[33] That this heritage could be perverted by the moneyed few was good reason, as the *Working Man's Advocate* put it, to "Awake, then, from your slumbers; and insult not the memories of the heroes of '76."[34] One orator took it a step further, making an explicit connection between the labor strike and the Revolution with the toast: "Our forefathers: theirs was a glorious strike for liberty."[35]

The previous remark, made as it was at a Fourth of July Temperance Society meeting during the Philadelphia general strike of 1835, points to another popular approach used by laborers, employers, and the "middling sorts" alike—Protestant millennialism. The Second Great Awakening had unleashed a new wave of religious fervor across the country. Stressing brotherly charity and the potential of man to create for himself a more heavenly social order, this surge in religiosity brought with it a distinctly millennial character.

The use of religion as an "opiate" by the emerging middle class to encourage submission among laborers has been noted in several historical studies. Advocating hard work, social harmony, and abstinence, authorities used Christian virtues to establish a moral framework of obeisance from their workers.[36] Still, it would be a mistake to conflate middle-class religion with working-class piety. Protestant Christianity also maintained currents of resistance to earthly authority and an aspect of liberty-loving communalism that could be wielded by workers in the service of their own class interests. E. P. Thompson has pointed out that the working class was present at its own making; its religious zeal could be channeled toward militancy as well as quiescence.[37] Conceivably, with faith and action, workers might help deliver the better world to come.

Biblical references suffused strike commentaries of the 1830s and 1840s. From calling for resistance to the seductive pull of mammon to equating labor organizing with "Holy War" (justified by the Gospel of Nazareth), the religious upbringing of most Americans made such moralizing familiar and persuasive. Although less common than explicit Revolutionary references, the language of evangelical Christianity cropped up repeatedly in descriptions of labor unrest, to the point that strikes could be envisioned as a form of justifiable Christian vengeance.

Words like "thou" and "forsake" appeared in major labor periodicals in regular reference to labor unrest during the 1830s and 1840s. The *Baltimore Mechanics' Banner and Working Men's Shield* reflected on a hatters' strike by noting that strikers were filled with "a spirit of holy enthusiasm" and it told those "who would question their heaven-born and blood-bought privilege to think and act for themselves, so far shalt thou come and no farther." Fall River, Massachusetts, workers refashioned hymns to include lyrics about the ten-hour day during their struggles, rhyming a ten-hour "banner" with "hosanna." The *National Trades' Union* warned master tailors to "forsake their evil ways and sin no more." The democratization of religion that seared its way through the Northeast in the 1820s and 1830s and inspired such widespread millennialist piety seems also to have burned through the language of labor.[38]

Other popular themes in antebellum strike writing included popular fears of "wage slavery" and of foreign intrusion. Wage slavery, or "white slavery," commonly served as a point of departure for social critics who despised the system of dependence on wages that they saw emerging in the 1830s and 1840s. With origins stretching back to older protests of Englishmen who "never, never, never will be slaves" and to Revolution-era declarations of freedom from British thralldom, slavery as a rhetorical device came to be part of a powerful binary that separated free white men from servitude and blackness. "Wage slavery" soon became a popular invective used to attack those who would deny workers their natural right to support their families.

After gaining momentum in the 1820s, the idea that a form of slavery could root itself in the North informed numerous censures of the emerging factory system and the increasing power of masters over journeymen in the developing market economy.[39] One "Ten-Hour Circular" explained, "we cannot bear to be the servants of servants and slaves to oppression."[40] In the same vein, Lowell women on strike a year later sang:

Oh! I cannot be a slave;
I will not be a slave.
For I am fond of liberty
That I cannot be a slave.[41]

With the rise of free labor ideology in the 1850s, cries of "wage slavery" became diluted as Northerners increasingly criticized the Southern system of chattel slavery and the Slave Power. Vaunting their free labor system by way of sectional comparison, Northern workers increasingly accepted wage labor as a rung on the ladder of success.[42] Still, the image of shackled labor remained a potent one throughout the antebellum period.

Strikes could also evoke the threat of insidious foreign influence. Xenophobia had first appeared in relation to fears of "aristocrats" attempting to subvert hard-won American liberties. The *Aurora* suggested that slavery itself had been "a barbarous [principle] of feudalism entailed on us by England," and editorialized during the first Philadelphia cordwainers' strike conspiracy case that employers were out to inflict this European-rooted institution on hitherto free Northerners.[43] A strike card issued to a New Jersey newspaper a few decades later similarly explained that an ongoing cordwainers' strike had been caused by conditions created by men who "endeavor to build up an aristocracy, better befitting the hot-beds of Europe than the atmosphere of free America."[44]

Warnings of the counter-republican influence of Europe could also be focused the other way. Employers issued "cards" of their own. During the Boston house carpenters' strike of 1825, a set of resolutions printed by master carpenters in the *Columbian Centinel* included, "RESOLVED, that we cannot believe this project to have originated with any of the faithful and industrious Sons of New England, but are compelled to consider it an evil of foreign growth, and one which we hope will not take root in the favored soil of Massachusetts."[45] Painting the opposing side with the brush of foreignness tapped into a dialogue of nationalism that incorporated fears of Catholics and foreign radicals. Following the 1848 revolutions in Europe, conservatives accused strikers of being directly influenced by undemocratic foreign ideas. At the same time, laborers would accuse police of using tsarist "Russian" tactics.[46] Future strikes would resurrect the foreign image in even more vivid ways.

Suffusing the Revolutionary references, the biblical moralizing, and the foreigner anxieties was the metaphor of war. The most powerful image of all, war served as a broad raft onto which the vagaries of worker protest could rest. It had mobilized Revolutionary rhetoric in the first place, and now it offered a language that could be employed to give special political meaning to strikes. To understand the power of war framing after the Civil War, it is necessary to briefly look at the varied application of the word *strike* before 1861.

The labor "strike" held a nebulous meaning throughout the antebellum period; its application in print was liberal and loose. A newspaper could use the term as both action and adjective, referring to the current "striking times," or to a work stoppage as being a "striking illustration of socialism." In the same breath, *strike* could be used as a noun, a protest event well attended by the city's workers and sympathizing elite. As a verb, its application was even less clear. "To strike" in the nineteenth century commonly meant a sudden blow made with an implement. Strikers and radicals were not hesitant to use the term in this manner, switching rhetorically between a justifiable community event and an organized attack when it suited them. During a mass strike in 1835, for example, the *Working Man's Advocate* reprinted a song with the verse

> Strike till the last arm'd foe expires,
> Strike for your altars and your fires,
> Strike for the green graves of your sires,
>   God and your native land.[47]

As this ditty suggests, organized violence held the most provocative connotation for the labor *strike*. Words grouped with the term often alluded to disciplined armed conflict. Particularly when strikes got violent, words like "ranks," "marching," and "procession" took on a warlike aspect. Because most concepts evoke other concepts, the metaphor of war with its interconnected network of combat language gave the *strike* the power of a structured battle.[48] In conjunction with the dominant meaning of "strike" as a blow, workers and observers alike had access to a dynamic idiom that could be used to spur concerted action.

War itself played an important rhetorical role in the conceptual world of antebellum America. Political struggles saw the reference employed with abandon—Andrew Jackson's "war on the bank" held the top story position for a good while. When the Workingmen's Party offered candidates in New York City in 1829, the *Working Man's Advocate* declared, "The working classes have taken the field, and never will they give up the contest till the power that oppresses them is annihilated." The language of war was less casually employed when used in reference to labor protest, however. The *Advocate* expressed its mission using a sublimated martial analogy:

> No weapons we'll use, nor for aught do we care
>   But knowledge and union to bring on the field;
> For those are the keenest and those we bear,
>   Whilst the press will inspire us and be our safe shield.[49]

The limits to explicit calls for war in this case reflected a deeper reluctance to stray from the political realm when dealing with class differences, a fact which particularly stands out when comparing American class language to that of French and British labor advocates, who employed a far starker vocabulary of bloody war references.[50] While radical labor leaders might fill their speeches with Old Testament–style warnings of labor's righteous wrath, most observers held a less-than-portentous view of strikes.

One of the first media pieces to recognize the novelty of mass labor insurgency and use the idiom of class war in relation to America was written by Scottish immigrant and social activist Frances Wright, who wrote in 1830 in her journal *Free Enquirer* that what "distinguishes the present from every other struggle in which the human race has been engaged, is, that the present is, evidently, openly and acknowledgedly, a war of class, and that this war is universal."[51] As the term "capitalist" came into wide use after the 1820s, it became more commonplace to pin social inequalities on capitalist connivance and even suggest a great future struggle between them and their subjects, as when Senator Robert Walker of Mississippi warned that rampant, unchecked capitalist land speculation would result in "a war of capital against labor."[52]

As tools used to comprehend labor unrest, evangelicalism, slavery discourse, Revolutionary memory, and war metaphors intersected with and supported one another. A strike of textile workingwomen at the Cocheco mill in Dover, New Hampshire, featured a Fourth of July parade in which the women combined celebrations of liberty with cries to resist "the shocking fate of slaves."[53] Following the ten-hour general strike of 1835, labor activist John Ferral combined protestant millennialism with anti-aristocratic sentiment, recalling how the "blood-sucking aristocracy . . . stood aghast; terror stricken, they thought the day of retribution had come."[54] During that event, which also has the honor of being the first general strike in American history, an estimated twenty thousand laborers took to the streets with banners and music. With the motto "6 to 6" (referring to the ten-hour workday, including an hour each for two breaks) on their placards and banners, workers and middle-class sympathizers paraded throughout the city in triumphant jubilation. A song written for the occasion, entitled "The Temperance Strike," combined war, the Revolution, religiosity, and temperance in provocative verse:

> Our Fathers—who may see their like!
>   When trodden down as cattle,
> For Liberty knew how to strike,
>   And win the righteous battle!
> ⸻
>
> Then strike who will for "6 to 6"
>   We flinch not in the war;
> For Temperance and for Seventy-Six
>   We strike—hurrah! hurrah![55]

Another example of this mélange of analytical tropes can be seen in a leaflet called the "coffin hand bill" (thus named because it represented the death of equality) distributed following a fine imposed on New York strikers in 1836. "Mechanics and workingmen! A deadly blow has been struck at your liberty! The prize for which your fathers fought has been robbed from you! The freemen of the North are now on level with the slaves of the South." Combining conflict, wage slavery fears, and the historical memory of the Revolution, the handbill solicited moral outrage at a basic cultural level. It is no coincidence that the format of the bill recalled the coffin theme of Paul Revere's Boston Massacre circular.[56]

As is evident in these few examples, the language used to frame antebellum strikes relied on popular concepts that could be reconfigured and adapted to suit a variety of agendas. This language did not evolve in a vacuum—the underlying social context revealed a society in a state of flux. The strike years of 1835–1836, which were particularly important in crystallizing popular ideas about the public order, inhabited a longer era in which a remarkable fluidity characterized American life. Increased capital concentration resulted in an employer-directed tightening of control over the labor process.

In many industries, what has been referred to as "proletarianization" at the workplace meant hiring more (often immigrant) journeymen and investing in technology that undermined traditional craft skills.[57] Furthermore, the modern system of state coercion was nearly nonexistent at this time; even New York City had no professional police force until nearly mid-century. A system of controls born in custom and the daily rhythms of face-to-face market interactions maintained social order. In these walking cities, riots and protests were ways that communities regulated themselves via extralegal justice. In the 1830s, such events increased in both size and frequency. During many of these incidents local politicians and newspapers (which were usually connected to one political party or another) sympathized with and even encouraged the acts.[58]

Strikes simply did not figure prominently in most of the published dialogue regarding social order before the Civil War. Generally, they were held to be unproductive and potentially dangerous to all parties involved, though justifiable in principle.[59] Although a few radicals suggested that an outright civil war of class against class was on its way, as when Seth Luther warned that "the next and last resort [after the ballot box] is the cartridge box," most laborites stayed within a rubric of restraint and clarity of purpose.[60] Frances Wright herself asserted that she had not intended to provoke "hostility . . . in class towards class" in her writings, but that she wished instead for a more peaceful and equitable political reorganization of society.[61]

The 1835 general strike of Philadelphia serves as a good example of the measured ambivalence accorded to work stoppages by the press. As workers marched in the streets with banners declaring "Liberty, Equality, and the Rights of Man," some newspapers, like the pro-Jackson *Pennsylvanian,* expressed sympathy with the strikers. "Politically it is of immense importance that a change should be effected," went one editorial. "Our institutions place all power in the hands of the very men who are now . . . debarred from . . . that cultivation which alone can render them capable of wielding their tremendous strength." The paper also recognized the connection made between the strike and the Revolution, noting that "freemen" were declaring "as our fathers did their independence."[62] The *United States Gazette* was more cautious in its reports on the strike, criticizing drunkenness and the alarming interracial aspects of the affair.[63]

As the labor movement built momentum, ambivalence turned into condemnation. The wave of labor insurgency that followed the 1835 general strike led to an increasingly distressed tone in the popular press, setting a pattern that would continue into the postbellum years: as long as strikes were peaceful, the press might be willing to recognize the economic factors that had inspired them. When disputes got more violent or simply continued for too long, a different picture emerged. During a tailors' strike in the tumultuous year of 1836, the *New York Herald,* an anti-union paper, recognized that although "no one has a worse opinion of Trades' Unions than we have . . . many trades and journeymen have some reason for revolting against the present state of things." Once violence broke out and the situation worsened, the *Herald* quickly changed its tune, declaring "we are on the verge of domestic riot, blood shed, and local revolution."[64]

The *Herald's* explanation for the current "diseased state of society" in which "the spirit of insubordination" was running amok reflected commonalities in much of Jacksonian strike analysis. Nature and political factors accounted for things. The *Herald* urged a cool reappraisal of the situation. The strike and resulting violence had been due not to "the poor devils of Irishmen . . . the popish religion, or . . . the fanatics and abolitionists," as many erroneously believed, but rather to characteristics both inherent and acquired. The "grasping nature of the human heart" and especially the "small aristocrats," such as master tailors who charged too much for their goods, had created the volatile environment. By the following Monday, the paper presented a seven-point plan to address the "Causes and Remedies of the present discontents" that blamed landlords colluding secretly with local politicians to raise rents, false reports by food distributors to raise prices, the "monopoly" held by the New York Gas Company, and of course the "miserable rum drinking agitators" behind the Trades Union movement.[65]

Enlightened disapproval of strikes increased in the press in the wake of the labor unrest of the mid-1830s. Hezekiah Niles, a hard-working advocate of nonpartisan journalism whose *Niles' Weekly Register* delivered a cornucopia of information to his subscribers, went from presenting a relatively sympathetic belief that "turn-outs" were a positive means to get "high prices for honest labor" to a more negative view by the spring of 1835, noting that strikes resulted in business contractions that hurt workers and employers alike. By 1836 Niles found the current wave of strikes to be "going a great deal too far." In an issue covering an 1836 strike in New York he explained, "It is truly painful to see such a procession, marching for such a purpose; and, in some instances with profane mottoes upon their banners. One of these mottoes was—NO SURRENDER BY THE ETERNAL!" Niles even printed a statement by a manufacturer that paternalistically commented that *his* workmen needn't worry about unemployment because they had not been affected by

> the brutal leprosy of blue Monday habits, and the moral gangrene of "Trades Union" principles . . . they and myself find just cause to felicitate ourselves . . . of the inconvenience, injustice, and nuisance of perpetual vexations, regular combinations, and periodical strikes from marauding gangs of transient and tramping Trades Unionists, who have proved themselves destitute of every moral principle, as they have become notorious for their wickedness and folly, their presumption, their insolence and audacity.[66]

The pro-business *Journal of Commerce* was just as condemnatory of the labor movement, if not more grandiose in its wrath. As unions became increasingly associated with strikes, the *Journal* declared that labor organizations were "not only inexpedient, but at war with the order of things which the Creator has established for the general good, and therefore wicked." Even the pro-union *National Trades' Union* sought to distance itself from strikes, which it determined to be not in its best interests.[67]

By the end of the Jacksonian period, strikes had become a matter of some concern. The flourishing of mass communication encouraged the publishing of working-class-related stories. Coupled with the increasing use of populist, Revolutionary language and a set of interconnected discursive themes that privileged conflict over more tempered analysis, newspapers and popular journals were now discovering a broad, literate, and paying audience for labor protest coverage.

The Rise of Mass Communication

Traveling across the country in 1831–1832, Alexis de Tocqueville noticed that Americans devoured the printed word—newspapers in particular—at a remarkable rate. In the second volume of his *Democracy in America,* Tocqueville wrote, "nothing but a newspaper can drop the same thought into a thousand minds at the same moment." For this French visitor, America's

newspapers and its democratic "associations" were connected. The latter
supplied business for the former, and vice versa.[68] While periodical literature
production had been rapidly accelerating since the start of the nineteenth
century, the advent of the penny press in the 1830s gave the masses full access
to a whole world of information.[69]

The opening world of mass print communications, combined with ever
larger strikes, brought class conflict into American homes on an entirely new
scale. Whereas earlier the press had provided information of a largely political
persuasion to a select group of middling readers, the penny press delivered
more titillating narratives to the urban and semi-rural masses, the day-laborers
and journeymen alongside the bourgeois strivers. More Americans than ever
read a different sort of "news." At once more alarming and compelling, this
news carried with it elements of an unmistakable, growing class rift.

The penny press, or "one cent miracle," represented the coming of a
new kind of information-oriented society. The price made the product widely
accessible and the prurient contents made it wildly popular.[70] The modern idea of "news"—a continuous narrative of broader national and global
events connected to the reader by way of the newspaper's "invisible frame"
of neutrally presented, pertinent information—was invented at this time.
Newspapers now presented an exciting panoply of knowledge to the reader,
disclosing a series of ongoing events in brief, exciting portions.[71] New technology in printing and more efficient distribution methods provided the news
business with the means to deliver their product to a ravenous reading public. Working-class readers reveled in the tales of crime and punishment that
perhaps gave them a sense that their rights were ensured by news guardians.[72]
Working people might well have believed the *Sun*'s democratic masthead: "It
Shines for All."

Laborers had other news options as well. Starting with the first labor
paper in 1828, the workingmen's movement had over sixty-eight labor periodicals seeking proletarian patronage by 1834, led by George Henry Evans's New
York–based *Working Man's Advocate*.[73] The *Advocate* sent a weekly rallying cry
to the "industrious" and "productive" classes to defeat the "aristocratic" elements of society bent on undermining America's delicate democratic system.
Like much of the rest of the language of class employed at the time, Evans's
paper structured its analysis in political and "natural order" terms, presenting
the workingman's troubles as the result of the hidden machinations of the
"parasitic classes" of society. Bankers and merchants, whose wealth seemed to
derive from simply living off of the labor of others, were primary targets.

Solutions to this aristocratic manipulation were simple and numerable.
Get rid of the class legislation that favored monopolies; promote democratic
public education and voting rights; prevent employers from working their
employees beyond their capacities for less than they could live on; and ensure

just property taxes and inheritance laws.[74] The natural order of things in a democratic society, concurred an optimistic coterie of political economists, must favor equilibrium. Aristocratic laws only needed to be eradicated to ensure that natural liberties, such as the guarantee of the whole of the fruits of one's labors, would not be threatened.

Such class analyses, rooted as they were in inherited Revolutionary memory, had an irresistible popularity. Jacksonian William Leggett's widely read *New York Evening Post,* for example, served as a platform from which vituperative calls against the "privileged" were sounded.[75] Because the answers to the tendencies of unjust accumulation of vast fortunes and the diminishing of laboring men's economic security rested in political solutions, labor protests were not generally viewed by the press in a favorable light, but rather as disruptions that could be just as harmful to those carrying them out as to those who were the target.

With a colorful argot of republican idealism, a far-reaching network of daily news publications brought strike news into many American homes by the 1830s. Presenting the literate public with a mixture of Revolutionary ideas, social anxieties, and historical memories, newspapers assembled daily events into an accessible and continuous national narrative. The democratic aspect of the press fed into broader currents circulating throughout the country. As "classes" replaced "orders" and historical folk memory replaced classical allegory (such as comparing Washington with Cincinnatus), the arena of debate concerning the legitimate uses of power took on a populist aspect.[76] Already inclined to frame its analysis with the cadence and informality of spoken language, the press catered to its emerging national audience with a folksy style that favored crudity and concision over cultivation. Connecting all the strands of thought embedded in this public language was the bonding agent of Jacksonian rhetoric: the model of the cleanly bifurcated society.

With the "producing" or "useful" classes in one camp and the "parasitic" or "aristocratic" classes in the other, Jacksonian commentators swept a complex society of capitalist farmers, small producers, merchants, slaves, journeymen, domestic workers, and investors into a world of absolutes. While a tripartite model of society that divided the population up between the upper, middling, and lower ranks also had much popularity in social analyses, the division of society into haves and have-nots carried a set of very compelling critiques. To denounce those who sought to undermine American equality, labor advocates, reformers, and even conservative thinkers agreed that, in the words of George Bancroft, there was a "feud between the capitalists and the laborer, the House of Have and the House of Want, [as] old as social union, [that] can never be entirely quieted."[77] George Henry Evans even undertook to distinguish between "useful" and "useless" occupations in order to clarify the opposition, which included "useless" lawyers, bankers, and stockbrokers.[78]

The expansion of the media, and the oppositional model that ran through editorial pages, printed speeches, and popular illustrations, would be essential in providing needed fodder for contemporary social critiques. Social division also inspired a renewed desire to fulfill the American promise, diffusing the conflict with myriad political measures. Ongoing, jarring changes in the economy would intensify this process.

Darkening Horizon

The Panic of 1837 spelled the demise of the nascent Jacksonian labor movement. The number of strikes declined and unions shrank considerably or collapsed altogether. The labor press, the emerging voice of working people, had taken a blow that it found difficult to recover from. Searching for other means of social redemption, many former laborites plunged into utopian schemes or retreated to reactionary critiques of incoming immigrant populations. Still, thoughtful commentaries on strikes continued into the 1840s, reflecting the persistence of the themes that had shaped strike analysis in the previous decade. The model of class conflict framed in terms of political causes and solutions remained a guiding, if embattled, social construct.

In one of the most trenchant antebellum expressions of class conflict, reformer and religious radical Orestes Brownson wrote with Old Testament foreboding that in America "that most dreaded of all wars, the war of the poor against the rich, a war which, however long it may be delayed, will come, and come with all its horrors. The day of vengeance is sure. . . . Every day does this struggle extend further and wax stronger and fiercer; what or when the end will be God only knows." The causes of this struggle, Brownson argued, were to be found in "social influences, the action of government, of laws, of systems and institutions upheld by society, and of which individuals are the slaves" and, he claimed, in the nefarious doings of the priesthood. The apocalyptic solution he hinted at would do away with the system of wages and "emancipate the proletaries." Contemporary labor radicals like New York's Mike Walsh agreed that "capital" had "enslaved" labor and that this demanded of workers a call to arms to restore equality: "Nothing but revolution or legislation can effect the indispensable change."[79]

Despite efforts by prominent political economists such as Henry C. Carey to explain to the public the essential "harmony of interests" between employers and the employed, many others voiced deeper fears. Radicals, trade unionists, social critics, and many community leaders warned of an emerging antagonistic system of permanent wage servitude, anathema at a time when working for wages was still viewed as a temporary condition. In a speech made before the Philomathean Society of Farmers College in 1847, Reverend Charles Boynton warned that the "whole tendency of our modern system of labor and

wages is to discontent and revolution. . . . It cannot endure, and, if not gradually reformed, will rock at last the foundations of society."[80]

Newspaper magnate Horace Greeley agreed, and in an editorial in his *New
York Tribune* he noted that strikes were "like Battles of any kind—sometimes
apparently necessary, but if so a grievous and desolating necessity" that
would never be more than a temporary fix. Strikes were ultimately not useful, Greeley believed, because the root of labor's oppression, the "Hireling
or Wages system," could not be easily corrected with work stoppages. Others
agreed that the wages system had taken a terrible hold on society. A speaker
in an address to the New York Typographical Society in 1850 declared, "It
is useless for us to disguise from ourselves the fact that, under the present
arrangement of things, there exists a perpetual antagonism between Labor
and Capital."[81]

Critiques such as these inevitably managed to leave some room for
reform. As Martin J. Burke has pointed out, a broader theme of reconcil-
able class conflict is apparent in antebellum industrial writing. For Orestes
Brownson, the answer rested in the dissolution of the priesthood and a radical
redistribution of inheritance. For Mike Walsh, Tammany Hall corruption and
Whig legislation that supported the "all-grasping power" of "capital" needed
to be uprooted. For Horace Greeley and George Henry Evans, the solution lay
in land reform and labor cooperatives. Still others had their own recipes. In
a speech reprinted in the Unitarian *Christian Register and Boston Observer,* a
lecturer explained that the "aristocratical tendencies of accumulated masses
of capital" could be easily remedied with "free schools, and a free press."[82]
Other writers were more dramatic in presentation, if less clear on specifics:
the Albany *Mechanic's Advocate* exclaimed, "fierce and blood-thirsty Capital
will swallow up the whole laboring class in its huge maw, unless measures
are speedily adopted to stay its ruinous progress."[83] Such comments revealed
that the emerging "labor question" needed to be addressed in ways that jibed
with the language of politics and natural law undergirding antebellum understandings of society.

As capital and labor overlay the older model of the industrious many
and the aristocratic few in the 1840s, American opinion makers struggled
to come to grips with an industrial landscape increasingly characterized by
large commercial cities, growing markets, a massive influx of immigrants,
and the inexorable spread of the wage system. *Hunt's Merchant Magazine and
Commercial Review* took a conservative, reasoned view in an article entitled
"Capital and Labor." "The rule is, that labor cannot wait, and is therefore
at the mercy of capital," the writer explained. While the "principle of free
competition" is good for those who are have "talent, means, [and] energy,"
it gives "no chance to the weak, the poor, the friendless. It develops great
energy, and produces great results; but it makes one part of society the tools

and instruments" of the other. Given that this economic system would fol-low such a course, strikes could be viewed as understandable, but by nature *irrational* reactions to an arrangement that placed unmotivated workers in a necessarily subservient position.[84]

A more common argument stressed that the shared interests of capital and labor made strikes antagonistic to a harmonious society. A writer in this vein brought piety and natural law neatly together: "Thus will strikes ever result in ultimate injury to those who engage in them. They may meet, and have met, with apparent success for a time, but being against reason, and opposed to that community of interest which Providence has instituted between the workman and the employer, they must in the end bring the sure penalty that attends every infraction of natural law."[85]

Describing an 1852 New York strike as part of an "epidemic," the con-servative *Scientific American* took an even more negative view of concerted labor stoppages. "Their effects are generally disastrous to all concerned, both employers and employed, and always more hurtful to the latter than the former." *Scientific American* would finally come to the conclusion that strikes damaged industry "irremediably."[86]

The theme of the futility of strikes was repeated in many periodicals.[87] The laborite *Mechanic's Advocate* agreed on the ineffectiveness of strikes in general, noting in several issues slight modifications of the phrase: "in nine cases in ten, the really injured party weakens itself, injures its cause, strengthens the bonds of its oppressor, and rivets tighter its own chains." However, in the particular, the journal revealed a disinclination to focus on natural absolutes in regard to individual strikes. In cases like that of the impoverished "slop shop" workers at the time, the *Advocate* encouraged workers to strike.[88]

Traditional modes of popular analysis were modified further by interna-tional events. The Revolutions of 1848 introduced a new group of European radicals to the American labor movement. Their influence would first be felt in the New York strikes of 1850, during which one émigré pleaded, "Many among us have before engaged in fighting for liberty in [the] Fatherland. Now, brethren . . . it is time to fight again, and to fight boldly; we must not flinch; we must be resolute."[89] With this new blood came a new vocabulary of radical-ism. In the 1848 revision of Webster's *Dictionary*, words like "communism" and "socialism" were formally introduced to the American lexicon.[90] While such language and influence could contribute to working-class solidarity, they also could represent insidious forces at work. Conservative newspapers like James Gordon Bennett's *New York Herald* fanned the flames of nativism, linking mass strikes with foreign ideologies. Labor organizations often complained that the stigma of "socialism" was being applied to their efforts with hurtful reckless-ness in the press.[91]

Despite labor condemnations of media bias, the press in large part continued to treat unions with a degree of sympathy. Popular fears of concentrated wealth and of insidious distant influences manipulating the law coalesced around strikes in this decade as never before, making strikes more politically volatile and less easy to condemn.[92] Nevertheless, during the strike years of 1853–1854, as the mainstream press reported strike after strike (about four hundred in all), the motif of war cropped up sporadically but with increased portent. Horace Greeley's *New York Tribune* saw a pattern by 1854, noting that each spring a fresh wave of strikes swept through the nation's cities. Although pro-labor in general, the *Tribune* delivered a message about strikes with new foreboding: "A strike is a declaration of Industrial War; and war should be the very last argument of republicans." One image of war recalled recent European revolutions; another was found in Indian resistance. For "Labor to . . . expect to starve Capital" via the strike was "as absurd as for a war party of Indians to undertake the siege of Gibraltar expecting to compel it to surrender."[93]

As the industrial world took on a darker hue and class lines hardened, changes in journalism portended greater significance for strikes.[94] In 1844, the invention of the telegraph allowed stories to instantaneously reach the nation's major news offices. Telegraphy was expensive, however, and found use primarily in relaying major national and international events and market reports. Innovations in printing technology also allowed for a much higher rate of news delivery in the 1840s and 1850s, with so-called "lightning" presses capable of putting out twelve thousand impressions per hour by 1849. Other innovations followed the Mexican War, such as multiple-deck headlines that neatly summarized the major story at a glance. Illustrations also became more commonplace, adding a visual dimension that presented an image with which to associate national events. The rising popularity of illustrated journals like *Harper's Monthly* and *Leslie's Illustrated Weekly* supplied the reading audience with visuals to go along with the story.

Perhaps most important for national strike coverage, newspapers began to pool their resources to more effectively cover different stories from across the country. In response to demand and to difficulties in reporting the Mexican War, several New York publications began running identical telegraphic dispatches on the conflict. By 1849 a group of major papers were sharing the costs of printing identical foreign and national reports. The advent of the Associated Press, with its capacity to deliver a story nationwide, would be as significant to spreading strike coverage as the newspaper revolution had been in the 1830s.[95]

Despite these changes, strike reporting reflected the endurance of older Revolutionary notions of community action and festivity. The largest antebellum strike, the Great Shoemakers' Strike of 1860, illustrates the staying power

FIGURE 3 This image of the Great Shoemakers' Strike of 1860, printed after a report on a championship boxing match, suggests this strike was conceptualized as a spectacle rather than a war. Note, however, the ways—in image and in text—in which this "riot" is portrayed as a disruption of the social order, something not to be taken lightly.

Source: *Frank Leslie's Illustrated Newspaper*, March 17, 1860.

of local political activism in the face of deeper class changes in antebellum America. The coverage of the event highlighted the calmness and orderliness of the strikers, occasionally adding bits about social events, such as picnics and parades, during the strike. Strike songs were composed that compared the workers to slaves and to downtrodden European masses, adding in a healthy dose of biblical and Revolutionary allusions.[96] Illustrations of the strike (at this time a novelty in American strike history) depicted organized strikers and militia marching peacefully in the snowy streets of Lynn, Massachusetts. A rare depiction of "rioters" showed a well-dressed crowd surrounding a wagon and unloading its goods.[97]

FIGURE 4 This image of the Great Shoemakers' Strike of 1860 depicts an orderly march, led by local militia, that captures the festive, communal atmosphere of most large antebellum strikes.

Source: *Frank Leslie's Illustrated Newspaper*, March 17, 1860.

Soon a debate over deeper significance arose as the strike wore on. Democratic papers like the *Bay State* concurred with Republican organs, such as the *New York Tribune*, that solutions to labor's problems rested in understanding the natural laws of supply and demand.[98] A few were not as sanguine about America's industrial future; a New York journeyman housepainter, for instance, said that now there was clearly "a war commencing between labor and capital."[99]

During the Great Shoemakers' Strike, Abraham Lincoln gave a speech in which he reiterated the right to strike while asserting that the law needn't be dramatically changed to "prevent a man from getting rich." Recognizing both the capital-labor model and the local nature of all strikes, Lincoln's remarks steered a middle course between the views of advocates of natural law who saw turn outs as pointless and harmful and those who advocated radical change via working-class militancy. Reaffirming the right of the republican workingman to work and withhold work as he chose, the president-to-be both vaunted strikes as evidence of a superior system of labor (juxtaposing it with *strikeless* slave labor) and set the public at ease by declaring "we do not propose any war on capital." Giving every man a chance to move beyond wages meant legitimizing his right to strike while he toiled among the working classes. Poverty, said Lincoln, was the condition in which most Americans, including himself, started life. As long as the aristocratic moneyed interests were kept at bay through legislation and democratic vigilance, the social order need not be as grim as radical laborites suggested.[100]

The Great Shoemakers' Strike of 1860, like the mass strikes of the 1850s and the Philadelphia general strike of 1835, was perceived primarily to be an affair caused by a distress in the system rather than an indicator of a broader conflict. While strikes could be framed as metaphorical wars waged by workers, the battles were firmly locked within a defined set of labor and community relationships. The debate continued to be mainly understood in socio-political—not class—terms, as strikers defined their activities according to broad ideals of individual autonomy and equal rights. Remaining a key source of labor militancy, the Revolution stood not as an exemplar of violent revolt but rather as a model of communal moral defiance. Though there was much debate over what the Revolution meant, it never stood as a bloodbath that warranted a full repeating. Interconnected with the popular historical memory of the generation of '76, moral suasion remained the primary publicity tool of strikers. Parades, dress, and regalia symbolically connected strike language with justifiable action. Similarly, the threat of foreign influence had not yet become a fear of full-fledged invasion, and the menace of a system of "wage slavery" worth striking against became diffused by remarkable Northern support for free labor as sectional tensions increased in the 1850s.

Strikes, then, belonged only peripherally to the wider realm of national class and sectional tensions on the eve of the Civil War. They were battles, but contained ones directed for specific moral purposes within local arenas. These limits generally kept them separate from violent riots and from abstract "labor" in the popular imagination. The media never framed strikes in such a way as to be more than local stories except with the occasional shrill editorial warning of impending disaster if the Trades Union movement went unchecked. Even following the invention of the telegraph and the resulting nationalization of the media, the Mexican War, the Gold Rush, the West, railroad accidents, political wranglings, and sensational murder trials occupied the center of national news coverage. Strike news was often secondary to boxing coverage and ads for miracle oils.

But between the cracks, an ominous narrative occasionally peeked through. Reporting on the worldwide phenomenon of strikes, some journalists recognized a deeper, troublesome trend in the 1850s. In London, unions were waging a "campaign of aggression" that had already "ruined" numerous industries. In America, a strike of iron molders was said to be causing "far more" injury to employers than employees. This was new. Before, the conservative press commonly depicted strikes as foolish battles that harmed those who depended on wages more than those who handed them out. Now it was suggested that strikes might give labor power unimagined in former times. The arrival on America's shores of a labor campaign along British lines, one journal insidiously implied, could be calamitous.[101]

The new fear of labor dominance swirled about a congeries of circumstances that gave industrial conflicts of the 1850s an import not previously possible. Businesses were expanding once again at a remarkable rate, led by the railroads and their armies of wage laborers. Furthermore, with technology capable of printing and illustrating single events on a mass scale and the new institution of the Associated Press capable of delivering a single story instantly to millions nationwide, the potential existed for major strike events to be quickly collapsed into a single account with a single set of accompanying images. While these potentially alarming factors lay dormant within a republican milieu of rights and community in 1860, soon the old strike framework would be in ruins, and mass stoppages would become something truly monstrous.

2

Drifting toward Industrial War

The Great Strike of 1877 and the Coming of a New Era

In the fourth year of America's Civil War, William Sylvis, president of the Iron Molders' International Union, addressed a group of laborites in upstate New York. Rejecting the older "harmony of interests" dictum, Sylvis told the audience that there in fact endured a "sort of irrepressible conflict" between employers and workers.[1] He had appropriated this phrase from the ongoing national discussion concerning the inevitability of the bloody sectional struggle. The notion of an unpreventable war between owners and workers resonated with his audience, a people accustomed to reading daily about great and bloody battles waged over the very definition of the republic. In the years to come, the phrase "irrepressible conflict" would prove a stubbornly popular description for the relationship between capital and labor, evidence of a remarkable cross-pollination of language and ideas initiated by the war experience.

Serving as both a template for nationwide upheaval and a supply house of appropriate words and ideas, the Civil War imparted to the industrial world a compelling idiom of struggle and conflict. As large units of organized labor and corporate capital coalesced following the war, martial language helped Americans to conceptualize class relationships in a manner appropriate to their late experience. Favoring conflict rather than consensus, war framing helped persuade the public to see labor and capital as antagonists vying for social control rather than as partners building a better world.[2] Incorporating industrial and union developments into a frightening mixture of postwar anxieties, war talk helped to make older republican understandings of progress and social order appear obsolete.

Fitting the various components of labor relations into the new antagonistic class understanding did not settle anything, however. The linguistic tools that total war supplied did nothing to assign causality to labor hostilities. As a result, a multiplicity of explanations for industrial conflict arose. Labor activists connected war metaphor to a sense of entitlement extending from labor's role in winning the great struggle against the slave system. Fortifying longstanding rhetorical themes of natural rights and social equality, war language was used to support the workers' goals of attaining a more equitable share of the economic pie.[3] For the reading public at large, the opportunities for social redress mixed with the horrors of the war to create a more ambivalent atmosphere. While the war fostered patriotic sentiments of liberty and rights, it also inspired feelings of caution and wariness.

Though a number of historians have explored the ways in which the Civil War helped spur American intellectuals onto "realist" reform paths, the wider cultural effect of the war in popular understandings of social relations has been generally overlooked.[4] The significance of this oversight is important, considering that labor violence in the postbellum years, particularly during the Great Strike of 1877, is commonly treated uncritically as the gateway to a new and unforeseen world of class conflict.[5] The role played by the Civil War itself, in providing the language used to describe this model of capital-labor antagonism, has since slipped quietly from view.

In this chapter, I will look at the ways in which the Civil War imprinted a disquieting image of battle upon the industrializing world of labor relations in the 1860s and 1870s. Following a general discussion of the cultural and institutional responses to the war and the ways in which the railroads inadvertently reinforced a martial model of labor relations, I will focus on the climactic Great Railroad Strike of 1877. This strike, the first national "labor war," would set the stage for a new era of industrial battles.

The Civil War and Popular Culture

The Civil War marked a transition in the American experience. In the words of philosopher Henry James, it "left a different tone from the tone it found."[6] Throughout the abundant textual and verbal discourse surrounding the event, the burden of adjusting to a world in which such an unheard-of scale of carnage and apparent self-immolation would occur weighed heavily.[7] Its bloody novelty collided with inherited notions of social stability and order. An entirely new grammar would be required to comprehend it. Walt Whitman, a sensitive observer who was skeptical of the capacity of words to do the job, wrote that the "*real* war would never get into the books."[8] A cursory survey of popular writings in the decades following the war, however, suggests that Whitman's prophecy would not go unchallenged, at least in the world of public life.

Languages of politics, business, and foreign affairs all became imprinted with a martial aspect that favored descriptions of events in grandiose, military terms. In the world of finance, James A. Ward notes, "corporate officers delivered 'ultimatums,' declared their 'neutrality' on certain issues, went on the defensive to protect their 'territory,' and sued for 'peace' when no other recourse was available." There would be "attacks" on the enemy as businesses sought dominance over each other in a quest for national "victory."[9] In politics, battle metaphors and gratuitous references to the late war became part of the *lingua franca* of electioneering. Republican strategists would have the goal of attaining "unconditional surrender" from the other side, celebrating the "Appomattox" that followed electoral victory.[10] Reformers framed their endeavors in martial terms as well—the temperance movement, for example, became "The Women's War." Foreign events also lent themselves to Civil War comparison. When the Paris Commune of 1871 erupted into widespread violence, it became known as the "Civil War in Paris" or the "French Insurrection."[11]

The media itself was transformed by the war. As battles went on in other parts of the country, the reading public proved ravenous for news from the front. Newspaper readership began to expand significantly in 1861 and remained very high in the postbellum years.[12] Journalists presented the war as an ongoing narrative, with a plot filled out with bold characters and decisive actions, sometimes handsomely illustrated, and always with accompanying lists of casualties. The formula sold marvelously. After the war, one publisher complained that the reading public craved a continuous supply of "conflagrations . . . calamities, . . . commotions, revolutions, [and] wars," and that they possessed a seemingly unquenchable thirst for the immediate telegraphic coverage of "exciting, thrilling, and astounding events." Giving the public what it wanted meant dispatch-style reporting, bold headlines, and a dramatic treatment of distant events.[13]

Journals and other periodicals in the postwar years commented on labor turbulence with terminology not unlike that found in William Sylvis's Civil War–era diatribes. *Old Guard* explained, "the real 'irrepressible conflict' of modern times is of a very different character from that which Mr. Seward is supposed to have discovered. It is the conflict of labor and capital." While another journal found the popular "idea of an irrepressible conflict between man and master" to be "erroneous," it revealed a declining faith in the old dictum of the harmony of interests: "perhaps, [we] can have only a millennial solution, when the lion of capital shall lay down by the lamb of labor." The conservative *Merchants' Magazine and Commercial Review* viewed ongoing eight-hour strikes as evidence of a "war of classes having been inaugurated." Other newspapers began using the heading "Capital and Labor" to account for strikes currently under way in other cities.[14]

Even political economists whose faith in the harmony of interests remained unaltered discovered themselves in a defensive position. In *The Science of Wealth* (1866), Amasa Walker criticized, among other things, the "popular language" that currently, and mistakenly, considered capital and labor to be antagonists. Henry C. Carey, oracle of the harmony of interests, found himself reiterating his protectionist theories with unexpected vigor. In a pamphlet issued in 1873, he worried about the popularity of the idea of "a war between capital and labor." Books like Albert Bolles's 1876 *The Conflict between Labor and Capital* further affirmed the commonplace assessment of pervasive labor-capital conflict.[15]

Martial imagery sold because there was a large market predisposed to find war in a variety of contexts. As discussed previously, war had long served as an organizing metaphor for conceptualizing strikes and labor unrest. But the Civil War experience did more than add a new referent to the mix; it profoundly redirected strike analysis by providing a far more visceral signifier for organized combat than had heretofore existed. The categories of analysis posited in chapter I—Revolutionary talk, millennial Protestantism, foreign fears, slavery, and combat—all underwent noticeable shifts in interpretation as a result of the war. Talk of rights and revolution became reminiscent of secession. Millennialism received a dose of Revelation-style calamity. Foreign-ness still bothered Americans, though the nationalism unleashed by the war helped briefly to assimilate outsider groups. Wage slavery discourse now had the precedent of emancipation.

The war experience also encouraged a new way of looking at unions. As labor organizations became more organized and national (which was in itself a consequence of the war), their struggles for recognition and wages came to be seen as national battles both in labor circles and in the mainstream press. As will be discussed below, the largest strikes would be viewed as *literal* battles in a much larger conflict. First, it is necessary to evaluate some of the material changes in labor relations that supplied the raw material for the new way of looking at the industrial world.

Labor Organizes Its Ranks

During and immediately after the Civil War, workers sought to capitalize on solidarity resulting from shared experience both on the battlefield and at the workplace. Pulled together by patriotic collectivism, laborers transposed efforts to fight a common foe in the fields of war onto a dynamic organizational drive at the workplace. A surge of workplace and political activism begun in the later years of the war continued well into the postwar period. Collective experiences of combat occasionally broke down ethnic rivalries, and veteran workers eagerly engaged themselves in broader labor campaigns such as the

eight-hour movement (led by war veteran Ira Steward) and the first nationwide collaboration of unionists, the National Labor Union (founded in 1866).[16]
The newly elected head of the organization, William Sylvis, put this militancy
in the bluntest terms: "Our late war resulted in the building up of the most
infamous moneyed aristocracy on the face of the earth. . . . We have made war
upon it, and we mean to win."[17]

Although the Civil War itself was more of a "middling" than a "poor" man's
fight (despite popular declarations to the contrary), laborers had good reason
to entrench themselves. During the war an ominous collusion of the state and
corporations in the suppression of strikes had taken place. Several generals
responded to corporate pleas during the war by issuing orders prohibiting men
engaged in war production from picketing or even joining unions. Soldiers
were used to protect strikebreakers and occasionally to prevent work stoppages
in industries deemed valuable to the war effort, such as coal mining.[18] In New
York, an antistrike bill introduced in the spring of 1864 designed to "Punish
Unlawful Interference with Employers and Employees" was met with a hailstorm
of protest from labor organizations. As one worker put it indignantly, "Why is
it that they seek to crush the workingmen? It is from the working classes that
they got men to fight the battles of the country and to sustain the American
flag. Shall these men suffer for the bread necessary to sustain them?"[19]

The mainstream press noted the newfound labor militancy and continued to chastise strikers as fundamentally ignorant of the laws of supply and
demand, although now a grudging recognition of the theoretical legitimacy of
strikes often accompanied these denunciations.[20] While labor activists agreed
on the futility of strikes in general, postwar context provided new justification
for labor protests, reflecting a new sense of empowerment.[21]

Following the Civil War, and with heightened rapidity in the years prior
to 1873, trades unionists organized themselves with a vengeance. Inspired
by wartime mobilization and a fear of the growing power of capital, workers
swarmed into local and national organizations, most notably the National
Labor Union and the Knights of St. Crispin. Union organizers stressed both
antagonism to war-profiteering capitalists and praise for the blood-earned
right to a greater share of America's rising wealth. Their demands were stri-
dent and clear. As machinist and labor advocate Ira Steward explained to a
gathering of laborers in November 1865, "we yet want it to be known that
the workingmen of America in future claim a more equal share in the wealth
their industry creates and a more equal participation in the privileges and
blessings of those free institutions, defended by their manhood on many
a bloody field of battle."[22] By 1870, David Montgomery has estimated, over
300,000 workers belonged to some fifteen hundred trades unions.[23] This
number would dwindle following the economic crisis of 1873, but the sense of
militancy would remain.

Journals aimed at working-class populations, such as Boston's *American Workman*, seconded the sense that a new age dawned, that a time for righteous change was afoot. In its June 26, 1869, issue, the *Workman* explained that the ultimate aim of labor should be to overthrow the entire "system of working for hire" via a series of worker-owned cooperatives. It observed that the money spent conducting the "many strikes which have been carried on in different parts of the country" could be better put to use in establishing a new harmonious economic order.[24]

William Sylvis maneuvered this new terrain ably, recognizing that while strikes were still frowned upon by most Americans, a fresh incentive to resist employer demands now existed. Publicly disavowing strikes, he privately told a group of unionists not to "strike until you are well organized, and then strike hard." *Strike* was both event and action here—Sylvis's straightforward use of the physical blow metaphor reflected militancy invigorated by the new context.

Just as workers found a new footing in their own war experience, a rising chorus of public voices reaffirmed a postwar fear in the direction taken by America's economy and industrial relations. By the end of the 1870s, a number of journalists, writers, and reformers had begun to methodically dissect the often corrupt accumulation of wealth among the capitalist class. The public had made Mark Twain and Charles Dudley Warner's *The Gilded Age: A Story of To-day* (a humorous and pointed indictment of a society betrayed by greed and corruption) a runaway bestseller in 1873. When Henry George published *Progress and Poverty* in 1879 and wrote of "want and suffering and anxiety among the working classes," the public took his word for it with little debate.[25]

Despite the shift in discourse, it would be a mistake to see the Civil War as the prime mover in changing popular perceptions of the industrial scene. Postbellum labor relations are best understood as a dialectic between the new martial vocabulary and the rapidly evolving industrial climate that bestowed upon strikes an increasingly national import. In the postwar years, the numbers of workers per business continued to rise as corporations came to dominate the business scene. This accompanied the "long boom" of capital expansion dating from the 1840s, in which employers tended to increase the number of workers rather than revolutionize the technological aspects of production. One consequence of this process was that workers organized more intensely along craft lines and shifted activism from neighborhoods to workplaces.[26]

National market convergences further separated labor militancy from its previous communal connotations by universalizing the impact of strike actions. Strikes in Pennsylvania's coalfields threatened cities like New York with a cold winter; strikes on eastern docks threatened Chicago's marketplaces; strikes along the railways threatened everybody. While labor leaders and the mainstream press continued to condemn strikes as counterproductive and harmful to all parties involved, individual strikes elicited varied responses from the public. Playing an important role in the drama of postwar class conflict, the railroads deserve special attention in this story. Railroads provided a concrete manifestation of an industrial enemy suitable for the times and also helped to generate the armies of wage laborers needed to make mass strikes nationwide affairs.

The Railroads: Carriers of Class Conflict

Indispensable to the new world of hostile industrial relations was the railroad. Railroads in the post–Civil War years defined corporate America, imposing their massive, hierarchical structures on everything from law to language.[27] They tested and stretched the possibilities of America's belief systems along with the urban spaces and rural landscapes that they rolled through. Magnets for metaphors, the great engines inspired comparisons to trees, rivers, mythical beings, even the human body. Locomotives were Cyclopes, behemoths, and iron horses; rail lines were arteries, branches, octopus tentacles. Optimists associated the speed and industrial output connected to the roads with America's potential. Others portended that these "dragons" augured a less comforting industrial future.[28] Railroad accidents had a terrifying life of their own in the media.

Those most affected by the roads were those who labored on them. Working on the railroads required centralized organization and regimentation—it is no coincidence that the phrase "army of labor" cropped up repeatedly in reference to the sizeable workforce required by this capital- and labor-intensive enterprise. The growth of this army was spectacular. A few thousand railroad employees in 1840 turned into over 150,000 by 1870, each having a specialized set of tasks required of him. For the vast majority of railway workers, this meant very long hours of strenuous work and the tight industrial discipline and extreme injury rates that went along with them.[29]

The snorting, puffing, smoking locomotive did more than take fingers and limbs from hapless employees. It tore through urban spaces with a vengeance, plowing through carriages and occasionally people, even sending sparks onto wooden roofs. Opposition to the inroads of rail on American life extended beyond city neighborhoods: farmers protested unprofitable and unfair rating schemes and merchants complained of usurious freight rates. The public resented the railroad moguls who lived in luxury and openly flouted the laws while millions lived in abject poverty. The recognized role of the railroads in creating the unstable economic landscape added fuel to the fire.[30] While strikes along the lines could be devastating to commerce and livelihoods,

FIGURE 5 As this hideous anthropomorphism suggests, the railroads could evoke unsettling images.

Source: *New York Daily Graphic*, August 14, 1873.

they also could be quite popular. Compared with the critical reception of distant miners' strikes going on at about the same time, urban newspapers responded to railroad strikes with decidedly less animosity. During a massive engineers' strike in 1873, the *Indianapolis Daily Sentinel* blamed the strike on the railroad "oligarchy," and the *Scranton Times,* among others, explained that public sympathy was clearly with the strikers.[31]

The 1873 strike itself, which happened in response to a wage cut, was part of a much broader action of engineers and firemen who struck simultaneously in a number of large midwestern and eastern cities. The ostensible target of the strike was the Pennsylvania Central Railroad, but because the line stretched through numerous prominent commercial centers, its results extended far beyond that corporation. The strike froze traffic for days, and the national press quickly ran nearly identical reports on the progress of the "Engineers' Strike" and its impact on national industry. For a brief moment, the transportation of goods that fed the national market was seriously impeded in major cities like Chicago, Pittsburgh, and Indianapolis. Some papers remarked on the "alarming aspect" the strike would assume if it became general. Reporters closely watched the "movements" of the strikers as they added soap to engine water and attacked replacement workers.

As the railroad strike of 1873 continued, newspapers ran editorials blaming everything from "labor fanatics" to the aristocratic railroad moguls to the lack of laws in place to contain working-class agitation. The media's mixed coverage of the strike reflected a deep ambivalence toward the railroads, possibly because of the obvious role the Iron Dragon had played in the industrializing process. Although the strike ended quickly, the combination of anti-railroad sentiment, wariness toward strikers, and fears of a much larger capital-labor conflict foreshadowed events to come. The most extreme voices of ominous portent came from the fringes, the pro-railroad corporate conservatives and the socialist radicals. The former referred to the strike as "flat rebellion, not simply against the companies . . . but against the law of the land," while the latter called approvingly for "Bread or Blood."[32] The center held, though the combination of this new kind of nationwide strike and the stark idiom of total war used to understand it provided the public with novel conceptual possibilities for class combat.

The Great Railroad Strike of 1877

America's largest and most dramatic labor uprising, the Great Railroad Strike of 1877 carried the language of the Civil War fully into the industrial world. The strike's causes had to do with the alienation of a large segment of American society, hostility to the railroads, and the ongoing and deeply unnerving effects of the prolonged depression that followed on the heels of the Panic of 1873. The immediate trigger for the walkout was a series of wage cuts, which inspired railroad firemen in West Virginia to desert and then seize their engines to prevent their use by others. While a major strike was not unexpected, its results were. Within weeks, hundreds of cities were battling raging flames, millions of dollars in damages had been inflicted, and more than one hundred lives were lost.

For contemporaries and future historians alike, the Great Railroad Strike would be viewed as a spectacular opening clash in a new era of class warfare, "as sudden as a thunder-burst from a clear sky."[33] If we look at public representations and discussions of the event, the self-evidency of this assessment is less apparent. Apprehensions of the strike were the result of older modes of analysis bent into a new shape, evidence of the impact of the Civil War and the ongoing effort to come to terms with a rapidly changing set of industrial relationships.

On one level, journalists and commentators framed the strike using language consistent with antebellum strike analyses. Aristocratic monopolists were hauled forth as having created an army of wage slaves to do their bidding. The American Revolution, long a cultural benchmark for assessing the causes and correctness of social upheavals, was recalled by some as a glorious precedent for current striker actions. Another longstanding theme of strike analysis, the fear of foreign intrusion, also found its way into newspaper reports. Protestant millennialism emerged as an apocalypse of Revelation-style proportions was shown to be under way. The most consistent framing device of antebellum strike coverage, the war metaphor, found triumphant use as scaffolding for the media's language.[34]

What made the Great Railroad Strike of 1877 unique was the apparent literalness of these evaluations. It was quickly seen as an *actual* battle between two massive armies, a true Armageddon cast down upon a sinning land, a catastrophic, foreign-style revolution. The myriad interpretations of the Great Strike were held together not by the political model of class assessment common in antebellum America but by a new one predicated on the language of absolute war. A new, antagonistic model of labor relations forced itself violently to the surface.

At the start of the strike, press coverage had much in common with that of previous large strikes. It was at first referred to as a mere "strike" or "riot" and was covered mainly on back pages. The *New York Times,* for instance, titled its July 17 article "Railroad Employes on a Strike. Foolish Firemen and Brakemen on the Baltimore and Ohio Cause of the Trouble." The *Chicago Tribune* had nothing on it in its July 17 issue and placed an article entitled "Riotous Strikers" on page five of the next day's paper. The *New Orleans Times* similarly had only a small article on page one entitled "The Season for Strikes" on July 18.[35]

Over the next few days, as the strike spread and clashes between strikers and militia ensued, coverage quickly cohered into a national narrative of destruction. By July 19, the *New York Times* had continuous front-page coverage of the "Railroad Men's War," and other major papers similarly reported in bold first-column headlines on the status of the "War on the Rails" or the "Strikers' War."[36] Other papers took a bit longer. The *Cincinnati Commercial Tribune*'s cycle of stories, for example, went from "Railway Matters" on July 18 and 19, to "Railway Racket" on the 20th, and finally to "Railway War" on the 21st.[37] Perhaps the *San Francisco Chronicle* best summarized the grip of the event on the nation, explaining in its July 23 edition that "There probably has been no time since the breaking out of the late unpleasantness in 1861 when news was so anxiously sought for and so eagerly gathered up when found as the present."[38]

In addition to time, geography was also a factor in initial differences in coverage. As the strike expanded outward from Martinsburg, proximity to the violence affected the tone and quantity of reportage. Papers in large eastern cities reported the strike as "civil war" and a "reign of terror" when the violence extended into their spaces or peripheries. When the strike hit Pittsburgh on July 19, the next day's *Pittsburgh Commercial and Gazette* printed a whole page (out of a total of four pages in the issue) on the "railroad war," whereas the event still occupied a minor space in most other major papers. When the roundhouse in Pittsburgh was occupied by retreating militiamen and scattered fires spread outward for three miles, headlines nationwide converged. Most major papers along the eastern seaboard and deep inland now reported on the strike with similar dispatches from the "seat of war" in Pittsburgh, adding speculations regarding the shocking suddenness of the event and the possible location of the next major battle. The *New Orleans Times* smugly explained how the South remained "solid" in the face of this Northern war.[39]

Despite clear differences in opinion and content, a remarkable convergence in coverage among the nation's most widely read news sources did take place.[40] The largest dailies, often using Associated Press dispatches (which used telegraph technology and a network of reporters to synchronize and distribute news stories throughout the country), printed closely aligned reports of war and riot. On July 27, for example, the *Chicago Tribune* led with a piece titled "Pitched Battles" about the "Steady War" between capital and labor. The *New York Times* breathed a sigh of relief with a war update: "Our dispatches record no extension of the strikes into new territory." In a *Times* editorial, an author reflected that it had become a "Drawn Battle," noting that there were no longer "any decisive advantages on either side." The *Cincinnati Commercial Gazette*'s July 27 edition suggested that the causes of the conflict lay in the debt and inflation that had led to the development of "two distinct classes" resulting from the "inception of our civil war." Whether explicitly connecting the strike to the Civil War, giving city-by-city coverage of the struggle, listing combat-related mortalities, or ruminating on the causes and effects of the strike, news outlets in effect coordinated their reports, framing the event in no uncertain terms—this was a battle of national scope.[41]

The continuous update of events, or "intelligence," throughout the two weeks of violence supplied readers from New York to California with a single narrative of catastrophic class conflict. Stark war imagery saturated every report, occasionally explicitly recalling comparison to the past war but more often simply using the style of war correspondence perfected a decade earlier and conferred ingenuously to this event. An "insurrection" was being carried out by "railway rebels"; casualty lists were placed next to maps of strike progress; images of conflict were presented not only depicting chaos but also showing two clearly arrayed sides facing off against one another, with ranks of soldiers firing or charging on disheveled lines of rioters. In one issue of *Frank Leslie's Illustrated Newspaper,* an image of the strike's "general," John Ammon (a minor leader who by all accounts controlled very little), is shown sitting "at his post" with his lieutenants, plotting the grand strategy of his soldiers.[42]

War guided the coverage at the most basic level of description. The following is a fairly typical front-page report of an incident of violence:

> Major Harry Gilmore, with a squad of men from company C, fifth regiment, formed a line at the head of the platform in front of the ticket-window. . . . At this a movement was made by the rioters from Barre street, but they retreated after ascending from the platform for a few yards. Anticipating the movement, the militia were ordered to load and make ready, which they did, but the retrograde movement on the part of the rioters prevented any extra measure at this time. The mob held possession of the depot yard, and occasionally fired shots and volleys of stones.

Making a train station into a battlefield gave this occurrence the sense of precision required to make surging masses capable of carrying out "retrograde movement" and leveling "volleys of stones" at soldiers, who in response tried desperately to gain possession of the field. The chaos of a mass of protesters swarming a railroad platform, undoubtedly less organized than this article suggests, had been made to conform to the logic of battle. The orderly descriptive structure delivered to the reader here and in numerous other strike articles imparted a familiar story—massed assault—and carried with it a set of images both frightening and understandable. This excerpt also reveals another device prevalent in the coverage. The side of law and order was described with specifics, while the strikers were described as a faceless mob. In this case, Major Gilmore and C Company of the Fifth Regiment represented order.[43]

War framing constantly reinforced the notion that the strikers were fully capable of concentrating, mobilizing, and rallying their numbers for the purposes of mass assault. Military and political leaders supported the dialogue. In a declaration published on July 20 from the War Department, Colonel Vincent of West Virginia announced that if the "insurgents" did not disband, he would enforce the president's will with arms.[44] As he and other military officers soon recognized, the insurgents did not disband so easily. They would gather threateningly in public spaces, form a "strong force" or be "reinforced" before firing a "fusillade of small arms" (or "volley" as another paper might

FIGURE 6 In this picture, Robert Ammon is depicted as a general directing his forces. In reality, Ammon had little control over the situation.

Source: *Frank Leslie's Illustrated Newspaper*, August 11, 1877.

put it) at the soldiers, who would then promptly—and legitimately—return fire. Reports from Washington, D.C., portrayed congressmen as willing to take martial measures long abhorred in the republic. As the *New Orleans Picayune* ominously reported, "There is a good deal of talk among friends of the Administration and in army coterie, of having hereafter a big standing army."[45] The impending and irrepressible conflict of capital and labor had become the reality it was foretold to be. Perhaps the most telling evidence of the transference of past onto present was the fact that in calling for military intervention during the strike, President Rutherford B. Hayes referred to the event as an insurrection rather than a work stoppage.[46] Here he exercised his powers as guardian against domestic revolt (as had Lincoln) rather than relying on the portion of the Constitution that dealt with restraint of trade, the traditional home of anti-strike legal maneuvering.

The sense of danger of course *was* very real, as was the blood spilled in struggles between protesters and the militia. The impact of the event, the seeming self-evidence of Civil War-style reporting, was grounded in the bewildering novelty of the 1877 strike. This strike was more violent than any in the past. It involved more workers, existed over more space, and drew in more direct observers than any work stoppage in the nation's history. Journalists themselves sometimes found their own lives in danger, giving readers a sense of the imminence of disaster. A reporter in Pittsburgh wrote at the end of one dispatch, "I must desert my post to get further west from the fire."[47]

The violence of the Great Railroad Strike was no fabrication of journalists' imaginations. Yet it was the very novelty of the strike that provided the opportunity for an interpretive scheme that did not necessarily address troubling aspects of the situation—namely, the seething popular discontent toward railroad intrusion into urban life, the unplanned nature of the riots, and the anti-capitalist rage evident in the search for locomotive and roundhouse targets.[48] News frames do not exist separate from "reality." They provide a narrative structure that directs public interpretation of an event in particular ways, and this can be effectively done only when linkages can be established between events on the ground and the experiences and mind-sets of the readers. Bloodshed did indeed occur. However, in employing a "total war" frame on the Great Railroad Strike, the media constructed a version of events that helped cast a specific, organized logic (the logic of war) to it, as evident in the John Ammon-as-"general" description. The fact of the matter was that no such organization was possible. The strike was largely unplanned and spontaneous. Unionists were probably a *minority* of the insurgents in most places.[49]

The mainstream press was not alone in its martial descriptive technique. The labor press, which experienced a renaissance after the war (with over 120 labor newspapers established from 1863 to 1873), also framed the event in war terms.[50] The *National Labor Tribune,* the leading labor periodical of the time, described the violence in Pennsylvania in a way not unlike the *New York Times* or the *New Orleans Times.* During the famous roundhouse battle of Pittsburgh, for example, the crowd had formed itself into "squads" after a round of "desultory firing" between themselves and the militia.[51] However, while the violence was condemned, ideological differences with the mainstream press were evident in the treatment of the causes of the strike, differences which the *National Labor Tribune* placed at the forefront of its coverage. Capital had initiated this war with wage reductions and oppressive tendencies, a process that had inspired the *Tribune* to note in an earlier issue that the "privations endured . . . are no less better than a civil war."[52] Now that a national strike was under way, the underlying causes needed to be brought to the surface to correct the mistaken belief that the strikers were the only party at fault. A headline in that issue asserted forebodingly, "History Repeats Itself."[53] The pro-labor *Irish World* similarly depicted the strike as a great battle, placing the blame firmly on the "rapacious Gold Ring" and "the Money Power."[54]

Past fears collided with the present in many ways in the summer of 1877. The riotous mixture of middle-class whites, youngsters, immigrant laborers, African American workers, and women involved in the strike proved very disconcerting to many in middle America who feared their older, simpler world was crashing down around them. For most mass-circulation periodicals, making the strike into a war was as much about reconstituting the dominant social order as it was about packaging the chaos for its audience. Naming the politicians, military officers, and locations helped give the side of law and order a recognizable face. Veterans were rallied once again to defend their country, and newspapers heaped praise on those who had fought on opposing sides in the prior war but came together in this one.

The strikers who were set against them, on the other hand, were depicted paradoxically both as an anonymous mass with neither mind nor motive *and* as an efficient army capable of executing strategy and field tactics. Reporting the conflict thus, reporters devalued the legitimacy of the strike and perhaps avoided alienating a section of their readership that might have played a role in the destruction. They also bolstered the war assessment by assigning agency to the opponents. In addition, naming participants in this manner bestowed humanity to one side while simultaneously dehumanizing the other, a tactic for justification that would be used liberally in media coverage of later wars.

Two "outside" groups in particular, nonwhites and women, were depicted as having key roles in bringing society to the brink of destruction. As shops were looted during the strike, numerous reports noted the presence of "Negroes" and women in the mobs. The presence of these groups reinforced the sense that this struggle was inverting the social order, pulling apart the fabric of ordered society as only serious civil conflict could. Coupled with war metaphors, reports of the involvement of women and nonwhites in the strike communicated a sense that the veneer of responsible republican society was being stripped away.

One reporter likened certain immigrant women in the riots to the "Amazons" of the French Revolution who led men to the barricades, noting, "The Irish women, who came and went with their clothes-baskets filled with hams, silks, and canned fruits, were not unlike their unsexed sisters of the Paris barricades." However, the writer made sure to note that the comparison did not mean that gender standards had been completely upended. This was still America, and it was simply "not possible to reproduce in our young Republic monsters such as these." Nevertheless, reports of women urging strikers on, standing up to militiamen, destroying property, and looting shops lent the coverage a tone of pandemonium and uncertainty. Similarly, reports of African Americans participating in the strike carried an alarming tone. One newspaper excluded blacks from "workingmen" altogether, suggesting that the presence of "negroes" was responsible for the "Rowdyism" involved in the strike.[55]

With the rise of the industrial war frame in 1877, antebellum themes of strike analysis took on new meanings. The popular antebellum theme of wage slavery provides a clear example. During the strike, editorials condemned the railroads for reducing their workers to the status of slaves, just as critics of wage employment had been doing for years, even to the point of arguing "slaveholders were models of mildness as compared with the average railway corporation in the treatment of its employes."[56] With a new kind of civil war afoot, such comparisons drew new relevance: could this current upheaval be a war of spontaneous liberation for wage slaves? Because the comparison of the corporation to the old slavocracy was so popular, the connection between the previous war of emancipation and a new one was both tempting and terrifying.

An article in the journal of the Brotherhood of Locomotive Firemen and Engineers expressed a popular sentiment: "the troubles have heretofore been confined to the employer and employe, and a fear has existed that the employe who has been treated more like a slave than a man, would assert his rights."[57] In St. Louis, a member of the socialist Workingmen's Party beseeched a crowd: "In the name of Lincoln, who freed 4,000,000 black slaves, labor must unite behind the Workingmen's Party to free 9,000,000 white slaves."[58]

The argument for a new American Revolution, one that would emancipate the wage slaves, was used mainly by radicals because the mainstream northern press seemed reluctant to promote revolution. This probably had to do with the fact that the Confederacy had used the Revolution to rationalize its own cause. Such revolutionary talk might have resurrected recent memories of the horrible cost of that conflict. Additionally, recent European revolutions (such as the Paris Commune of 1871) were quite bloody affairs. Nevertheless, the strike dangerously helped to strip away much of the reluctance of native workers to support socialist organizations previously deemed foreign and atheistic.[59] Employing a combination of Revolutionary equal rights language and more modern socialist concepts, radicals capitalized on discontents festering since the depression of the 1870s had begun. A moment had arrived in which ongoing industrial critiques could claim the power of popular mandate, and radicals were determined not to miss the opportunity. In a speech made by a young socialist named Albert Parsons on a day in which workers marched through the strike-ridden city streets carrying banners that read "Down With Wages [sic] Slavery," he concluded that voting for a nationalization of railroads would take away from men like Jay Gould

> the means by which they now enslave us. . . . It rests with you to say whether we shall allow the capitalists to go on exploiting us, or whether we shall organize ourselves. Will you organize? (Cries of "We Will.") Well, then enroll your names in the grand army of labor, and if the capitalist engages in warfare against our rights, then we shall resist him with all the means that God has given us. (Loud and prolonged applause.)[60]

A colonial could not have put it better.

Biblical reference, a common mode of prewar social conceptualization, similarly received renewed urgency. The Civil War had encouraged religious reflection and heightened millennial apprehensions, and during the Great Strike people assembled such perceptions into a powerful, if not novel, critique of contemporary industrial society.[61] As violence rolled across the Midwest and into the South, religious leaders came to the fore in condemning the chaos as God's punishment for the failure of his flock to "look after the religious condition of the lower classes." It could also be viewed as divine punishment exacted on railroad companies for forcing workers to break the Sabbath.[62] Despite this, mainstream religious organs emphasized a conservative view of things, to the point of the Christian *Independent* advocating "bullets and bayonets, canister and grape" to be used on strikers.[63] Beyond the church, a broader millennial apprehension was evident throughout the coverage, particularly in editorials. In the *Chicago Tribune,* for example, one editorialist harangued an "omnipotent" railroad corporation and explained that it could not continue to "pursue systematic injustice and oppression without experiencing a day of reckoning."[64]

Anxiety over foreign influences in American life, a bugbear haunting strike coverage throughout the nineteenth century, took on a new and terrifying life during the Great Railroad Strike. The Paris Commune of 1871, an event initially framed in civil war language by American newspapers, became one of the most common points of reference in 1877. Just as papers like the *Niles' Weekly Register* had blamed the origins of the 1835 Philadelphia general strike on foreign agitators, the railroad strike was easily blamed on European socialists.[65] The difference now was that the foreign threat included recent precedent for bloody social revolution (a term used by more than one contemporary to describe the strike) and a fresh lexicon of rebellion. The current war called for the brutal suppression of the alien "unwashed" mob. For a few extremists, this meant a return to a paternalistic monarchy. For many more it meant the funding of a strong standing army to put down this and future uprisings. The *New York Sun* echoed this reactionary refrain by suggesting a "diet of lead for the hungry strikers."[66] Perhaps the most disturbing call for order came from the treasurer of the Gatling Gun Company, who wrote to Governor Garrett of Pennsylvania after the strike that "one Gatling, with a full supply of ammunition, can clear a street or track, and keep it clear."[67] This horrifying solution took the vitriol to the level of specifics.

By the second and final week of the strike, the press largely united to present a tale of two armies. On one side, a nameless mob made up of foreign rabble, youth, and tramps, occasionally mixed with "Negroes" committing silly thefts of hams or alcohol, was presented as attempting to tear down society.[68] Opposing them stood the side of law and order, filled out by war veterans, stolid governors, the police, and the militia. The triumph of the latter side was nothing less than testament to the nation's "love of the law." The causes of the battle were less clear. Something of a cottage industry in the editorial pages, speculations on the causes of the strike were mostly organized around the mixed premise of a critical view of railroad monopolists and a critical view of the trades unions.

After only a month, there were so many different explanations for the strike that the *Galaxy* complained, "no two [editorials] agree as to the cause of the difficulty."[69] Typically major papers varied from blaming imported radicals from Europe (often relating the event to the Paris Commune of 1871) to the Civil War itself, which gave rise to the development of "two distinct classes, the . . . bondholding class, and the overwhelming larger class . . . who have to provide the means for satisfying the claims of the wealthy minority."[70] The flock of "instant histories" that appeared after the strike reinforced the war narrative. Books authored by J. A. Dacus and famed detective Allan Pinkerton (the latter possibly ghost-written) gave readers vivid accounts of strike battles and military defense, complete with dramatic pictures of armed combat.[71] The public's continued fascination with the strike was evident in the coverage of other strike "wars" in mining regions, in the republishing of strike coverage in collector's editions sold directly from newspaper offices, in a book of stereograph photos of the strike entitled *The Railroad War,* and most outlandishly, in advertisements boldly announcing things like "FIVE STRIKING SPECIALTIES."[72]

A Terrible New Vision

After the Civil War, and especially after 1877, Americans read of labor conflicts in martial terms. Especially during massive strikes, reporters and popular labor commentators would position capital and labor as opposing armies facing one another across a national battlefield. The newly national scale of industrial relations bestowed legitimacy to the popular assumption that capital and labor had come to the field to fight for dominance, and with the Great Railroad Strike of 1877, the struggle took center stage. Without a trace of irony, later historians would continue to write of the Great Railroad Strike as a "rebellion" without commenting on the climate of thought at the time.[73]

A rebellion without the moral weight of patriotic righteousness, the Great Railroad Strike became frozen in historical memory as a wake-up call. A strong sense that the strike had awakened a sleeping nation to the realities of a dangerous new industrial landscape prevailed in the media in the months that followed.[74] Whereas before, Americans had been complacent, even boastful of their country's growing wealth and stature, there was now an awareness of a debt to be paid for unchecked economic growth. *The Nation* wrote that the "faith that outside the area of slave-soil the United States had . . . solved the problem of labor and capital to live together in political harmony" had been proven erroneous. Ignorance and hubris prevented the enlightened classes from seeing the "profound changes . . . which have during the last thirty years been wrought in the composition and character of the population."[75]

The *New York Times* was even more explicit: "Whatever else the disturbances have done, at least they have opened the eyes of the American people to the order of things which has grown up among them so gradually as to be unobserved."[76] J. A. Dacus's widely read history of the Great Strike, published immediately after the event, summarized this sentiment on the opening page: "An epoch in the history of the nation is here marked."[77]

The new epoch was that of industrial war, symbolized by massive corporations and the subterranean rumblings of working-class discontent.[78] While the kind of reasoning that inspired this analysis required that the strikes and economic crises of the previous years be conveniently forgotten, it captured popular anxieties in a way that only a massive national conflict could. Just like the Civil War, the Great Railroad Strike sent Americans reeling from its shocking and unprescribed suddenness. Removing the moral component of the Civil War, Americans applied familiar words of national upheaval to grasp the ephemeral terror of the Great Strike, without imposing any of the honor that the former event's memory allowed.

In the "instant histories" published following the strike, the Civil War invariably served as a starting point of comparison. Like that war, the Great Strike was shown to be an event of national calamity that revealed America's true grit. Descriptions of specific locations of worker unrest supplied battle chapters in the larger story of the strike. Despite this style, overt comparisons to the Civil War typically stopped after a few pages. The past war was noted, but only as an initial point of reference—the internal dynamic of *this* story was essentially that of a cautionary tale rather than a triumphal one. The world as it had been known would be different now.

Evidence of the new world could be seen in the push to erect armories in the hearts of major metropolises. In New York City, a drive to build a new armory for the Seventh Regiment had completely stalled before the strike, after only $80,000 had been raised. In the wake of the strike, money began pouring in, as newspapers such as the *New York Evening Mail* exhorted readers to financially express their "gratitude" to their "brave defenders." By late 1878 the regiment had raised over $200,000, with more on the way via special state legislation. By the time of the new armory's completion in 1880, the regiment had received over $589,000, or double what had been raised for the Statue of Liberty at the time.[79] The public message of this structure, and the many others like it rising in the wake of the strike, was clear: vigilance would be permanently required.

Caution provided the basis for a new model of labor relations, in which addressing the elements responsible for the recent industrial battle would be top priority. The antebellum mode of politically framed class analysis which conceptualized the world as divided between producers and parasites was found wanting in substance and method. A new analytical framework was needed to fully grasp a new world defined by a real and ongoing conflict of industrial organizations. The economists who supplied this framework found historical European models to be most applicable. The present climate of national unrest had inspired a wave of scholarly inquiries into the nature of social change and of the historical progress of capitalism, and this opened the vista to new ways of looking at things. Scholars such as pioneering sociologist (and war veteran) Lester Frank Ward found that the "law of force" governed human civilizations. Labor economist Richard T. Ely received much attention for his call for a "proclamation of emancipation" from classical economics.[80]

The language of total war suffused early works of labor studies, helping to impart a frightening shape on the project of labor scholars in the decades afterward. Such academics recognized that organized battle had become the defining character of industrial affairs, and sought to find peaceful solutions. Founders like Richard T. Ely and Henry Carter Adams searched for ways of restoring the dream of harmony via cooperation and federal intervention. Others, such as economist John Bates Clark, attempted to reformulate the theory of profit to avoid "drifting toward industrial war for lack of mental analysis."[81] Despite such efforts, the problem worsened, as strikes and violent clashes persisted with unnerving regularity. All this enforced the growing belief that the Great Railroad Strike was not a defining battle, but rather a horrific portent of things to come.

3

The March of Organized Forces

Framing the Industrial War, 1880-1894

In the decades that followed the Great Strike of 1877, the master frame of total war guided much of strike reportage. By the mid-1880s the public read daily how workers formed "ranks" and took to the "field" during work stoppages. Strikes became "movements" in an ever- advancing labor front. This front was never static; in more prosperous times industrial war coverage receded from the top headlines, only to reemerge during periods of uncertainty. Despite these ebbs and flows, the idea of industrial war remained a constant worry for Americans through the end of the nineteenth century. As corporations and unions expanded and seemed to entrench themselves in preparation for greater conflicts to come, writers and speechmakers employed martial rhetoric to provide compelling narratives regarding the state of society.

In this chapter I will explore some of the ways in which labor confrontations came to be popularly depicted as organized combat in the final decades of the nineteenth century. Following a discussion of the pervasiveness of war language in conceptualizations of labor conflict, I will look at how groups representing capital and labor became armies locked in battle. Several key national strikes will then be examined, in particular the Great Southwest Strike of 1886 and the Pullman Strike of 1894. The first event is significant in that it presented the public with a spectacularly violent conflict between well-organized and clearly identifiable forces of railroad workers and owners. The second, a national strike of even greater proportions, lent credence to the belief that the industrial war was escalating beyond control.

The Blossoming of Industrial War Language

In the 1880s, the media's ubiquitous use of war language provided the reading public with numerous frightening accounts of labor unrest. "Capital and Labor" columns, now regular segments in major papers, included information regarding various forms of working-class riot and offered dramatic descriptions of strike activity along with authoritative snippets from the mouths and pens of industrialists, union leaders, and assorted analysts. A close focus on the damage done (fiscal and physical), pithy quotes from belligerent owners and strikers, and geographic, battlefield-style coverage of the largest strikes gave credence to the stark assessment made in the journal *Unitarian Review* in 1887 that "Strikes are simply a form of warfare."[1]

An issue of the *New York Times* during the massive Great Southwest Strike of 1886 (to be discussed in depth below) illustrates this martial format. In an article entitled "Losses by the Strike," several of the regions affected by a massive Knights of Labor–led strike are described. The writer pays close attention to the costs wrought by the walkout and the various activities of the "army of strikers." The organized nature of both the union and the manufacturing interests takes special precedence in the piece, which is written in a succinct, dispatch style. The Knights of Labor represent labor, and capital finds representation in a manufacturer's organization. Although the article does not include reference to any identifiable union leadership, a short piece on another page refers to Terence Powderly as the acknowledged leader of the Knights. Beneath the ostensibly objective tone of the article there lurks a narrative of strike as battle. In this case, the Knights clearly supply labor's "army." While it is less clear who capital's troops are, the journalist stresses the leadership element of both sides. The coherency of the story pivots on accounting for the participants in an organized, militaristic fashion.

A survey of other labor-related articles in the *New York Times* during this decade suggests that the "Losses" format was quite standard, even in regard to concurrent but unrelated strikes. In 1882, for example, an article entitled "The Labor Agitation" described unrelated strikes in Massachusetts, Cleveland, Boston, Cincinnati, and upstate New York collectively as "Working Men's Movements." "Movements," used in this case as a verb rather than a noun, implied not social organizations but rather troop maneuverings, reflecting a style borrowed directly from Civil War coverage and ever-present in the years since 1865. Numerous editorials describing unions as entities bent on striking reinforced comparisons to armies, which also had, essentially, one purpose—combat.[2]

Importantly, not everyone embraced the idea of class war. Many educated people sought to demonstrate its illusory nature. In an 1893 article on strikes in the *American Journal of Politics,* a legal scholar explained that although "We hear much about war between capital and labor," such talk is in fact a "mis-use of language." In reality, the two are "parts of one whole," much like the "brain" and the "heart." By anxiously recapitulating the harmony of interests, the author tipped his hand to the current state of popular concern. While the war metaphor popularly used did not reflect reality, the writer found himself defending his position using another metaphor—the body. This model also had deep roots in socio-economic analysis, dating back to the dawn of the Enlightenment. Unfortunately, war metaphor at this point overshadowed it.[3]

The popularity of the war frame would be reinforced by redundancy. The growth of the Associated Press, the close ties among the major editors in cities like New York, and the consolidation of the major media outlets meant that the reading public would be exposed to the same or closely similar accounts of a single event. In the 1870s and 1880s, shared telegraph wires began send-ing identical Associated Press reports to New York, Washington, and Chicago. The same descriptions of strike violence in Pittsburgh would be read as far off as Los Angeles, Denver, and Philadelphia within a very short span of time. This cooperative effort, which led to a borrowing of coverage of major events among the regional news media for the sake of efficiency (in addition to the flourishing of telegraph technology), permitted industrial conflicts to quickly become singular, nationwide events.[4] Unified national news coverage allowed such events to become the concern of all.

Newspaper content also reflected a widening readership, one less con-cerned with political matters than with intimate stories of crime, social affairs, and unusual happenings.[5] The rise of "new journalism," a movement characterized by vivid "sensationalistic" coverage, illustrations, fiery edito-rials, and increased advertising helped the media provide the public with exciting industrial war stories. Iconoclastic and enterprising editors like Joseph Pulitzer brought their papers to new heights of popularity by focusing less on politics and more on the grittiness of urban life, uncovering for their audience the vice and turmoil at the root of the new class discord. Pulitzer was unapologetic, declaring that complaints about his newspaper's "low moral tone" were "very unjust." His paper did not "manufacture" the sordid events of the day, "it just tells them as they occur."[6] Pulitzer purchased the *New York World* in 1883, and the paper soon had a great following. In 1885 he called for the ordinary folks who read his paper to each contribute pennies for the pedestal for the Statue of Liberty, and he raised $100,000 in just five months. As Michael Schudson notes, "this enabled the *World* to picture itself as the champion of the working people, to criticize the 'luxurious classes,' and to promote simultaneously the city of New York, the mass of ordinary citizens, and, of course, the New York *World.*"[7] Pulitzer's innovations had met with an eager audience, and between 1883 and 1887 his paper shattered every publishing record.[8]

Other newspapers quickly learned to follow his lead, lest they be left behind. A young Harvard graduate and beneficiary of his father's mining fortune named William Randolph Hearst watched Pulitzer's rise with envy, and set out to build his own empire of print. After assuming editorship of his father's *San Francisco Examiner* in 1887, Hearst turned it into a highly profitable, widely circulated outlet for sensationalistic, often crusading stories. He then moved to Pulitzer's turf in New York City with the purchase of the *Morning Journal* (along with the hiring of many of Pulitzer's own staff). The ensuing battle saw newspaper prices dive and circulation numbers rise.[9]

Other factors also contributed to rising newspaper readership. As public school attendance rose, illiteracy declined by 50 percent over the course of the final third of the nineteenth century (down to about 10 percent of the population in 1900). For millions, newspapers provided a daily bread of accessible information. In New York City (albeit the biggest producer of newspapers in America) in the year 1889, the ratio of people to morning newspapers was 2.5. By 1899 it was down to 2.0.[10] Long a nation of readers, the United States now devoured the news at an unprecedented rate. Access to newspapers continuously improved, beginning with the rise of "newsboys" and improvements in the postal system earlier in the century. By the late 1800s, papers were cheap, widely available, and read nearly everywhere. Newsboys prowled the streets for customers, taverns set out copies for their patrons, and in some cases, laborers read papers aloud while their cohort worked.[11]

Vivid war framing is evident throughout all of the industrial coverage I have examined in many of the nation's leading papers and journals. Regardless of the news source—be it the sensationalist *New York World,* the conservative *New York Herald,* or the reformist *Puck,* striking workers would typically be portrayed in "ranks" as active participants in union "armies." They might be described as occupying "posts," "taking the field," or leading "skirmishes" against shop equipment and replacement labor. During a national telegraphers' strike in 1883, for example, newspapers regularly reported on the union's effort to "capture" telegraph offices and rout opposing company "officers."[12] While conservative newspapers like the *Chicago Tribune* might be more inclined to characterize labor as the villain in industrial battles than would "worker friendly" papers like Pulitzer's *St. Louis Post-Dispatch,* there were far fewer differences in terms of the basic, non-editorial coverage of strikes throughout the mass media.

During the largest strikes, union leaders found themselves cast in the role of generals. Beginning with the Great Southwest Strike of 1886, strike leadership came to be held responsible for all strike-related violence. As strikers became troops, leaders would be depicted as having control and authority over them. When the Knights sabotaged a train in Texas, the *Waco Daily Examiner* likened the organization's leader to "a mighty general" sending his troops out "in times of war."[13] In reality, such control would have been quite impossible, given the decentralized nature of the Knights' organization. A fiction created by the logic of war language, "generalship" fitted better to the story of industrial battle than to the reality of it.

"Generalship" was not the only loose fit. Labor and capital, each occupying a distinct position in the battle, did not always receive coherent, accurate representation during strikes. Journalists would often describe the battle without delineating clearly the opponents involved. Strikers might be first shown to have specific agendas, such as preventing replacement laborers from crossing their ranks, and then be collapsed into the "mindless mob" when violence broke out. Sometimes, labor's interests would be included with "crowd" activities even when no clear correlation existed between the two. Similarly, periodicals would often remark on "capital's" interests without differentiating between small and large businesses, financial institutions, or any other concrete form of combination. The fact that strikers had decided to wage battle typically meant that their target would be portrayed as a representative of capital. In editorial pages and in journals, it remained both expedient and consistent with the dominant trope of war to fit labor militancy and management retaliation into a battle framework, even if it did not fit the reality. Alternative explanations were not necessary.

The impact of a national strike in a core industry was no fiction, however. Part of the magnitude of national strike-battles in the 1880s had to do with the increasing interconnectedness of industry and communication. As one newspaper remarked at the onset of the nationwide 1883 telegraphers' strike, "Strikes used to be local. But now the spread of the means of transport and communication is giving a continental expansion as well to the ills as to the blessings of civilization."[14] Depicting these "ills" as battles made sense because their results could be so devastating to the social order. It is important to recognize the interrelatedness of discourse and reality here. While war language flourished as a result of the Civil War experience, it continued to apply because labor relations so often seemed to fit the frame.

While one newspaper might accuse the employer of inaugurating the fight and another pin the blame on the workers during a strike, the commonly used lexicon of combat provided daily readers with a vivid sense of battle. Specific newspapers did often take sides, as was most evident in the editorial sections, but no paper, apparently, could afford to ignore strikes or to report them as anything less than skirmishes in the capital-labor war. Never before had the reading public been so large or so united by the market.[15]

The emergence of a broadly united readership would be significant. Reformers, unionists, and editorialists could appeal to the "public" without defining the group in any clear way. Political association, ethnicity, and gender became invisible in the "public appeal," despite the implied white middle-class identity of most readers. As the following analysis of the Great Southwest Strike of 1886 suggests, the public was becoming a significant source of appeal for advocates of reform who required a popular mandate to implement their proposals. Just as advertisers increasingly appealed to a generalized definition of "the masses" to maximize sales, journalists and activists looked beyond party and class to garner approval.

An investigation of labor-related articles in popular middle-class journals in the 1880s shows how national magazines appropriated the newspapers' war style. Surveying a range of pieces of the industrial scene, it is apparent that *strike* and *war* had become equivalent terms, and that journal opinion pieces across the ideological spectrum stayed firmly within the rubric of war when suggesting remedies and offering judgments.[16] The reformist *Unitarian Review,* for example, referred to strikes as "rumblings of vast pent-up forces" in one of a long series of articles portraying the industrial world as a battleground. In an essay on labor "agitators," *The Chautauquan,* a journal targeting the rising middle class and its craving for self-education, explained that the nation had found itself in the midst of a "pending contest" in which ongoing strikes threatened, among other things, non-unionized labor. While George E. McNeill, writing for the pro-labor *Arena,* portrayed unions positively as "recruiting centers in the war of humanity," most commentators writing for mainstream journals agreed with *The Chautauquan* in looking upon strikes as assaults on the public welfare.[17] Typically, labor conflicts created fear for social peace in the hearts of the middle-class editors of popular periodicals.

An article in the middle-class *Andover Review* vocalized the deeper conflict lurking suggestively in the background of much strike analysis. The writer warned that capital and labor were "drawing off into separate camps, and organizing their forces for active hostilities." In perhaps the most striking example of this sort of analysis, minister Lyman Abbott reflected on the state of industrial affairs mid-decade in the popular journal *The Century.* Arguing from the perspectives of both author and observer, Abbott noted that "Every morning paper brings us the report of some strike or lockout, which is like the shot of a single picket along the line."[18] This comment represented no fanciful interpretation of events; it made sense in light of a standard reading of the daily press.

Two Sides Arrayed

The pertinence of labor-related war language spoke to the strongly held belief in a divided society. Created much earlier and injected with new life in the aftermath of the Civil War, a bifurcated social model let observers divide the polity into two antagonistic groups. Although numerous conceptual models existed, and distinct classes of "artisan," "farmer," "laborer," and so on filled the writings of scholarly and layman texts alike, bisecting society provided newspaper editors and commentators with an especially powerful rhetorical tool. From the "republicans" versus the "monarchists" in Jeffersonian diatribes to the division of "haves" and "have-nots" in the Jacksonian period, presenting two inherently conflicting groups imbued moral arguments with a Manichean finality.[19]

The post–Civil War division of capital and labor rested on a more uncertain notion, one that implied that something in the very nature of the economy might be at fault. According to one 1881 article in a popular middle-class journal, it was "rapidly becoming a conviction that the disorders and wrongs of civilization are not the mere accidents of our social system, but its legitimate and inevitable results."[20] For many, "aristocratic" corporations had created an entirely new social climate, one that bred class conflict and subverted democracy.[21]

The sense that something had gone awry, however, needs to be placed in a longer context of social division. "Industrial war," a phrase used in many editorials regarding the state of labor affairs, appeared self-evident largely because it represented an updated, if greatly intensified, version of an older model.[22] During the antebellum period, as noted previously, the idea of social division pervaded much of laborite rhetoric. The Civil War did not create a new climate of war so much as it inspired a vision of social antagonism of unprecedented magnitude. Building on concrete changes in workplace organization and on the evidence of violent social upheaval, the "industrial war" model seemed so convincing because the world of the present appeared to be in such stark contrast with the antebellum world of wistful rural innocence.[23]

Within the new context, strikes became the flashpoints at which the social partition expressed itself. Like battles in a larger conflict, each strike connected to the grander narrative of industrial war via certain standard thematic cues. For example, several individual strikes from around the country might be lumped together under a single heading. The organization of strikers themselves, decentralized and uncoordinated as they often were in reality, typically took on the aspect of militaristic precision. Newspaper accounts could portray an identifiable central leadership coordinating the "movements" of the strikers with martial uniformity. Following the 1877 railroad strike precedent, the cost of major strikes would be tallied on "casualty" lists that recorded lives taken, wages lost, and damages incurred.

The media did not act alone in stimulating war apprehensions; unions played a role in contributing to the growing sense that class conflict constituted the new industrial reality. Labor activists employed battle descriptions in their explanations of the industrial climate, as evident in the public discourse of two of the most significant labor organizations of the 1880s, the Knights of Labor and the Federation of Trade and Labor Unions. Each counted on a divided society to inspire loyalty and action among their followings. Each helped to supply middle-class participants in the ongoing "labor question" debate with concrete evidence that unions provided foot soldiers for the industrial war.

The Federation of Trade and Labor Unions was an organization whose rhetoric embodied the belief in a society divided by class. Formed in 1881, the Federation grew to become the American Federation of Labor, the most enduring labor organization in American history. Charging its official writings and speeches with a stark language of class division, the Federation's leadership openly embraced strikes and consistently reiterated a principle of a two-sided social struggle. In its 1881 preamble, the organization declared that "a struggle is going on in the nations of the civilized world between the oppressors and the oppressed of all countries, a struggle between capital and labor." For some, the Federation's position on strikes and class war was far too extreme. One newspaper editorialized that the preamble "breathes the spirit of conflict rather than pacification."[24]

The Knights of Labor, a far more mainstream labor organization in the 1880s, was less stark than the Federation of Trade and Labor Unions. This organization, the largest in America at the time, conceded the existence of a divided society but argued that the social division was reversible. Its appeal and career reveals much about the ways in which ordinary Americans came to terms with the new climate of hostile industrial relations. Formed secretly in 1869, it expanded rapidly following the Great Railroad Strike of 1877, growing to extraordinary size with close to 1 million members by 1886. Like labor organizations in the antebellum period, the Knights argued in its national publication *Journal of United Labor* that society was divided between producers and parasites. They invited all "useful" producers, a category broad enough to include everyone except bankers, liquor dealers, industrial monopolists, and lawyers, to join them.

The main difference between the Knights and antebellum labor organizations, aside from its broad "industrial" as opposed to narrow "craft" base, was its overtly martial quality.[25] The Knights of Labor extolled the values of military-style honor, waging an ongoing battle with the corporate/capitalist dragon imperiling the land.[26] Its material culture, iconography, literature, and poetry all tapped into a warlike sentiment of manly resistance. In initiation rituals, Knights swore to "defend [labor] from degradation."[27] An excerpt from the Knights' most popular song illustrates the point:

Storm the fort, ye Knights of Labor
Battle for your cause:
Equal rights for every neighbor
Down with tyrant laws.[28]

The Knights capitalized on the belief in a society rent by social war. As proclaimed in its manifesto, there existed an "inevitable and irresistible conflict between the wage system of labor and the republican system of government."[29] The organization situated itself on the side of moral righteousness in a battle between those who produced with honor and those who robbed behind the mask of distant corporations. The Knights relied on social pressure exercised by the mass of its membership to advance its constituents' interests. Unfortunately, war metaphor did not provide the organization with a coherent plan of attack. Seeing labor soldiers and capitalist predators at war was one thing; designing a workable battle strategy was something else entirely. The ambivalence of the Knights toward strikes suggests that the possibility of escalating the industrial war did not appeal to them. Making their stand in the moral realm rather than the more frightening one of strikes, the Knights revealed the limits of relying on war rhetoric to inspire action.

Contrary to the fiery language of the Federation of Trade and Labor Union's preamble, the Knights declared that peaceful arbitration should be the mechanism for resolving industrial disputes. In part because it relied on the popular idiom of war without extending the logic of combat through to coercive action, the Knights garnered a broad base of support without an accompanying centralization of power. The organization counted on its moral and numerical strength in fostering community support for its activities, engaging capital as "men of honor" at the arbitration table. The leader of the Knights, Terence Powderly, often boasted that he had never personally inaugurated a strike. Even at the local level, efforts to ban strike funds revealed a keen distaste for open conflict with capital.[30] Yet in practice, strikes *made* the KOL. One of the first actions taken by the Knights at their inception was to create a national strike fund. Following an initial membership surge in the wake of the 1877 railroad strike, the number of recruits skyrocketed as strike rates increased, regardless of their outcomes.[31]

Labor historians typically play up the ideological differences between the Knights of Labor and the Federation of Trade and Labor Unions. Indeed, there is much evidence demonstrating clear ideological dissimilarities between the two groups. The Federation's leadership had been influenced by Karl Marx, as is clearly evident in its talk of worldwide class struggle. The incendiary character of its speeches, texts, and actions all suggest that historical materialism reigned as the organization's earliest articulated philosophy.[32] However, the broad working-class appeal of both the Knights and the Federation reveals similarity as well, in much the same way that ideologically diverse periodicals could all tap into the same rhetorical reservoir of combat to sell their product to a vast audience.

Both the Knights and the Federation relied on the belief in a society divided against itself. They both positioned themselves as locked in an industrial struggle, fighting valiantly for the side of labor. The media and the politicians had long capitalized on and contributed to the language of class war; it is of little doubt that the literate mainstream of union rank-and-file membership also absorbed this popular discourse. If divided on the ultimate nature of the struggle—for the Knights leadership it was a reversible one; for the Federation, it was evidence of a permanent class conflict—both groups could agree that strikes were battles, that industrialization entailed a war of clashing forces, and that conflict, not harmony, embodied the current state of industrial affairs. Whether or not war constituted an anomaly to be remedied or an inevitability to be worked around depended on the individual. Much as in the Civil War–era "irrepressible conflict" debates, participants in the industrial war dialogue might disagree over the causes, but not the essential character, of the situation.

Often with a high level of enthusiasm, members of both the Knights and the Federation participated in the dramatic labor contests of the decade. As David Montgomery has noted, laborers made great strides in terms of organization and strategy in the 1880s. Unions increasingly took the offensive, calling more strikes than ever before in efforts to compel recognition from owners.[33] They carefully applied resources to aid strikers, timed strikes to cause the most damage to target industries, increased the use of the sympathy strike and the "rolling strike" (in which a series of strikes keeps pressure on the industry while minimizing individual striker financial loss), and coordinated massive boycotts.

Worker militancy often came as a reaction to actions taken by employers to reduce labor costs. Employer maneuvers, such as the hated "drive" method of supervisor-controlled work acceleration, along with the development of technology to reduce dependence on skilled craft workers, met with shop floor militancy and intensive organizational campaigns.[34] Control efforts by the unions meant keeping strict tabs on the amount of work expected to be done, coupled with an expansive vocabulary of pejoratives to keep over-eager workers in line.[35] As a result of this climate of militancy and increasing workplace hostility, the 1880s saw a marked increase not only in the number of total strikes but also in the number of strikes ordered by unions and rooted in the enforcement of union rules and union recognition.

In the midst of these hostilities, one group actively worked for peace. Labor economists such as Charles Adams, Richard Ely, and Carroll Wright, some of whom who had seen combat during the Civil War, endeavored to steer America away from the precipice of class war by supplying valuable information and appropriate guidance. In their desperate efforts to demonstrate

TABLE 1

Number of Strikes and Percentage of Strikes Ordered by Unions, 1881–1889

Year	Number of strikes	Percentage of strikes ordered by unions
1881	471	47.3
1882	454	48.5
1883	478	56.7
1884	443	54.2
1885	645	55.3
1886	1,432	53.3
1887	1,436	66.3
1888	906	68.1
1889	1,075	67.3

Sources: Data taken from U.S. Commissioner of Labor, Twenty-first Annual Report (Washington, D.C.: Government Printing Office, 1906) and Florence Peterson, Strikes in the United States, 1880–1936 (Washington, D.C.: Department of Labor Bulletin no. 651, 1938), 32, 33. Compiled by David Montgomery and published in his article "Strikes in Nineteenth-Century America," Social Science Quarterly 4 (February 1980): 92.

the veracity of the "harmony of interests" dictum, such men reflected the powerful influence of war metaphor on American political economy.[36]

The (Dashed) Hopes of Political Economists

When economist John Bates Clark explained in the journal New Englander in 1879, "If it be incendiary to proclaim only an irrepressible conflict between capital and labor, it is imbecile to reiterate that there is no possible ground of conflict between them," he summed up the recognition of endemic industrial strife evident in most labor-related scholarship of his time.[37] Clark and other social scientists strove to make sense of the industrial war. They charged their self-appointed peace mission with diplomatic rhetoric and a strong desire to remedy the current socio-economic ills that plagued the nation. Outside of the constraints of vested interest, they viewed (in the words of labor economist Henry Carter Adams in 1891) the "movements of society from a height," finding the root causes of the industrial war and calculating solutions that best suited the problem.[38] Analyzing railroad profits, wage levels, and commodity prices, these academics supported their earliest public appeals for peace and understanding with a mountain of data. They provided detailed accounts of labor's ongoing battles with organized capital and offered suggestions that typically involved some form of legal action, such as fixing wages and legitimizing unions.[39]

In one of the first attempts to construct an American labor history, Richard Ely sought to reconfigure social relations in such a way as to mediate the worst possibilities of escalating labor conflict and to recapture the ideal of social harmony. In his 1886 book *The Labor Movement in America,* he advocated a political economy that supported the cause of organized labor and worked toward eliminating the divisive wages system. He recognized at the start that the labor movement was engaged in a great battle for its future, it essentially being a "systematic, organized struggle of the masses." In the first chapter, aptly titled "Survey of the Field," Ely explained that "no previous age was more eventful in the life of economic and industrial society than that in which we are now living." The present situation saw the labor movement as a "force pushing on" for a more harmonious civilization, one in which the struggle against capitalists would eventually be replaced by shared ownership. Ely's prescribed path to the harmony of interests recognized conflict as the current state of affairs. Strikes, being efforts by workingmen's organizations to withdraw labor until they received just remuneration, would actually be necessary in ultimately attaining this harmony because they provided a counterweight to capitalist depredations.[40] The irony of peace via battle would not be lost on him for long.

Henry Carter Adams, Ely's contemporary and successor as the preeminent American labor economist, similarly recognized the conflict at the core of contemporary society. He believed that the labor movement was neither good nor evil, but instead the inevitable product of industrial capitalism. By the standards he set, responsible labor would be worth integrating into a durable system of industrial relations. A cofounder of the pro-regulation American Economic Association, Adams believed in limited federal intervention, when necessary, on both the capital and the labor sides of the conflict. He hoped to build a modern system of industrial relations on a truce between currently opposed interests. In an important address, Adams asked that the current "fearful" struggle—which was due to labor's loss of influence in the workplace—be solved with such a new "social philosophy."[41]

Despite their efforts, men like Ely and Adams saw their hopes for peace consistently dashed by violent strikes. Following a massive cycle of strikes in the mid-1880s known as the Great Upheaval, Ely despaired that "[unions] are as a rule based on strife. They aim to prepare their members for industrial war. Now we must hope for peace."[42] He rescinded his support for strikes by the end of the 1880s. John Bates Clark's 1886 treatise *The Philosophy of Wealth* painted a similarly frightening picture:

A contest is here in process on a scale of magnitude impossible in earlier times, a battle in which organized classes act as units on the respective sides. The solidarity of labor on the one hand, and of capital on the other, is the great economic fact of the present day; and this growing solidarity is carrying us rapidly towards a condition in which all the laborers in a particular trade and all the capitalists in that trade, acting, in each case, as one man, will engage in a blind struggle which, without arbitration, can only be decided by the crudest force and endurance. The strained relations of the parties in the contest, the surliness and desperation, the threatenings of literal war, are already a phenomenon of it.[43]

Whether or not "strife" or "battle" would be a permanent part of industrial society or merely a phase of growth, a discussion that took a central place in many economic works, the tone of analysis echoed Civil War–era debates regarding the "irrepressible" nature of that conflict. This is not to say that labor economists in the 1880s merely reread a script written during the Civil War; rather, they adapted it. A close look at the most violent strike of the 1880s, the Great Southwest Strike of 1886, offers a glimpse into the discourse of class war that frustrated the peace efforts of the best academics.

The Armies of Rail Commence Battle:
The Great Southwest Strike of 1886

The period 1885–1887, also known as the Great Upheaval, represents the nineteenth-century high-water mark for strikes and social unrest. Farmer movements, anarchist threats, and unprecedented union militancy all contributed to a growing sense that the industrial war had come to a climax.[44] A centerpiece of the Upheaval, the Great Southwest Strike of 1886 presented the public with a spectacular battle between large and apparently well-disciplined units of labor and capital. It situated the Knights of Labor, which according to much of the press embodied the working-class army, against a massive rail system controlled by Jay Gould. The strike, which began in March 1886, resulted in a struggle that some believed would culminate in the "final adjudication of the relative position which labor and capital are to occupy in this country."[45]

Like other major strikes of the period, the causes of the Great Southwest Strike of 1886 extended from deeper processes of capital accumulation and the degenerating relations between workers and employers. In the 1880s, a boom in western expansion featured a tremendous growth in western rails. Most rapidly extending into southwestern regions such as Missouri, Kansas, Arkansas, Texas, Colorado, New Mexico, and the Indian Territories, railroads brought farmers, boomtowns, and extraction industries into yet-unexploited places in the West. Between 1880 and 1886, total railroad mileage in the Southwest nearly doubled to some twenty-five thousand miles of track. Cities like El Paso, Texas, and Sedalia, Missouri, expanded dramatically with the rise of large-scale mining, cattle, machinery, and goods distribution industries. The West was becoming a deeply integrated part of the national industrial economy.[46]

The railroads, however, brought uneven gains. Over-construction and wild industrial speculation had resulted in serious unemployment at the start of the decade. Following an economic downturn in 1884, several railroads controlled by Jay Gould reduced wages. A successful strike led by members of the Knights of Labor along the Missouri Pacific, the Missouri-Kansas-Texas, and the Wabash lines resulted in the cut being rescinded. Later that year, the Knights led another successful strike against the Wabash Railroad after some Knights were fired once their membership had been disclosed. The Knights' success in these strikes gave it an image of organizational might. Their rapidly growing numbers demanded the attention of employers everywhere.

By March 1886, the Knights were not just the largest labor organization— they were seen as representing organized labor itself. As membership surged beyond a half million, the sense that organized labor had amassed an industrial army grew. Newspapers began to publish concerned, detailed reports of the strength of the Knights. In a famous article first printed in the *New York Sun* and reprinted frequently elsewhere, a journalist noted that the Knights of Labor, through strikes and boycotts, "can array labor against capital, putting labor on the offensive or the defensive, for quiet and stubborn self protection, or for angry, organized assault, as they will."[47] Reading the popular press, one might have thought the Knights untouchable. The Great Southwest Strike of 1886, a strike that involved thousands of workers both along the lines and in dependent industries such as rail and coal production, sparked fears of labor conquering the industrial kingdom. Coupled with the rising significance of the Southwest and borderlands in the growing industrial order, the larger implications of a nationwide Knights-led rail strike during this period of serious labor unrest would be enormous.

Opposing the Knights stood a corporation under the influence of the infamous Jay Gould. Not a well-liked man, Gould made appearances throughout the decade in the major dailies as a greedy capitalist whose wealth depended on the deliberate manipulation of corporate stock and governing boards. Reporters kept readers well aware of Gould's various encroachments on the public welfare. In the early 1880s, *Puck* often caricatured Gould as a Semitic-looking Fagin (though he was not a Jew), a man whose avarice had resulted in the ruination of honest Wall Street speculators and later in the justifiable walkout of his telegraph company employees.[48] For labor leaders and reformers, he represented the worst of capitalist depredation. Many businesses resented their dependency on his vast enterprises. This resentment fortified public sympathy for the Knights even as journalists criticized the organization as becoming more insidious and militant. This mixture of opinions made the strike an even more divisive affair.[49]

The strike began in the spring of 1886, after the railroad summarily fired Knights Master Workman Charles A. Hall for absence. He had been attending a Knights meeting at the time, and despite the fact that the foreman had given him permission to go, he was dismissed.[50] The local Knights, led by Martin Irons, demanded that Hall be reinstated. The railroad refused, possibly because Gould wanted an excuse to draw the Knights into a costly strike that could seriously damage the union. The strike got under way on March 6, 1886. Eventually, the stoppage stretched over numerous western states and involved thousands of workers.

With a few minor exceptions, the strike fast proved unpopular in the press.[51] Unlike the forgiving treatment afforded some previous strikes, newspapers depicted this one as based solely on the actions of a single worker and the unbridled arrogance of labor's power. A *Puck* illustration depicts this point, showing a haughty-appearing man on a platform carried by workmen, standing beneath a banner that says, "I was discharged and I shall be reinstated, if all my fellow-workmen have to suffer."[52] The strike soon became violent, which further tilted editors against the union (despite the fact that a widespread court injunction had contributed greatly to the laboring men's distress).

Ominous projections regarding the impact of the strike abounded in the popular media. The *Waco Daily Examiner* noted early on that the strike "caused great alarm as it is supposed to be the inaugural step of a great strike on the Gould system contemplated by the Knights of Labor." In a brief interview with Terence Powderly in the same issue, the Grand Workman first condemned strikes in general but then uncharacteristically slipped from his traditional position, referring to the larger battle in no uncertain terms. While arbitration is "always" best, he said, "when it is possible, strike, only as a last resort but when that point is reached, strike hard, strike in earnest, and never surrender except to just concessions."[53]

The strike quickly spread throughout the Southwest rail system, which included Texas, Kansas, and Missouri. Within a week the press represented the event almost uniformly with war language.[54] In major newspapers, dispatches from different regions came in curt bites of information. Strikers had become engaged in a "railroad war." They captured positions and "killed" engines in what the *Washington Post* declared to be a "trial of strength between the organization and the railways, which will veritably be a battle of two giants."[55] The armies engaged in this "fierce contest between capital and labor," the Knights and Gould's railroad company, both refused to surrender and said as much through their respective representatives. The *San Antonio*

Daily Light predicted that this strike would be destined to become a grand "fight between [all] railroad corporations and organized labor."[56]

While newspapers critical of the Knights dedicated much editorial space to denouncing the organization, pro-labor news outlets did not substantially alter the tone of the daily coverage of the strike. Western newspapers critical of the railroad "barons," such as the *San Francisco Chronicle,* maintained that the strike was a cataclysmic battle between capital and labor. Though Pulitzer's labor-sympathetic *Post-Dispatch* pinned the ultimate blame on Gould himself, it characterized the Great Southwest Strike as a battle to the finish in which "mobs" of strikers carried out "movements" against replacement laborers. The *National Labor Tribune* handled the strike more obliquely, blaming the current "labor troubles" on management. The *Tribune* also criticized the mainstream press for not dealing with labor conflict in a more unbiased manner. The *Tribune*'s quarrel, however, was not with the overtly martial descriptive method in general use, but rather with the assessment of blame for the "strike fever."[57]

Using war framing, media outlets of various ideological positions allotted alternative degrees of blame to the combatants. Clearly hostile to the Knights of Labor, the *Nation* described the strike as a "rebellion" against authority in general. Along similar lines, the *Waco Daily Examiner* found the violence to be evidence of invading "communism." Less hostile to organized labor, the *New York Times* criticized both Gould and the Knights for prolonging this "war." Joseph Pulitzer's *Post-Dispatch* included commentary from legendary laborite John Swinton, who blamed the "unprecedented magnitude" of the current "labor struggle" on capital concentration and working-class "intelligence." As the strike wore on and episodes of violence spread, the mainstream media found less and less cause to advocate a "truce" that would satisfy both sides of this battle; the Knights, argued the *New York Times,* had scant public support in this instance.[58]

As the strike continued and the violence associated with it escalated, the media's war language grew more intense. In St. Louis, strikers moved aggressively to "Capture the Stronghold of the 'Scabs.'" This headline implied massive organization and rapid troop movement, despite the fact that the "Stronghold" had not been a fort created and defended by replacement labor but instead a traffic thoroughfare in which nonunion scab labor operated the engines. In another incident, strikers exchanged fire with federal marshals following an arrest of one of their own outside of Fort Worth, resulting in a hail of gunfire that killed at least one officer. The remaining strikers fled. The event would be described as a "Baptism of Blood" for Texas, an incident in which the authorities had "outgeneraled" the strikers.[59]

Coverage of the Great Southwest Strike reflected the media's self-appointed role as battlefield dispatch service. While the press saw itself as faithfully and

FIGURE 7 This illustration of the Great Southwest Strike of 1886 shows a classic "retreat" combat image, complete with stylized death-throes and defiant fist-shaking.
Source: *Harper's Weekly*, April 17, 1886.

accurately relating the facts, the mode of analysis imposed on the violence an organized aspect that did not reflect the reality of the situation, placing sporadic violence and isolated episodes of sabotage into a grander, simpler narrative of battle. Headlines such as "Wage War" and "Warring Workers" over-emphasized the strategic control of the Knights. Despite the *Washington Post*'s assertion that Powderly aimed a "concentration of all the force of his order" upon Gould's system, Powderly himself had little or no control over the various district assemblies in the Southwest.[60] Further, the efforts of these assemblies to boycott targeted lines and otherwise influence strikers proved ineffective— control was too diffused and decentralized, and the power of the corporations (along with a friendly state, countless hired guns, and thousands of replace-ment laborers eager to work) was too great. The "war" was more a desperate set of uncoordinated, though violent, incidents.

Regardless of its disorganized character, the Great Southwest Strike took on a life of its own in the media. Towing out the old warhorse "Irrepressible Conflict," one newspaper went so far as to explain how the entire national American business enterprise was "Organizing Its Forces" for an inevitable and imminent showdown. The article claimed that "some time next month" a national meeting of industry leaders would gather to devise a "means towards defense against the power of organized labor." As to what this "defense" would entail, the paper remained silent. It seemed newsworthy enough that this strike could inspire a militant reorganization of capital's forces.[61]

Offering a slightly more nuanced take on the strike, the *Fort Worth Gazette* (a periodical, in the words of an historian, "not unfriendly to the Knights of Labor"[62]) suggested that the real villain was Martin Irons. Under the telling heading "A House Divided Against Itself," the *Gazette* editorialized that Powderly and Irons each represented a different direction for the Knights. "Powderly would bring industrial and social relief by working upon and obliterating the causes of social and industrial ills, Irons would cure the disease by killing the patient. . . . The men who are for peace stand by Powderly. The incendiaries, anarchists, and the ignorant elements sustain Irons." The *Gazette* argued that the Powderly faction was not in control currently, and that it would be up to him to cleanse the organization of its violent elements and rein in Irons.[63]

For the mainstream press, the strike was as grand as any disruption in the past, bigger even. The *Waco Daily Examiner* exclaimed that the Civil War would be a mere "bagatelle" compared with the "oncoming revolution," which could "end in the complete destruction of our social fabric." Yet details regarding the nature of this revolution, the specific goals of labor's forces, and the constituency of capital's defending army remained a mystery.[64]

Longstanding themes of strike analysis also presented themselves in the reportage. Revolutionary memory reappeared in a comparison of Martin Irons to George III in his "quartering" of strike soldiers along the struck lines. The word "tyrant" shot fast and loose across editorial pages, as journalists and editors complained about Powderly's immense powers as head of the Knights. Similarly, "tyrannous" capital received its share of blame in quotes from interviewed strikers. The Knights of Labor emphasized older themes to its advantage. In a circular submitted to the major papers, the labor organization declared that it fought for the side of "liberty" against "King" Gould.

Although the specific authors of this circular remain anonymous, the text provided a remarkable recapitulation of Knights rhetorical themes of moral battle against the aristocratic foe of capital. Gould was depicted as a "money monarch," a "fiend" whose ambition was to crush workingmen's lives and families. Exhorting laborers to "marshal yourselves on the battlefield," the circular relied on a republican language of righteous defense, weaving in pleas for manhood and the inevitability of millennial reckoning.[65] A poem submitted to *John Swinton's Paper* echoed the sentiment in rhyme:

> But men of America, to liberty born,
> Shall hurl back the insult and menace in scorn [. . .]
> And cursed be the dog that submits to be ruled,
> By a plundering usurper like old King Gould.[66]

Millennial themes appeared in the media in declarations that the bloody retribution now under way was the result of prideful capitalist excess. For some religious leaders, the upheaval portended a brighter future. In a *New York Times*–published speech by the typically anti-union Henry Ward Beecher, the strike seemed to be a good thing, akin to the stone that rolled away from Jesus' tomb and released Him to Heaven. Like that stone, the current destruction foretold a release of tensions and a brighter future; it was "evolution" rather than "revolution," declared Beecher. The Knights likened themselves publicly to David, fighting the "Goliath" of rail. In the strike circular they swore to "Heaven" that they would prevail in this battle of biblical proportions.[67]

Slavery too appeared in a variety of ways. Some insinuated that Jay Gould, by defeating the Knights, wished to reduce the labor force to a state of enslavement. On the other side, *Harper's Weekly* printed a Thomas Nast cartoon depicting a white worker in shackles (labeled "Irons Grip") and a black man standing above him shaking his head, saying, "No sooner am I really set free than you enslave yourselves, and at the expense of your families, too."[68] The pity of a black man surely inflamed the white-dominated labor movement. Using the slavery pejorative against the Knights, the pro-business press suggested that the Knights had compromised their white manhood by following Irons in this strike.

The perceived threat of a biracial strike also cropped up occasionally in the press, because some of the Knights' southern assemblies were African American in composition. Warned the *Texarkana Independent* in April 1886, "adventurers and meddlers" were out "organizing some kind of secret societies amongst colored men in the country." Other articles similarly feared outsider, even "Communist" influence in upending the racial hierarchy during the strike. The main criticisms of the strikers, however, focused less on race than on the strike tactics in general, such as "engine killing" and physical violence.[69]

By its fourth week, the media routinely reported the strike as something of an ultimate battle between organized foes. Leaders from each side, especially Martin Irons and his opponent Jay Gould, were shown to be in absolute control of their forces. Cartoons and illustrations typically focused on these men to the exclusion of their respective constituencies. One image of Terence Powderly showed him sitting on a barrel of gunpowder (with only the "powder" part showing in a play on words), holding "red hot irons" dangerously in one hand as a patrolling soldier approached in the background.[70] The message, that the leader of the strike held national security in his hands, could not have been more clear.

Proposals for arbitration, an idea touted as a peaceful solution to the war of capital and labor by the political economists, often emerged when the two sides seemed at loggerheads during prolonged strikes. Here the papers tossed arbitration advice about freely until the violence that inspired military calls for order drowned out calls for mediation. The unlikelihood of arbitration succeeding in the face of two such powerful and intransigent opponents was depicted in a contemporary *Puck* cartoon, in which a strike-hammer-wielding workingman stood opposite a monopoly-club-wielding capitalist in a room facing out to a bustling industrial scene. Between the two now-bent warriors stood a miniature Powderly, holding an arbitration bill, telling them he is glad to see that both are "willing to stoop to *This*."[71]

The Great Southwest Strike of 1886 proved to be a devastating failure for the Knights of Labor. When the strikers finally folded on May 4, they found themselves out of work and with no action being taken to remedy their grievances. The same day, a bomb thrown into a mass of policemen at Haymarket Square in Chicago would be connected to the Knights, tarring the organization permanently with the blackness of anarchy. Membership declined precipitously.

The coverage given to the Great Southwest Strike made apparent noticeable changes in the major themes of strike analysis since the Civil War. Most conspicuously, martial imagery and a detached journalistic style prevailed as the dominant mode of analysis over older references to republican rights and imminent enslavement. The growing tendency to depict the forces of capital and labor as regimented organizations with leading commanders reached new levels. On one side, the Knights of Labor, led by Terence Powderly or Martin Irons, represented the whole of organized labor. On the other side, the railroads under Jay Gould's leadership portrayed capital. Importantly, organized labor received the lion's share of negativity. Supporting Gramsci's hegemony thesis, the media's frightening war framing tilted perception in the direction of union-led anarchy and destruction, even while some space was given to a critique of monopoly. As Eugene V. Debs (albeit not an "unbiased" observer) would later remember, "The press united in fiercest denunciation. Every lie that malignity could conceive was circulated. In the popular mind Martin Irons was the blackest-hearted villain that ever went unhung."[72]

The stakes for the Great Southwest Strike proved to be very high—the very largest labor organization had tied itself to a losing battle, and now was sinking fast. Gould gloated that the Knights were finished, even suggesting (along with a few journalists) that Martin Irons *intended* to discredit the Knights' national leadership.[73] Many in the Knights' leadership took the loss to mean that strikes were to be avoided at all costs, and that the political realm needed to be the new arena for labor's struggle. As one Kansas Knight explained, politics had to be the path to meaningful change, since "in strikes capital is the stronger."[74] At the Knights' National Legislation Committee meeting that June, the organization determined to flood Congress with petitions for new laws (such as land reforms) in an effort to counteract rumors of its demise. Despite the political shift, the organization shrank precipitously as employers refused to negotiate with Knights-affiliated workers.[75]

Although the Knights lost status as organized labor's most imposing army, the battle between capital and labor raged on. Driven by a narrative of calamity, industrial relations by no means seemed more peaceful, even as the grandest army of labor collapsed. Class conflict remained, yet its permanency and meaning remained unsettled ideas. In the decade that followed, a great depression and a revitalized industrial union movement set the stage for a new and even more grandiose struggle between the industrial armies.

An Escalating War: The "Crisis of the Nineties" and the Pullman Strike

Beginning in 1893, a severe depression gripped the economy. In its wake, scarce jobs and shrinking wages provided the catalyst for a series of major strikes that would provide the backdrop for what is known as the "crisis of the nineties." For many reasons, this historical description serves as an appropriate title for the final decade of the nineteenth century. Industrial violence, economic depression, waves of "new" immigrants, and structural transformations in the economy made this period justifiably unsettling to many contemporaries. Coming to terms with all of this proved a daunting task, one simplified greatly by the guiding idiom of war between capital and labor.

Throughout public discourse in the 1890s, war framing provided a flexible scaffolding of analysis for politicians, social scientists, and laborites alike. The Populist journal *Farmers' Alliance* asserted, "The actual state of society today is a state of war, active and irreconcilable war on every side." A congressman opined that laws needed to be passed in the industrial realm to provide "a narrower field for agitation" for "demagogues" on both sides of the conflict. A popular union song was titled "Battle Hymn of Labor." All of this illustrated how war framing carried the day. Tapping into a broad stream of military language, different opinions and ideological programs could be fashioned to give different groups their own moral monopolies.[76]

Reviewing popular journals and mainstream urban newspapers for this decade, one finds that strikes, as key episodes in a growing industrial war, reaffirmed and augmented social division. Striking unions would represent labor at such times, while hired soldiers, National Guardsmen, and employer-enlisted strikebreakers provided ample evidence that capital was just as strongly involved in the fight, even when relying on local government authorities for aid.

In the 1890s, strikes also took place on a wider field, with large numbers of disputants and effective coordination increasingly being the norm. Between 1890 and 1900, there were never fewer than one thousand strikes in a year; they totaled anywhere from 164,000 workers out in 1892 to 505,000 workers in 1894.[77] Extensive business consolidation had helped to create a truly national setting for capital-labor conflict, and large corporate enterprises would be the sites of the most significant national strikes by the turn of the century.[78] Some groups of firms, such as the railroads, formed alliances such as the General Managers' Association in order to provide assistance to member businesses during strikes (typically in the form of replacement laborers). Workers responded with their own nationwide alliance—the American Federation of Labor—as well as a new industrial union that threatened to engage a vast number of railroad laborers within the ranks of a single organization. This organization, the American Railway Union, would be at the center of the largest national strike of the decade, the Pullman Strike of 1894. The Pullman Strike alerted millions to the possibility of an even greater escalation of the industrial war, and is worth closely examining.

BY THE SPRING OF 1894, among those workers blighted by the depression were factory workers of the Pullman Palace Car Company, who found their wages reduced, but not their cost of housing or utilities. George Mortimer Pullman, the tycoon who owned not only the factory but also the adjoining town that bore his name, had decided to cut wages without providing rent relief. Workers living in the town protested, Pullman refused to negotiate, and they went on strike, appealing their case to a fast-growing industrial railroad workers' union.

George Pullman himself was something of a visionary who believed that labor and capital could coexist peacefully if the proper environment were created. His town was clean, well-organized, liquor-free (with the exception of the hotel lounge available to its wealthy clientele), and racially homogenous. He worked ceaselessly to publicize his creation, not just to boost his company's image or to attract workers but because he believed he had set an example for the rest of the world. During the World's Fair of 1893 held in Chicago, he distributed thousands of free copies of pro-Pullman literature, including works such as *The Story of Pullman* and *The Town of Pullman*. These titles extolled the orderly splendor of his model town in pictures and easy-to-read prose. Special trains took visitors from the fairgrounds to the model town. Pullman became one of the most high-profile capitalists in America.[79]

During this same period, industrial workers—native and otherwise—found themselves squeezed by the fierce depression and facing severe hardship if not outright starvation. Many felt that organization offered the only solution, and the American Railway Union seemed to be a savior for the Pullman workers. The ARU, the largest union of its day, had sprung into existence in 1892 as a result of an organizational drive to gather all railroad workers into a single union. While the idea of one big union stretched back at least

several decades to the Knights of Labor, the ARU was different. A true industrial union, the American Railway Union aimed at uniting all white workers
within a single industry. Its president, a man named Eugene Debs, had a gift
for passionate appeal and thrived in the limelight. Debs believed that labor
would lose the industrial war without large organizations like the ARU, and
his infectious eloquence threatened his union's enemies.

Much like the rationale for military might in the twentieth-century arms
race, Eugene Debs saw a massive union across craft lines as an "army [that]
would be impregnable. No corporation would assail it." It would be so powerful
that it would consign the whole idea of the strike to "the relic chamber of the
past." A union to end all strikes, the ARU grew rapidly following a successful
walkout against the Great Northern Railroad in April–May of 1894. With some
150,000 members in an industry that operated along a finite corridor easily
accessible to the union, the ARU represented a uniquely powerful labor organization. In the middle of its first national convention, the Pullman strikers asked
the ARU for assistance. After initial hesitance, Debs agreed to help the strikers,
and on June 26, 1894, the official boycott of Pullman Palace cars began.[80]

Once the boycott began, events quickly escalated as workers refused to
attach Pullman cars to trains and then struck when ordered to do so. The
New York Times made the significance of the ARU's decision clear: "while the
boycott is ostensibly declared as a demonstration of sympathy in behalf of
the strikers in the Pullman shop, it in reality will be a struggle between the
greatest and most powerful railroad labor organization and the entire railroad
capital."[81] Indeed, the sides did quickly coalesce; soon after the strike began,
the railroads united behind the General Managers' Association, an entity
created during the Great Upheaval in 1886 to rationalize the transportation
process and to counter the influence of organized labor. The largest industrial
union now faced the most coordinated alliance of capitalists.

As with other mass strikes, coverage was not entirely anti-union at the
outset. George Pullman's benevolent reputation had been questioned for years.
Now the media held him at least partly responsible for the current hostility of
his workers. Area newspapers such as the *Chicago Inter Ocean* and the *Chicago
Herald* criticized him for contributing to the suffering of his employees during
the depression. Farther away, the *Boston Transcript* proclaimed that "public
opinion" sided against George Pullman for refusing to allow even the question
of arbitration to be discussed. News correspondent Nellie Bly of the *New York
World* went to Pullman town and wrote a series of articles highly sympathetic
to the plight of the workers. She explained the low esteem many held toward
George Pullman to be the result of his own hubris: "No man ever had a better
chance to benefit mankind than had Pullman. No man deserves more the condemnation of the world." The *Chicago Daily News* even set up a store in town to
provide the strikers with basic supplies for survival.[82]

Such pro-unionism in the press underscores the difficulties of capitalist editors in pressing their own agendas on strike coverage and the possibilities for more ambiguous representations of industrial war. While the large newspapers were published by capitalists who, however subtly, often influenced the course of coverage and believed that unions were dangerous, it was no given that all labor publicity would be negative. Similarly, ostensibly "pro-labor" editors might suddenly turn against unions and let their staff know as much. For example, when Joseph Pulitzer, the "hands-on" owner of the *New York World* who supported the Homestead strikers in 1892, read an op-ed piece in his newspaper that supported Debs in his defiance of Grover Cleveland's federal intervention, he summoned the offending journalist to his office. He berated him, demanding that he acknowledge his erroneous judgment. The reporter did not back down, and he could not be fired by dint of his union contract. Pulitzer could only ban him from writing further editorials.[83] Even with this accomplished, Pulitzer's paper still did not provide a consistently negative coverage of the strikers. Nellie Bly, the reporter sent by Pulitzer to cover the strike, explained in the *World* that the strikers "are not firebrands; they are not murderers and rioters; they are not Anarchists. They are quiet, peaceful men who have suffered beneath the heel of the most heartless coward it has ever been my misfortune to hear of."[84] Still, even as she wrote this, other editorials in the *World* condemned the strikers.

Other periodicals similarly found owner ideology influencing, though not entirely directing, strike coverage. The three major Chicago papers, the *Chicago Tribune, Chicago Times,* and *Chicago Daily News,* were all owned by wealthy, politically sensitive businessmen who were, on some level, dedicated to the social harmony that made things safe for business. The *Tribune,* owned by prominent, conservative Republican businessman Joseph Medill, was the most reactionary, making sure that Debs was referred to as "Dictator Debs" and the strikers strongly associated with anarchism. The *Daily News* was a bit more sympathetic, it having been founded by a pro-reform, community-minded entrepreneur and published in the 1890s by nonpartisan businessman Victor Lawson. The *Times,* on the other hand, was consistently pro-striker, being under the direction of "insurgent" Democrat Carter Harrison II. Despite these differences, as David Paul Nord argues in his study of these three periodicals in the late nineteenth century, during the Pullman Strike all three newspapers conformed to a "firm commitment to commercial order, social harmony, and social control."[85] From Nord's study, plus what we can learn about Joseph Pulitzer during the strike, one can see that despite individual differences that did have an impact on the coverage, an overall story arc emerged in the press that the nation was confronted with a serious challenge to the social order.

Nevertheless, days after the inauguration of the "fight" between Debs's ARU and Pullman's railcar company, circumstances would place considerable pressure on Debs's shoulders. The boycott had inspired numerous strikes throughout the West and Midwest, and attempts to move trains through often failed in the face of efforts by organized and intransigent workers. American business, so intimately connected to the rails, seemed imperiled. Given the magnitude of this strike, Eugene Debs seemed to be the most commanding labor general the nation had yet seen. Debs, it seemed to a great many observers, held unprecedented power.

Eugene Debs tried to maintain public support with a characteristic public appeal. In an eloquent call to arms that included references to Lincoln, manhood, the "great public," and the striving of labor for "living wages," Debs explained that the strike had "developed into a contest between the producing classes and the money power." He felt that the strike had indeed become a climactic battle, but from his perspective labor represented the side of good while the railroad corporations signified the powers of corruption and greed.[86]

The largest newspapers printed Debs's speech on the front page. He had tapped into the rich rhetorical vein of nineteenth-century republicanism and white men's rights, waxing eloquently on the sublime importance of this strike as a great, millennial stand against the oppression of unfettered capitalism. While his speech did make clear to the public his moral position, when combined with the violence that quickly ensued and the media's presentation of the strike as a battle, it also provided fuel for the media's central story of industrial war. The axis of the coverage turned not on the notion that the strike had been a justifiable endeavor but instead on the thrilling and well-selling story of class conflict on a national scale.[87]

Editors instantly recognized the special nature of this strike. Once the American Railway Union leadership announced its intentions, the newspapers spun the decision into the inauguration of a national struggle between capital and labor.[88] The standard style of strike reportage, which placed a premium on charges, marches, volleys, and conquests, reached new levels of extravagance in July 1894. The anti-union *Chicago Tribune* printed boldly on July 2 "Strike Is Now War." Later in the issue, it elaborated that the violence currently breaking out between the strikers and the militia reflected the true nature of all strikes, which were in actuality a "kind of warfare that cannot be carried on peacefully for more than a few days."[89] Other periodicals less inclined to make such blanket anti-union statements quoted Debs and followed brusquely with announcements that the strike had become an ultimate battle between the largest capitalists and all of organized labor. The *Journal of Political Economy* pointed out that the Pullman Strike stirred far more public alarm than had either the 1877 strike or the Great Southwest Strike.[90]

Labor leaders threw fuel on the fire. President M. H. Madden of the Chicago Federation of Labor announced, "We all feel that in fighting any battle against the Pullman company we are aiming at the very head and front of monopoly and plutocracy. . . . As the question now stands it will be solved only by a struggle to the end to demonstrate which has more coherency, capital or labor." Grand Master Workman James R. Sovereign of the Knights of Labor urged a general strike for all of Chicago. Populist leader Moses Oppenheimer declared the "working class desire to assert that they are willing to rebel against the arrogance of the monopolists. . . . This is no longer a strike—it is the great Western rebellion."[91] The universality of such grandiose gestures across political divides helped bring into existence an urgent nationwide dialogue of escalating war.

As walkouts quickly spread from city to city and tied up rail traffic across the Midwest, the press shifted gears, arguing that this was more than a battle between union and corporate interests; it was an assault against the United States itself. Uncle Sam, a figure who since the early nineteenth century personified the federal government, played a key role in embodying editorial opinion toward the supposed dangers of the ARU's actions. As Debs called on his constituency to fight the General Managers' Association, the image of a vengeful, rail-thin, Lincolnesque Uncle Sam appeared regularly in major newspapers to represent a righteous, reactionary federal response.[92]

In popular cartoons an indignant and quite violent Uncle Sam would be shown picking up a scruffy striker by the nape of the neck or even lighting a fuse on a "Debs" stick of dynamite. Uncle Sam could also be shown as a disciplinarian father, about to spank an infantilized Debs. Standing in for the combined public/federal interest, the pin-striped mascot served as delegate for government-sanctioned violence. The appropriation of the Uncle Sam icon reflected the media's appeal to a self-defensive patriotism for the sake of social order. While patriotic calls ran in the other direction as well, such as when the pro-ARU *Railway Times* parodied the "Star Spangled Banner" saying "O'er the land—eighty three per cent of it—of the userer, plutocrat and thieving politician / And the home . . . of the slaves,"[93] the lion's share of media analysis focused on the patriotism inherent in trades union repression.

When President Grover Cleveland sent in federal troops to secure the safe transport of the mail and violence ensued, the American Railway Union was wholly demonized by the majority of the mainstream media as fomenting an uprising against both federal authority and the public. When Illinois governor John Peter Altgeld refused to send in the National Guard, the press accused him of being "anarchistic" and the "friend and champion of disorder."[94]

Civil War references that framed the ARU in negative terms abounded, strengthening the view that a new rebellion of labor threatened to subvert social order. The strikers were "rebels," and their "general," Eugene Debs, more than once found himself compared to Jefferson Davis. His union had "made war on the Federal Government and the State Government. Their assault on the former was as unprovoked as the Confederate firing upon the flag at Fort

Sumter." The Grand Army of the Republic (an organization composed of Civil War veterans) even volunteered to help, declaring, "The soldiers of 1861 are as ready to fight Anarchist rebels north of Ohio as they were secession rebels south of it." Southern newspapers also used the Civil War comparison, but with a twist. The *Louisville Courier-Journal* promised as "solid" a South *behind* President Cleveland as it had been *opposed* to Lincoln in the last war.[95]

Configured into a treasonous attack against the United States, the Pullman Strike opened the gates to "total war" references and yet again led everyday readers to believe that organized labor posed a threat to social order. The presence of federal troops on the scene, by this point dispatched to strike zones to maintain order (typically at the expense of legitimate protest) and to ensure the safe passage of mail, cemented the combat picture. Troops would be shown to "Take the Field" and to struggle to "gain possession" of key rail areas such as stations and switchyards in great "pitched battles."[96] Newspapers explained that these battles had transformed the boycott into a "rebellion."[97] Recalling the events of 1861 and connecting them with the ARU—increasingly portrayed as being far more organized than it actually was—provided a crucial link to the previous insurrectionary activity of the old Confederacy. The country had now been swept into a new civil war, one perhaps more threatening than the prior one because this was based on class instead of regional antagonisms. As a piece in the *Railroad Trainmen's Journal* later put it, the Pullman Strike was a "civil war" of the "worst kind. Not a sectional but a class war."[98]

Papers that continued to support the strikers also found much similarity between the events of 1894 and those of 1861. Rather than emphasizing the violence of the current struggle, these periodicals cast the strikers in the moral role of the North in ending slavery. The pro-ARU *Chicago Times* (which gained 16,032 new readers in one week of strike and would gain many more by strike's end) editorialized, "There is a war against slavery progressing in Chicago today. . . . The members of the American Railway Union are fighting for the victims of Pullman as thirty years ago the white men of Illinois fought for the black men of Alabama and Virginia."[99]

As in 1877, the labor side understood its forces to be fighting for the same cause as had those who died for their country in the 1860s. The ARU's *Railway Times* compared Debs to Lincoln, now fighting for the "white slaves."[100] Casting an alternative take on the Civil War analogy allowed pro-labor periodicals to navigate the common martial idiom while assigning an alternative moral direction. A reporter for the *San Francisco Examiner* articulated this use of the Civil War most fully:

> It took many battles to win the war between the States, but at last came Appomattox. The surrender of the slave-owners there insured the perpetuity of the Union; in this war between money and men there will

also, I think, be many battles, but there will come another Appomattox and a surrender of the slave-makers, which shall give guaranty that the Union will be worth preserving.[101]

A battle in a broader war, the Pullman Strike could be configured, depending on the source, as either between "money and men" or "Americans and Anarchists." Most of the periodicals reviewed here tended toward the latter view. Organizing violent incidents with battle language and explicit references to the Civil War, the media delivered strike coverage along a highly readable, highly persuasive plot line of union-led insurrection.

In terms of general reportage, the Pullman coverage further revealed the establishment of the "new journalism" in ongoing coverage of the labor war. Joseph Pulitzer's *New York World*, a newspaper ostensibly in favor of labor's cause against capital, combined dramatic illustrations with vivid, detailed description to offer a graphic depiction of labor's most significant battle. In one issue, the *World* dedicated space to describing the "riot shot gun," a shotgun capable of firing a wide-spreading blanket of pellets to hit as many targets as possible with minimal lethality. While other newspapers referred to this latest weapon casually, the *World* printed images of the gun in obscene detail, describing its exact dimensions and the innermost workings of its firing mechanism.[102]

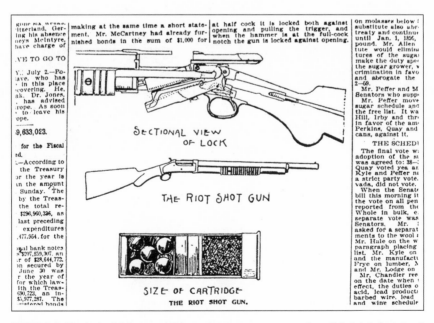

FIGURE 8 The industrial war would require new weapons, such as this "riot shot gun."

Source: *New York World*, July 3, 1894.

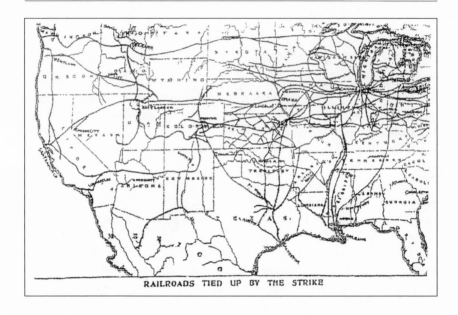

RAILROADS TIED UP BY THE STRIKE

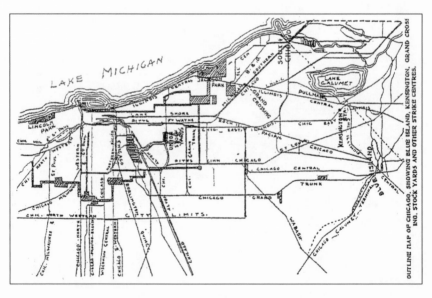

As in 1886, printed images further helped exaggerate the magnitude of the Pullman Strike in the public mind. While the ARU had centrally orchestrated the nationwide boycott and Debs encouraged sympathy strikes, individual strikes and episodes of sabotage and violence in different regions were local affairs. Similarly, the General Managers' Association was in practice no omnipotent force; it relied on an amenable government and judicial system, which in

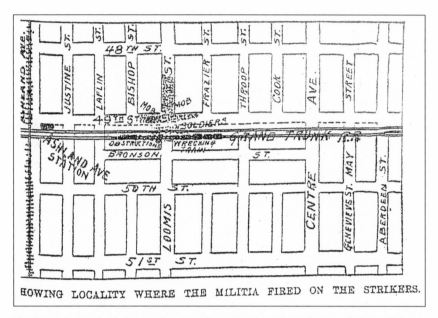

SHOWING LOCALITY WHERE THE MILITIA FIRED ON THE STRIKERS.

FIGURES 9, 10, & 11 Assorted national, regional, and local maps (of the Chicago area) were deemed necessary to grasp the enormity of the Pullman Strike.

Sources: *New York World*, June 29, July 7, 1894; *Chicago Tribune*, July 8, 1894.

turn applied its compulsive influence according to the independent operation of various courts, troop units, and commanding officers. Illustrations provided the war metaphor with a concrete representation of the "leaders" of the battle, compressing the various interests and agendas within a single rubric.

To illustrate the respective commanders' positions, papers printed stylized busts of Debs and Pullman akin to "classical portraits of kings and generals."[103] Equating the actions of thousands of rioters and strikers with a single image of Debs helped to simplify the story, and the busts gave a human leadership element to each side. Images of army officers and railroad officials (particularly George Pullman) contrasted with portraits of Debs, often above panoramas of the participants and the most important scenes of battle. Unlike the Great Strike of 1877, in the Pullman Strike each side could be clearly identified and represented as having a specific agenda and a core of key personalities. Maps had more detail in this strike as well, with comprehensive pictures of both city blocks and the nation at large appearing alongside the coverage.

The key to configuring this strike as a treasonous attack against the United States was making Debs appear to be the leader of an ignorant army of foreigners. The worst violence of the strike took place in and around Chicago (where at least thirteen people died), an entrepot of "alien" immigrant groups such as Hungarians and Poles. Chicago's strikers were "a mass of evil, angry, hungry foreigners," explained the *New York World*. In a particularly xenophobic piece by Frederic Remington in *Harper's Weekly*, the famous artist reported that a "malodorous crowd of anarchistic foreign trash" had instigated all of the violence. He went on to explain that the "real," native workingmen wished that the occupying soldiers would kill these foreigners.[104]

Pro-labor periodicals by contrast offered mixed opinions of the situation, praising the union's ambition, if not always its actions. The *Railroad Trainmen's Journal*, a union periodical that criticized the ARU for robbing it of membership, sympathized with the strikers while denouncing Debs's tactics as senseless. The union paper *Boston Labor Leader* agreed that while backed by a "chivalrous purpose," the ARU's disastrous "mighty battle" highlighted only the weakness of industrial unionism as compared with a more defensible craft unionism.[105] In a published statement that supported the strikers while denying support for a sympathy strike, the AFL explained that the media had falsely painted the "working classes [as] now arrayed in open hostility to Federal authority."[106] Less critical of the ARU was the pro-labor *Arena*, a popular reformist journal that condemned "All the Tory plutocratic newspapers" that denounced the union's struggle. In several articles, *The Arena* argued that the ARU operated along the most honorable principles. At one point it compared the Pullman boycott to the Sons of Liberty's boycott of British goods in 1773. Even more favorable to the strike for obvious reasons, the union's own *The Railway Times* took every opportunity to criticize the corporations and praise the brave and manly strikers.[107]

After Debs refused to obey the court's injunction to cease striking, he was arrested. Without a leader and in the face of mounting federal and popular pressure, the strike fizzled. The anti-union *Chicago Tribune* cast Debs as a defeated Lee, triumphantly declaring, "Debs Has Reached His Appomattox." The nation was again safe, the forces of American order having prevailed over an insurrection led by a dictator and carried out by a foreign mob. A poem published in the *Tribune* the same day summarized the triumph of business and order, as well as illustrating the mighty appeal of Civil War reference. Written by "Golden Rod," the following piece was entitled "After the Strike."

> Way back in the sixties
> Honest men in blue
> Fought to crush rebellion
> With brave hearts and true.
> Now they "volunteer" again
> (To [Governor of Illinois] Altgeld's great dislike),
> Willing to do battle
> To put down the strike.[108]

Debs's "Appomattox" had arrived, and the press took full opportunity to delve into the historic consequences of the surrender. In one of the most significant examples of this, the *New York World,* the paper with the largest circulation in the country, published a town hall–style discussion on the meaning of the strike in its July 15, 1894, issue. Culling responses from a wide range of discussants, including major newspaper and journal editors, politicians, labor leaders, and businessmen, the *World*'s piece reflected a desire both to make sense of the recent chaos and to further establish the popular press as the proper forum for the national industrial dialogue.

In the *World*'s town hall article, the respondents might well have been talking about the close of a recent internecine war. With carefully measured, hopeful language, the editor of the *Chicago Herald* noted that the strike would benefit the nation by underscoring the necessity of peaceful arbitration in the face of escalating industrial conflict. The *Chicago Times*'s pro-union editor found that while the strike had "widened the breach between capital and labor," it had also taught the working man the benefits of unity, a "lesson" that would further the march of peaceful industrial evolution. The editor of the anarchist *Arbeiter Zeitung* agreed that workingmen had become more unified as a result of the strike. For this respondent, however, there would be more darkness before the light. This strike had merely been "the first battle" in a longer war, one yet to be fully waged by nationally organized "lines" of capital and labor.[109]

The common use of the term "Appomattox" in relation to the Pullman Strike reflected the gravity of national strikes at the close of the century. This Civil War referent, which appeared repeatedly throughout press reports on the Pullman Strike, alluded not to the reconciliation of two geographic sections but of two equally powerful national forces, each capable of waging destructive war. Debs's Appomattox was not to be a truce between the warring armies, but rather a pause for reflection. The industrial war would continue to escalate unless the federal government again adopted a role in securing a lasting peace, just as it had during Reconstruction. To accomplish this, a new player in the conflict, the public, would be required to come to the fore.

4

The Emergence of the "Great Third Class"

The "People" and the Search for an Industrial Treaty

Escalating labor conflict in the 1890s reinforced popular fears of imminent, apocalyptic class war. For many reformers and editorialists, the answer to the problem of labor conflict rested in appeals to the "public," a body that became a tentative player in strike analysis in the 1880s and to a much greater extent during the depression years of the 1890s. The widely discussed antagonistic division of capital and labor had done more than provide a foil against which reformers could articulate their ambitions; it drove a wedge of anxiety through the hearts of millions of Americans. Each national strike reinforced a powerful desire for a peaceful remedy.

Situated between the opposing industrial armies, the "public" first served as a rhetorical device with which newspapers could sort out the forces involved in a mass strike by setting them apart from the rest of the people. By the last decade of the nineteenth century, the public would be called upon to serve another purpose: mediating body. As the ongoing industrial war made it seem ever more futile to suppose that capital and labor could settle their differences by themselves, this "great third class" was regularly beseeched to leverage a truce between the warring forces.

The emergence (or more accurately, reemergence) of an active "public" in social relations involved decades of exhortations and political wheedling. In this chapter, I will analyze how the role of the public was first perceived (at least as far as labor observers were concerned) as a force to be reckoned with at the turn of the century. Focusing on the "public" as it came to be viewed as an autonomous actor in the industrial scene, I will explore the multiple meanings of the term during key strikes in the 1880s and 1890s. This will be followed by a look at some well-publicized institutional attempts at giving this group a concrete role in solving class conflict, namely the U.S. Industrial Commission of 1898 and the even more high-profile National Civic Federation. Finally, I will examine the Anthracite Coal Strike of 1902, a news event in which the "public" found itself at the center of a plan to resolve industrial hostilities in one of the largest and most central of American industries, coal.

The Rediscovery of the "Public"

The appeal to popular democracy to solve social ills was nothing new in late nineteenth-century America. The nation had been founded with a document headed *We the People,* and since Revolutionary times the "people" had provided the underpinning for American politics and the underlying ideology of popular sovereignty. As a result, the masses were often portrayed as having a certain wisdom and responsibility, particularly by politicians. Public figures had long depended upon this body in making legitimate their various policy appeals, from Madison, Hamilton, and Jay's "Publius" in the *Federalist Papers* to Lincoln's calls for support of his "People's Contest."[1]

During the Progressive Era, the "people," or "public," as it came to be called, took on a special prominence. A loose group of reformers who gave voice to a sense that society had entered a crisis period (class violence, political corruption, and the perils of New Immigrant invaders being some of the reported culprits), Progressives sought to rehabilitate the nation and set things right via thoughtful legislation.[2] Roughly between the 1880s and 1920, Progressives celebrated the journalistic fearlessness of muckrakers such as Jacob Riis, Upton Sinclair, Ida Tarbell, and Lincoln Steffens, and they counted on the expertise of professional social scientists to develop laws that might counteract the dangers posed by unbridled industrial capitalism. In developing a useful shorthand to describe the victim of these dangers, Progressives found the concept of the "public" irresistible.[3] As the ultimate victim of class hostilities, the public embodied the multitudes that would be endangered if social order became fragmented by a major strike. Sheer repetition of the "public" expression, coupled with the common assumption that class war could prove socially devastating if not checked, helped develop the public's role as the ultimate judge and arbitrator in industrial relations.

The public played its first significant role as an entity unto itself in relation to warring capital and labor in the coverage of the Great Southwest Strike of 1886. There were several reasons for this. Although massive, the Great Southwest Strike for East Coast Americans might have seemed something of a distant affair. The newspapers recognized that bringing the significance of this struggle home to daily readers required the establishment of an intimate connection between themselves and the strike. Establishing this connection proved relatively easy. Far-off labor battles on a grand scale often resulted in shortages of goods, higher prices, fewer jobs, and transportation inconveniences. Associating these discomforts with frightening images of labor conflict was simple, and probably fiscally lucrative for the reporting papers.

Extending from this palpable impact came the broader consequence of a national rail strike: the disruption of social order. Railroads occupied a central position in the national marketplace, being responsible for the steady transport of goods and people from place to place. Consumers counted on goods brought great distances by rail. Thousands of Americans worked directly for the railroads, not only as laborers but also in the growing echelons of management and clerking. Indirectly, many other workers depended on the railroads for jobs at stations, in the coal mines that produced fuel for locomotives, and at docks where rail lines ended. Widening the sphere, small business owners and large segments of industry whose livelihoods had grown interconnected with those living in other parts of the nation might also find their fortunes threatened by cessations in rail traffic.

When violence erupted following the collapse of a supposed agreement made between Knights of Labor president Terence Powderly and rail tycoon Jay Gould during the strike, references to the impact of the strike on the wider public increased in number and intensified in content. *Harper's Weekly* raged that if more railroaders joined in, the damage to the "public welfare" would be disastrous. *Puck* noted that whereas before the strike "public sympathy" had been on the side of the Knights and against Gould, now the tide had turned. Americans would not stand for the despotism of Knights, asserted the journal. On the labor side, the *National Labor Tribune* referred to the "robbery of the public" carried out by the corporations to win support.[4]

Nearly a decade later, during the Pullman Strike, the "public" would again be alerted to its interest in the outcome of a national strike. Early on, the *New York World* warned that the American Railroad Union would "not command public sympathy" with its boycott. The *Baltimore Sun* similarly explained, "If it were simply a matter between employer and employe, the public might let them settle it for themselves. But it is not. The public are deeply concerned, and the people have the right to insist upon a remedy if one can be found."[5] The *Chicago Tribune* railed on numerous occasions that Debs and his union were alienating the "public," at one point printing an image of a man wearing a "general public" hat looking down on ARU members who are busily tying his ankles with railcars.[6] Other mainstream papers included references to the public at every available opportunity, particularly when addressing the supposedly revolutionary qualities of this strike.

The public also played a role in the minds of labor leaders. Eugene Debs first recognized that winning a strike that affected the entire country

HOW LONG WILL HE STAND THIS SORT OF THING?

FIGURE 12 The public is recognized by the media as the party negatively affected by the Pullman Strike of 1894.

Source: *Chicago Tribune*, June 30, 1894.

required a large measure of public sympathy. As the Pullman Strike got under way, Debs appealed to the masses in a speech published in numerous major papers. He pointed out "the great public is with us." He believed that the moral righteousness of his struggle against the plutocracy of rail would, if phrased appropriately, find resonance with a group whose love of democracy outweighed its narrow interests as consumers. He capitalized on his high profile, tacitly recognizing his status as "general" of his forces, to plead his case to the largest possible audience.

But who precisely was the "public"? Clearly, the *Chicago Tribune*'s "public" and Debs's "public" were not the same entity. The vagaries of the expression allowed for a variety of possible definitions of the term; its use depended as much upon the intended audience as on the author. For *Puck, Harper's*

Weekly, and *Nation,* journals whose readerships were small but whose influence in culture and politics were large, the "public" likely referred to those voting, middle- and upper-class whites who feared the power of organized labor in disrupting America's economic advance. In 1883, prominent Yale social scientist William Graham Sumner bemoaned the fact that "even amongst the people of standing, to whom we must look to establish the body of public opinion," no clear-cut, unified explanation was provided to explain the causes of industrial conflict.[7] Here Sumner tipped his hand, suggesting a sort of trickle-down theory of the public. Men of high social rank (such as he) were to provide the essential knowledge, and from their writings and lectures would flow the basis of enlightened opinion for the reading classes, who in turn created and implemented legislation and in whose hands ultimately rested social order. Significantly, journals aimed at the educated elite did not necessarily give capital free rein. As Louis Galambos has shown, distrust and ambivalence marked the majority of business-related journalistic coverage in this era.[8] Being critical of big business allowed such periodicals to create room for a "public" interested in the cessation of hostilities between workers and owners. Their public took no sides in the conflict; it was a peace-loving, democratic body that believed in the rights of all citizens to do as they wished within legal bounds. Overt support for unions or capitalists (except when one or another group was responsible for a strike) was generally avoided for these reasons.

For the national labor press, the *National Labor Tribune* being the most prominent example, the "public" referred both to organized labor *and* to working people at large, a projection that often seemed to overlap with the middle-class press's definition of "public." Widening the public to include everybody but capitalists gave such journals a moral advantage by claiming that union interests combined with the interests of all those not involved directly with the "plutocracy." This dubious distinction, bestowed upon certain capitalists whose empires seemed particularly large and oppressive, served to unite the "public" further by implying that such men intended to subvert the whole institution of popular sovereignty via sinister, wealth-based cabalism.

Major newspapers like the *New York Times* spoke to an even larger "public," suggesting in editorials on the industrial war that the "public" included everyone *not* active in the particular strike under discussion. Such newspapers tended to be nebulous regarding the actual composition of the public. Selling papers meant alienating as few customers as possible while making as strong an argument as one could. This effort gave the newspapers' "public" the appearance of a large, vague, and outraged (nothing sells like indignation) segment of society. The *Times* itself, having been rescued from serious decline by Adolph Ochs in 1896, aimed to provide, according to Ochs, "a forum for the consideration of all questions of public importance." Though a conservative man, and never having the populist pretensions of a Hearst or Pulitzer, Ochs would present his "public" with critiques of both aggressive workers and rapacious bosses in the strike coverage provided by his paper.[9]

The most specific definition of the public came from a labor economist, John Commons. The most influential labor scholar of the early twentieth century, Commons sought to account for the two parties engaged in the industrial war. As the struggle worsened, he attempted to quantify a third agent, what he called the "great third class, the public." In the symposium "Is Class Conflict in America Growing and Is It Inevitable?" published by the American Sociological Society in 1908, Commons put the three-part model into words. He reasoned that there were about 6 million non-agricultural, wage-earning laborers, who by nature of their position opposed 1.5 million "employers and investors" in "the field [of] class conflict." The rest of society—at the time, about 82 million people (including farmers, clerks, professionals, and "other laborers")—presumably constituted the public. Although these numbers were small compared with the total population, their "strategic" position in the economy made them extremely important. They could be capable of causing great damage, as all of the major strike battles of the time illustrated.[10]

For Commons, the solution to the "growing" but "not inevitable" problem of class conflict resided in the public's willingness to mediate the conflict through legislation. As the government expanded from one characterized (in the words of one historian) by "courts and parties" to a more complex, bureaucratic entity at the turn of the century, enlarged federal power would be rhetorically connected to the will of the people.[11] In the American democratic narrative, the "people" supplied the ultimate mandate for political action. In order to justify federal involvement, political activists (and now social scientists working for the government) would be compelled to make the "public" their ultimate source of legitimacy. The selective appropriation of the public by advocates of state intervention also helped to make capital and labor appear to be entities separate from, but operating in the same arena as, the third and increasingly powerful group.

When John Commons wrote this article in 1907, efforts to implement mediative labor legislation for the public interest were already under way. The U.S. Industrial Commission, established by President William McKinley in 1898, investigated industrial relations with an aim at finding practical solutions to ongoing labor problems. With the depression of the 1890s over, the commission found that massive corporations had become a permanent fixture of the economy, and that the long-term answer to labor conflict rested in the rising standard of living and in the state's support of anti-trust and worker safety laws. As for current strikes, the commission supported voluntary mediation between corporations and "responsible" unions. This designation, applied typically to the American Federation of Labor, meant a union interested not in initiating a grassroots industrial movement like Debs's ARU, but instead in working with federal and local authorities to arrive at limited employment agreements with management. AFL president Samuel Gompers, who served as a witness to the commission, played an influential role in forming these recommendations.[12]

Both Samuel Gompers and John Commons were also members of a more high-profile private organization aimed at creating a labor concord—the National Civic Federation (NCF). Designed to bring employers and workers to the bargaining table by way of a public trust organization, the NCF embodied the first voluntary effort to bring together the three major elements of society, capital, labor, and public, in an attempt to bring peace to the industrial world. The federation's justification for existence, especially in its early years, was mainly to resolve the class war. As John Mitchell, the leader of the United Mine Workers and a member of the NCF, told an audience at the organization's 1904 annual dinner, the federation was a "peace movement."[13]

The dream of the NCF began with a group of urban trade unionists and reformers in Chicago. Ralph Easley, a reformer and newspaperman who moved to Chicago in the 1890s, witnessed the shocking changes wrought by industrialization on that sprawling city and determined to find a way to channel public opinion in progressive ways. The goal was to ameliorate what he saw as the evils of poor government, violent social conditions, and industrial unrest. Born in 1893, the Chicago Civic Federation quickly found itself at the center of the Pullman Strike. Gathering together representatives of capital, labor, and other groups of interested "professions," the Chicago Civic Federation accomplished little but held such promise that leading industrial theorists and writers flocked in to help draft new mediation strategies. Easley soon corresponded with reform-minded individuals ranging from Theodore Roosevelt (then assistant secretary of the navy), Senator Mark Hanna, AFL president Samuel Gompers, and editor of the *Review of Reviews* Albert Shaw to the young economist John R. Commons.[14]

Easley quickly imagined a Civic Federation on a national scale, a "people's congress" that would replace ineffectual political solutions with a "forum" for leading thinkers and reformers. This would be a place for university presidents, academics, church leaders, and union heads to meet, sidestepping politicians and rallying the public toward a new system of industrial relations.[15] As the *Chicago Tribune* reported of the NCF's first national meeting in 1900, this was "perhaps the most important discussion ever had in this country of the broad and urgent subject of how to promote industrial peace."[16]

During a national conference in 1901, NCF president Mark Hanna described his organization's mission succinctly. He explained first that both "trusts" and "organized labor" had evolved to become permanent actors in the industrial world. Accordingly, the best way to ensure economic progress would be to institute an enduring "industrial peace." Peace would help both business and labor by ensuring the smooth, continuous operations of production. Tying a labor truce to American progress, Hanna endeavored to settle the problem of industrial war by persuading representatives of major firms, national unions (particularly the strike-prone, if conservative, AFL), and representatives of the public to sit down together and settle on favorable terms.

The leading voices of the National Civic Federation held a number of suppositions in common. First, unions were essential to the harmonious functioning of industry. As Easley later explained in a personal letter (that apparently went unsent) to a leader of the National Association of Manufacturers, competitive industry could not afford to simply grant better conditions, and so unions were "absolutely necessary if the conditions of the workers were to be improved." Without them, ruinous competition among employers and employees alike would inevitably arise and bring about more and more poverty, class conflict, and shuttered businesses. Managing the industrial world along rational lines of organization would bring benefits to all.[17] As John R. Commons explained, the only workable industrial system was a democracy, but "not Democracy in the historic meaning of a majority overruling the minority, but representation of organized voluntary but conflicting economic interests."[18]

The second presupposition was a conviction that industrial peace could be achieved by ratcheting up public pressure on both capital and labor. The government had thus far proved inadequate. Now was the time for experts and interested parties to be brought to a public table. John Mitchell, president of the largest and most significant union at the time (United Mine Workers of America) and, in the words of a modern biographer, "by far the best known and most celebrated trade unionist of his day,"[19] had faith in the power of the public. In his book *Organized Labor*,[20] Mitchell devoted a chapter to "Public Opinion." He explained, "one of the chief purposes of trade unionism is to appeal constantly, directly, and openly to the general public." This is because the "force of public opinion, acting directly through the newspapers and other channels of publicity, has forced one or the other side to submit" during major strikes.[21] In another chapter titled "Labor and Capital at War," he warned labor leaders who did not strike from the "the highest, noblest, and most disinterested motives" that they would be "comparable to . . . Benedict Arnold." In labor's struggle, the appearance of lofty motives was of supreme importance.[22]

AFL chieftain Samuel Gompers would later reminisce that he had initially been skeptical about joining the NCF, since he was "not in the habit of meeting with employers except for the purposes of avoiding labor troubles or effecting labor agreements and adjustment of labor difficulties." However, he would come to see it as rendering an "undoubtedly . . . constructive service" toward resolving "industrial disputes." By bringing together "labor, employers, and the so-called public. . . . [I]t helped establish the practice of accepting labor unions as an integral social element."[23] Mitchell, Commons, Hanna, Gompers, and other NCF leading lights all found the new organization essential in bringing the public interest as a positive force to the industrial battlefield.

Important limiting factors revealed the NCF's precarious position as peacemaker and representative of the new tripartite social division. First of all, the organization did not accurately represent either the people or labor. Its "public" representatives were not popularly elected, and included many business leaders (such as Andrew Carnegie) and pro-business politicians (such as ex-president and Pullman Strike–crusher Grover Cleveland). This is not to say that business as a whole supported the NCF—it did not. Social scientists such as John Commons also played a role in the "public" segment, offering the NCF a vision of social peace gleaned from academic study rather than popular mandate.[24]

Second, the NCF did not operate under federal authority. The federation sought to solve the problem of industrial war through voluntary cooperation, bringing together the interested parties in a peace effort that would not necessitate federal troops or restrictive laws. Given that both organized labor and major corporations were historically uncomfortable with state interference, the organization's mission seemed safely unobtrusive.

Acting as representatives for the "public interest," reformers understood that their legitimacy relied upon the degree to which they could convince policymakers and politicians that their jobs would not be adversely affected by promoting governmental interference in the private realm. The public, they explained, demanded a degree of interference from the state in the cause of industrial peace. Because this public understood labor conflict to be an ongoing, and escalating, story of dramatic skirmishes and forward marches, reformers had a new opportunity for political influence. State-guided diplomacy seemed a logical solution.

Labor economist Henry Carter Adams argued persuasively that a permanent peace might be realized if capital and labor agreed to operate in a government-mediated, economist-prescribed system of law. The key to birthing such an armistice, Adams claimed, lay in the midwifery of enlightened social scientists. Neutralizing the worst byproducts of industrial growth, that is, monopolies and socialism, would require specialized knowledge and careful planning.[25] As members of new tripartite panels of capital, labor, and the public, reformers such as Adams played up the necessity of an enhanced "public" role, their authority resting upon the scientific knowledge they had of the public's best interests.

Although the NCF and McKinley's commission would prove only marginally effective, the tripartite social division they embodied would prove an enduring model of class conflict resolution. At the dawn of the Progressive age, divining the "public interest" had become inextricably linked with solving the problem of class war, and these bodies gave the public the appearance of having a concrete role in formulating a solution.[26] National strikes, such as the Anthracite Coal Strike of 1902, would be the testing grounds for the new institutions of social stability.

A Tenuous Truce: The Anthracite Coal Strike of 1902

The Anthracite Coal Strike of 1902 pitted a massive industrial union, the United Mine Workers of America, against a tightly organized consortium of rail and coal corporations. It would result in the "public" claiming an unprecedented authoritative role in shaping the most significant labor truce yet. A close look at the media's conceptualization of this strike, in terms of both its similarities to and its differences from past national strike coverage, reveals the ways in which the public had come into its own as a third, and ultimately superior, actor in the industrial drama.

Following the depression of the 1890s, the anthracite (or hard coal) industry had experienced a major period of consolidation. This was due to the J. P. Morgan–controlled Reading company combining with the Central Railroad of New Jersey to acquire some two-thirds of the unmined coal in Pennsylvania. Morgan's actions, along with those of a small number of coal operators who controlled the rest of the coalfields, instilled in the public the sense that the entire supply of anthracite coal in America depended on the decisions of a handful of wealthy men.

Opposing the coal oligopoly stood the United Mine Workers of America (UMWA), an organization that endeavored to consolidate the anthracite workforce into a cohesive unit and had won a strike for higher wages and better conditions. With the relatively brief, and massive, turnout of 1900, the UMWA secured its victory after NCF member Mark Hanna pressured mine owners into signing an agreement for a 10 percent increase on wages.

The owners were not pleased with the new power of the mineworkers, or with the political pressure that had forced them to back down. In 1902, following a UMWA convention that resulted in demands for an eight-hour day, official union recognition, and further wage increases, the owners decided to resist. As a new struggle came to a head, John Mitchell convinced his union to ask the NCF to mediate the situation before the strike began. As previously noted, Mitchell understood the prime importance of making an appeal to this public organization. In doing so, he stepped onto a national platform to air his union's grievances. Because the corporations remained intransigent and unfazed by the NCF's purely voluntaristic authority, these meetings went nowhere. The union pressured Mitchell to call a strike. Covered by having made the appearance of seeking public-minded mediation, Mitchell concurred with his constituency and called a strike on May 12, 1902.

The Anthracite Coal Strike of 1902 immediately took on national importance. Hard coal, while not the only source of energy in the country, played a significant role in rail and domestic heating industries. The loss of this resource could mean a degree of commercial stagnation and economic hardship. As winter approached, the prospect of a drawn-out industrial battle involving a major source of heating became even less palatable.

As with past national strikes, this one seemed to require war language to comprehend it. To this end, the media delivered a battle as exciting as anything in the past. "Reports from the field" depicted "ranks," "squads," even "armies" of strikers, carrying on a battle in the coalfields of Pennsylvania. Keywords such as "charge," "retreat," "volley," and "assault" filled the pages of strike coverage.[27] Though it raged on in only a few isolated locations, this battle occupied the front pages of a number of major newspapers.

The press made it clear that Mitchell and George Frederick Baer (the owners' spokesman and also the president of the Philadelphia and Reading Railroad) constituted the generals of the opposing sides. Well into the strike, the Pottsville, Pennsylvania, *Weekly Miners' Journal* reported, "It is acknowledged all around that President Mitchell has his forces well in hand and that the ranks are as solid as they were five weeks ago." From strike "headquarters" in Wilkes-Barre, Pennsylvania, Mitchell and his high-ranking "officers" worked on their field strategy. The *New York Times* portrayed President Baer as a "General" who represented the worst of organized capital.[28]

A month into the strike, the "lines" remained "tightly drawn," with miners and the operators' henchmen facing each other across closed pits. Both sides refused to "surrender." Because each army had its own sources of cohesion, it was easy to see them as singular, entrenched units. Many (but not all) miners lived in communities isolated from the complex world of the urban centers, enclaves based on shared and often dangerous experience. Their union became a remarkably cohesive unit, and their big strike fostered kinship through its many social events, such as marches and festive parades.[29] The coal companies fought back with hired guns called the Coal and Iron Police (essentially a private militia), and also with the vigilante efforts of the so-called Citizen's Alliance they had recruited.

As in past national strikes, more than just war language was needed to frame the event. When violence erupted, some newspapers condemned the foreign element within the miners' ranks. Italian miners, belonging to a particularly "vicious" class of immigrants, received special notice when two hundred of them opened fire on a colliery on June 16. "Slav" miners, who were perceived to be from a rough and brutal stock of people, had assaulted a coal company agent in West Virginia a month earlier. Periodicals ranging from large papers like the *New York Times* to smaller ones like the *Lancaster Examiner* placed most if not the entire onus of strike-related violence on the shoulders of "foreign" laborers such as these.[30]

The foreign aspect of the miners' army was not the only way that the old fear of outsiders made its way into the reportage. The *United Mine Workers' Journal* referred to the Coal and Iron Police as "Hessians." When violence erupted, several newspapers used the expression "Reign of Terror" to relate the events to readers. The French Revolution reference also went the other way—the *New York Times* explained that the operators' appeal to their "sacred" right to property made as much sense as Louis XVI's appeal to the "divine right of Kings." Indeed, President Baer's infamous "Divine Right of Capital" letter, in which he argued that God had assigned men such as he to control the nation's property, drew much ire from the public when the papers published it in August. After the letter went to press, famous lawyer Clarence Darrow dubbed President Baer "George the Last."[31]

Slavery intruded its way into the coverage alongside the "foreignness" critiques of Baer. The coal president was another Simon Legree (of *Uncle Tom's Cabin* infamy), explained one journalist, intent on driving his wage slaves to early graves. The slave-driver indictment resonated with readers. Men with experience in the mines supported this assessment. In one letter to the editor, a retired miner explained that the mine operators intended to keep "American wage earners in bondage."[32]

While the keynotes of strike analysis—war metaphor, slavery, foreignness, and so on—filled out much of the coverage of the Anthracite Coal Strike, the new entity of the "public" was used in this event to a greater degree than in any previous national strike. By separating the public from both capital and labor, the media furthered a broad national discussion on the labor question in which strikes were understood as conflicts between distinct and socially isolated interests. It also placed the "great third class," that is, the public, in the role of arbiter.

As it went on, the press made sure readers realized the enormity of a drawn-out coal strike. Winter was coming, and a "coal famine" could be disastrous. Agitation for compulsory arbitration, in which both sides would be forced to the bargaining table, increased, as did calls for the public ownership of the industry to prevent strikes in the future. Major newspapers such as the *New York Times* urged the public to awaken to its necessary role and act on its interest in a peaceful solution to the labor conflict. In one early editorial, the *Times* pointed out that as the public learned more about the strike, it would arrive at the "conviction" that it must "find a way to enforce respect for its rights upon both parties to labor quarrels."[33] In order to prevent class war from hurting its interests, the public would need to be mobilized and educated.

Labor leaders also recognized the importance of appealing to the public. The National Civic Federation had been urging labor to join with public and business officials in crafting a cooperative industrial order. Following the "civic" or public-minded nature of the organization, it suggested that a truce could be implemented using only popular pressure. The president of the United Mine Workers and NCF member John Mitchell focused on swaying public opinion in his union's favor. Putting labor's demands in folksy legalistic terms, Mitchell likened the public to a jury, one he declared to be "90%" in agreement with the strikers' side. He also used statistics to show that the rising cost of living demanded higher wages and that the operators could afford to pay.

Capitalizing on popular fears of a coal famine, Mitchell told the press that the owners had a "moral obligation" to the "public interest which is suffering beyond calculation" to arbitrate immediately.[34] Here Mitchell associated the "public interest" with his union's cause. The "suffering" brought on by the higher coal prices and the potential public hardship from a coal scarcity in the future went hand in hand in his analysis. When President Mitchell helped to prevent a massive sympathy strike of the nation's bituminous miners, the mainstream media swung fully on his side.[35]

Mitchell's publicity campaign, coupled with a Dickensian disregard of public opinion by the mine operators, worked to make the strikers very sympathetic to the mass audience. My study of regional and major urban periodicals during the 1902 Anthracite Coal Strike reveals that most major outlets sided overtly with the miners.[36] According to an editorial in the *Scranton Times*, "We have no hesitation in placing the responsibility for this industrial war where it justly belongs, upon the coal carrying companies."[37] The owners appeared despotic, refusing to arbitrate with a well-run, responsible union headed by the businesslike John Mitchell. The plight of the miners received a generous amount of sympathetic press. Depicted as hard workers, whose terrible occupational climate won them little pay and no union recognition, miners garnered support from a public conditioned by a pervasive discourse of antimonopolism to view aggregate wealth with distrust.[38] Throughout the strike, the press exposed the owners as greedy and arrogant men, a select group of plunderers whose refusal even to listen to arbitration implied that they could not deny the legitimacy of the union's requests. George Baer seemed particularly tyrannical.[39]

On October 3, 1902, President Theodore Roosevelt called a meeting of union leadership and owners at the White House. Although that meeting would end inconclusively, Roosevelt had made an unprecedented move. As the nation's youngest president, Roosevelt was thrilled to cast himself in the role of the virile, activist guardian of public welfare. His was a personality attracted to the glory that accompanied decisive action taken in battle, and this episode of industrial war tested his self-made image. In his private correspondence, Roosevelt explained that he did not want to operate on the "Buchanan principle."[40] (Former president James Buchanan's inaction in the face of sectional collapse on the eve of the Civil War served as a lesson to Roosevelt, convincing him of his country's need for decisive leadership in the face of this strike battle.) He now likened himself to President Lincoln, a president who, in terrible times, made tough decisions despite contradictory advice and kept his nation together. In Roosevelt's case, the advice ranged between the extremes of sending in federal troops to crush the strike and forcing the operators to comply with the strikers' demands.[41]

Efforts to force a "treaty" gathered momentum as the months dragged on. A month into the strike, the *New York Times* criticized the coal operators for trying to "conquer a peace by forcing the unconditional surrender of the miners." The newspaper advocated a "settlement" between the two sides, mediated by the government if necessary. In countless editorials, the *Times* explained that public indignation toward the operators and the strike in general had grown. Consumers wanted a steady supply of coal, and the operators needed to work with the unions to make this happen. If the operators expected the miners to "surrender," explained one editorial, they needed to give them fair "terms."[42]

Peace advocates took many approaches. In his published "Sermon on the Coal War," one reverend prayed for a truce between the two sides, asking whether the church should step in and mediate a peace between the "contending forces of Capital and Labor." Another minister explained that it would be an "unpardonable sin against the public welfare" for either side to demand "unconditional surrender" without any compromise. A *Wilkes-Barre Times* editorial referred to the strike as a "war a la outrance," one that demanded not just victory for one side but a permanent system of arbitration. The suggestion of compulsory arbitration, in which both parties involved in a strike would be *forced* to the table, also circulated throughout newspaper editorial pages.

Other peace proposals similarly took on the sense of urgency only war can bring. Some advocated immigration restrictions to shut off the dangerous elements filling out the strikers' ranks. Others suggested that the federal government seize and run the mines itself. Whatever the solution, it was time for something to be done. Charles Foster, a former secretary of the treasury and the ex-governor of Ohio, captured popular sentiment when he explained that the time had come "when capital and labor must cease fighting and work together."[43]

After six long months and countless false hopes, President Roosevelt convinced J. P. Morgan to force the operators' hand. After a number of "peace conferences," the operators agreed to arbitrate. A jubilant *New York World* explained that the decision to arbitrate represented "practically a surrender to public opinion" on behalf of the mine owners.[44] A mediating Anthracite Coal Strike Commission was established, and the miners went back to work.

The Anthracite Coal Strike Commission itself consisted of seven men, each representing an interested party in the strike. Members included a military representative, a mining engineer, a judge, a mining businessman, a Catholic bishop, a labor leader (who had to come in as a "sociologist"), and the commissioner of labor, Carroll D. Wright.[45] The appointments reveal both the new efforts to include the public in the mediation process and the efforts of the state to create a peace between capital and labor via an ostensibly democratic process. While there was no "public" representative per se, Roosevelt created the body with the explicit intention of garnering widespread public approval for its resolutions, and operated under the pretense that the very formation of such a committee embodied the public will.[46] Unlike President Cleveland in the Pullman Strike, Roosevelt acted not to ensure federal property against the depredations of labor but instead to assert the federal role in ensuring that the public interest be served during factional contests.

Significantly, the commission's decision was to be binding, not voluntary. Under the president's guidance, the government's compulsive power was informed not by the arbitrary use of federal force but by the mandate inherent in a "publicly" interested committee. Reformer Henry Demarest Lloyd recognized the novelty of this, proudly declaring, "There has never been a labor strike equal to this one, and no labor arbitration has ever seen the cause of the workmen presented as this will be."[47] While the NCF's tripartite model did not precisely translate, the spirit of the model did. In future conferences, the three-way configuration would be more literally applied.

The pro-labor *Arena* believed that the Anthracite Coal Strike had created an opportunity for a peaceful resolution to America's industrial struggle. After explaining that the "industrial battles and sieges we call strikes" operate along the same "principle" as any war, it argued that the public, with its "vital interest in peace and order," had more to lose than either capital or labor. As a "non-combatant" (in the words of the *Mauch Chunk Coal Gazette*) the public clearly suffered the most during national strikes. A structure of permanent arbitration would ensure that this group did not face serious hardship whenever capital or labor decided it wanted a fight.[48]

After deliberating, the Strike Commission ruled that the miners' wages should be raised, their hours shortened, and a permanent system of arbitration instituted in the coal industry. Unfortunately, despite the momentousness of these changes, the ruling did not lead to the industrial peace that reformers and businessmen had wished for. Because the commission did not grant union recognition, the operators' continued refusal to deal with the miners' union remained unchallenged by the state. Further, ever since the Great Railroad Strike of 1877, courts had enforced a "government by injunction" (in the words of William E. Forbath) that drew the power of the law down heavily against a variety of working-class protests.[49] In effect, then, this apparently "neutral" government intervention did not guarantee that representatives of labor would be recognized in the future. This refusal spelled disaster for organized labor's larger objective of taking a permanent place at the bargaining table. It meant that the government's actions did not imply any greater victory for American unions.

However, change seemed under way. The "public" had become more than merely an abstract concept. It had now received concrete representation in the form of a federal surrogate of its will. The federal government had shown signs that its intervention into the industrial war would take the form of an explicit alliance with this third party, whose interests it would represent via labor secretaries and social scientists. While local and state institutions such as the National Guard often played a more immediate and decisive role in settling conflicts, with the Anthracite Coal Strike it was strongly suggested that the federal government had a decisive part to play as a placeholder for the great mass of noncombatants. This in turn supported the belief that the capital-labor war was a national, not a local, phenomenon. Not unlike during the Civil War, the federal government had the ultimate responsibility of ensuring social peace.

In 1902, the "public" moved decisively from its role of simple war casualty toward the more complex role of class arbitrator. A group whose interests overrode those of either capital or labor and ultimately guided society, it now had the power to step in and alter industrial relations under the aegis of its elected spokesmen in the federal government. Labor supporters of the NCF such as Samuel Gompers might have even seen in 1902 a glimpse of a new, positive federal role, one not beholden to the "tyranny" of the courts and rule by injunction.[50] In the next chapter, I will explore the ways in which the federal government began to fulfill its new role of public guardian in the early decades of the twentieth century.

5

The Fist of the State in the Public Glove

Federal Intervention in the Early Twentieth Century

On August 31, 1910, in the opening effort of a new run for the highest office, Theodore Roosevelt gave a memorable speech entitled "The New Nationalism." His speech was full of references to the Civil War, an event that Progressives had learned to enlist in the cause of social justice. He claimed that Lincoln, who had successfully "faced and solved the great problems of the nineteenth century," also offered light on solving the major problem of the twentieth century. He quoted: "Labor is prior to, and independent of, capital. Capital is only the fruit of labor, and could never have existed if labor had not first existed. Labor is the superior of capital, and deserves much the higher consideration." Not wanting to appear biased, Roosevelt explained, "If that remark was original with me, I should be even more strongly denounced as a communist agitator than I shall be anyhow. It is Lincoln's. I am only quoting it; and that is one side; that is the side the capitalist should hear. Now, let the workingman hear his side: 'Capital has its rights, which are as worthy of protection as any other rights. . . . Nor should this lead to a war upon the owners of property. Property is the fruit of labor; . . . property is desirable; is a positive good in the world.'"[1]

Roosevelt's summoning of Civil War memory and comparing it with the ongoing labor question reveals the power of industrial war framing into the twentieth century. The former president proposed a solution in the form of his "New Nationalism." The foundation of his argument was that, as in Lincoln's day, the federal government was needed to resolve a serious crisis in the social order. He explained: "This New Nationalism regards the executive power as the steward of the public welfare."[2]

Roosevelt's speech reflected a growing concern in America. By the dawn of the twentieth century, it had become apparent that settling the industrial war would require federal intervention. Given longstanding American traditions of popular sovereignty and a limited, unobtrusive state, promoting an expanded governmental role in mediating labor conflict required recognition of the primacy of the "public" over either capital or labor. Only if portrayed as the living embodiment of the popular will could the national government play a decisive part in structuring a permanent labor truce. Needless to say, enlarging the federal role would take time.

Two factors operated to spur along this process. The first was a sense that the class conflict was escalating beyond control. The second was an event—the First World War—that served to connect social order with the government's agenda for industrial peace. In this chapter I will focus on each of these in turn. The first section deals the escalation of industrial war before World War I, in particular the rising threat of syndicalism and the pervasive belief that the government had a significant role to play in settling differences between capital and labor. The second part explores the consequences of wartime nationalism in the years that followed. Focusing in particular on the steel strike of 1919, this section will deal with the heightened sense of national citizenship engendered by the war that made the "public" group seem the most significant element of society, as well as with the expanded role the federal government would be expected to play in enforcing an industrial cease-fire.

Escalation and Reaction, 1900–1915

By the early 1900s, the "public" had already been identified as a distinct and separate interest apart from capital and labor, and had been given representational form during McKinley's Industrial Commission and in the president's 1902 Anthracite Coal Strike Commission. According to a rising chorus of reformers and muckraking journalists, creating a permanent industrial peace required that the public clearly understand the causes of the class war, and that the federal government be responsive to its desire for social order.

Calls for peace resounded in this period of rising unionization and labor militancy. Especially after 1903, evidence of increasing class conflict was abundant, as a dramatic upsurge in strikes and workplace violence heightened the sense that the public stood naked and exposed to the clashing wills of labor and capital. (Between 1900 and 1919, the strike rate only rarely dropped below five hundred walkouts a year, with some years witnessing over three thousand strikes.)[3] Frederick Winslow Taylor, the famous exponent of scientific management, understood that a sense of class war characterized the workplace. In his famous *The Principles of Scientific Management,* first published in 1911, he argued that employers needed to focus on countering labor's "soldiering" efforts (a term, he noted, that seemed unique to America) to control the pace of work. While he vigorously repudiated the notion of an unavoidable conflict between capital and labor, Taylor focused especially on the current state of affairs, noting that "throughout the industrial world, a large part of the organization of employers, as well as employés, is for war rather than for peace." His answer, the careful measurement and readjustment of work routines, was but one of many circulating about at this time.[4]

Taylor's influence rode on the reaction to a wave of union militancy and the trope of industrial war that facilitated a national dialogue regarding the nature of industrial society. Reflected in the mélange of industrial war–related literature and radical ideas circulating after the turn of the century, words such as syndicalism (roughly meaning union-centered militancy) and socialism came to be understood as indelibly connected with labor's bellicosity by the contemporary press.[5] A closer look at the rhetoric and behavior of two of the most visible union organizations at this time, the Industrial Workers of the World and the American Federation of Labor, sheds light on the popular perception that the industrial war was getting out of hand.

The Industrial Workers of the World (the IWW, or Wobblies), an extreme syndicalist organization founded in 1905, saw itself on the "Fighting Front" of the class war. In its original preamble, the IWW opened: "The working class and the employing class have nothing in common. There can be no peace so long as hunger and want are found among the working people. . . . Between these two classes [workers and employers] a struggle must go on until all the toilers come together on the political, as well as the industrial field." A voluminous, if transitory, membership, which might have included up to 2 million to 3 million people during its first two decades of existence, testifies to the persuasive logic of its writings and speeches.[6] After the Wobblies gave up political action in favor of concentrating on the "industrial field," strikes became their most potent weapon.[7]

Striking was something of a martial art to the Wobblies. As with any fighting technique, it needed to be studied and cultivated. In one article in the organization's *Industrial Worker* periodical, four distinct types of strikes were described. Ranging from the "passive" to the "general" strike, work stoppages represented "skirmishes with the enemy," necessary attacks in the battle for industrial dominance. To claim victory, a final strike would eventually be required, a great general strike of all industries throughout the country. The millennial aspect of this plan is undeniable, evidence of the persistence of an older theme of strike analysis carried through to a new century. Driving home calls to battle with song and verse, the IWW appealed to many unskilled and otherwise alienated laborers. Among this number were many members of the supposedly conservative American Federation of Labor.[8]

Although the AFL leadership roundly criticized the Wobblies as radical deviants (having committed the sin of "dual unionism"), similarities between the two groups suggest a compatible *lingua franca.*[9] Like the Wobblies, the AFL scorned independent political action in favor of the specific and concrete gains to be made by striking. Using an idiom of total war, AFL president Samuel Gompers understood strikes to be part of his union's "strategy," telling one union secretary to "Strengthen your position so that you may have a good chance of victory before you strike." Although historians have long emphasized Gompers's cautiousness, his understanding of strikes as strategic maneuvers in an ongoing war with capital suggests that his wariness was more a product of caution than antipathy toward battle. In the pages of the *American Federationist,* Gompers stressed his position that strikes needed to be carefully directed "movements." His war was a gradual operation, dependent on precise maneuvers and incremental gains. Gompers's quarrel with those he referred to as the radical "irreconcilable impossibilists" had at least as much to do with method as with philosophy.[10]

Simply stated, the IWW and the AFL shared in and capitalized on the same frame of class conflict that supplied the public with vibrant accounts of industrial struggles. One consequence of this popular means of analysis can be seen in the appeal of militant class struggle vernacular for mainstream union members. While the content of the action differed according to each organization, the AFL's call for the mobilization of its "movement" against different "enemies" suggests that the militant rhetoric pervading union literature was not so distant from that of the Wobblies. News outlets and politicians similarly used this language to communicate information regarding the industrial world. Widely understood as labor "battles," strikes carried the connotation of organized combat.[11]

Industrial war discourse touched a popular nerve in the early twentieth century. Socialist organizers, perceiving society as being plagued by an ongoing war between workers and capitalists, found more success during this period than at any other time in American history. With over three hundred socialist periodicals in print nationwide, the Socialist Party of America garnered a wide audience from a variety of economic and regional niches, from poor, discontented farmers in the Midwest to urbanites in the East. Electorally, socialists found themselves a more pronounced presence. Socialist Eugene Debs, who described the nation as the setting for "a series of bloody and historic battles in the class war," received an impressive 6 percent of the popular vote in 1912.[12]

Mainstream politicians could not afford to ignore the pervasive fear of class war. In Theodore Roosevelt's speeches and public writings during this period, the conflict between "organized capital and organized labor" would be addressed again and again. He pleaded to Congress that the struggle between the two "federations" needed to be remedied through recognition of the "interest of the general public" or disaster would ensue. His use of the term "federation" seemed to equate organized labor (the American Federation of Labor, perhaps) with industrial capital. They were equally powerful entities, dangerous if left unchecked by the government. He told the New York Chamber of Commerce in 1902 that it would be up to the lawmakers as well as capital and labor to ensure "industrial peace."[13] Woodrow Wilson, among many other politicians, followed his lead. Wilson's addresses often referred to a division between unscrupulous capitalists and the common man, or of the "contest" between opposing ideals of positive change and reaction.[14] Wilson recognized keenly the political advantages of recognizing and proactively addressing the industrial struggle, as his October 1919 First Industrial Conference would later illustrate.

The disconcerting climate of industrial war, quantified most concretely in the rising number of strikes between 1909 and 1919, left a powerful imprint in the minds of academic reformers as well.[15] Positioning themselves as diplomats for the public in the industrial war, reformers now saw government as having a key role in restraining what leading labor economist John Commons referred to as the unchecked "weapons" of the strike and the lockout.[16] Moving beyond the voluntarist approach to industrial peace advocated earlier by the National Civic Federation, social scientists increasingly sought to include the government in labor relations by stressing its representative function.

Linking the government to the popular will, hence making themselves "public" representatives, reformers attempted to fashion peace in a way that mediated both populist critiques as well as laborite and managerial fears of unwanted federal interference. In this way, social reformers helped to supply rhetorical links between the government and the general public. By affirming the danger strikes posed to the "welfare" of the people, men such as Commons could implement interventionist policies without having to acquire an actual public mandate at the polls or violating their own voluntarist philosophies.[17]

Even if only to awaken both "federations" to the necessity for trade agreements, the state's involvement in the industrial world required public authorization in some form or another. In the first volume of John Commons's landmark *History of Labour in the United States* (1918), contributor Selig Perlman credited regulatory labor legislation to an awakened "public" that had, as result of the Anthracite Coal Strike of 1902, "become accustomed to view the labour question in a non-hysterical light" and had pushed the federal government to make wise arbitration laws. Commons himself became actively involved in founding an organization of social scientists, the American Association for Labor Legislation, whose goal was to advocate responsible, publicly minded labor laws.[18]

The federal government had ostensibly been active in creating a labor-oriented body since the establishment of the Bureau of Labor in 1884, which gathered data on working conditions and wages. Headed by former director of the Massachusetts Bureau of Labor Statistics (and Civil War veteran) Carroll D. Wright, the bureau signaled an effort by the federal government to analyze industrial work, if not empathize with organized labor (union activists wanted Terence Powderly for the top job). In 1903, the largely innocuous Bureau of Labor was absorbed into the Department of Commerce and Labor, in an effort to incorporate labor's interests within a broader framework of power-sharing with capital. However, the Bureau of Labor occupied but one of eighteen agencies represented in this department, and it received a scant 1 percent of the budget. Gompers would later refer to this as a "setback" that "whetted our appetites and desires and our insistent demand." In 1913, an independent Department of Labor was finally established in the wake of the 1910 Democratic congressional victory. The new department, designed to "foster, promote, develop the welfare of the wage earners of the United States," demonstrated, symbolically at least, that labor had come to be taken seriously as a player in the industrial world.[19] A different federal organization, however, would have a much bigger impact on the public discourse of class war.

In 1911, a collection of social workers and activists circulated a well-received petition to institute a new federal investigative body to provide the public with the latest information regarding the industrial war. The petition began ominously: "Today, as fifty years ago, a house divided against itself cannot stand."[20] Perceiving the nation as facing a conflict akin to that which had confronted Abraham Lincoln, the petitioners urgently demanded federal intervention. Drawing on Civil War memory, which at this point seamlessly and without further explanation could be employed to illustrate the magnitude of the industrial situation, reformers made their project immediate and essential.

Later that year, the U.S. Commission on Industrial Relations was born, the most conspicuous effort yet by the federal government to deal with the industrial war. Its role, as one of its staunchest congressional supporters explained, would be to "show the employer and employee alike the necessity of getting together and thrashing out their differences over the table instead of in the industrial battlefield of strikes."[21] Beyond educating the combatants, the commission would educate the masses; "public representatives" were to be given equal billing with capital and labor in its information-gathering procedure. The public representatives included such labor-sympathetic personas as NCF participants John Commons and Mrs. J. Borden Harriman (a pro-union activist). Pro-labor attorney Frank Walsh chaired the commission. While the "public" body was only minimally representative of wageworkers, it better represented the voting public than the NCF had. The representatives recognized the necessity of enlightening *all* of America to the folly of class conflict, and they scripted their project accordingly.

From the start, the commission worked diligently to shed light over the industrial terrain. Its composition reflected the new tripartite understanding of society: representative members of capital, labor, and the community all testified on the extent of the problem and possible peace solutions. Supplying the general public with a window through which to view the extent of the class war, the commission sought to appeal to the broadest possible base of concerned listeners. It marked a new phase in generating public awareness; the government now advertised itself as an unbiased information broker. As the embodiment of popular will in an age of increasing state presence, its activities necessitated a careful appeal to its constituency. The effects of the new process of information gathering and dissemination would be important; it was soon reported that the situation was even worse than hitherto imagined. According to the commission's findings, published in 1915, social inequality—perpetuated by criminally "unjust" wages, endemic unemployment, and a feeling among workers that they had been denied social "justice"—had created the conditions for the escalating labor conflicts.[22]

The U.S. Commission on Industrial Relations's findings sent ripples of shock through the country. One newspaper accused the commission of issuing an "indictment against organized capital" itself. Whether or not others shared this view, the escalation of hostilities first evident during the Gilded Age were made undeniable by this highly popular body. Supplying testimony for the commission's *Final Report* in 1915, William Haywood, secretary-treasurer of the IWW, reiterated what had by now become a commonly heard assessment. He explained that "there can be no identity of interest between capital and labor. . . . We say . . . that the struggle between the working class and the capitalistic class is an inevitable battle." He ominously portended the struggle to continue "in spite of anything that this commission can do."[23] The specter of irrepressible conflict had yet to be exorcised.

The commission's *Final Report* galvanized reformers, laborites, and employers alike. The *Report* itself had been tendered in three parts, due to quarrels among the groups involved in the commission. In the first report, signed by Frank Walsh, the onus of the industrial conflict rested with those employers whose draconian repression of unions left workers poor and with a bitter taste of injustice in their mouths. In the second report, written by Commons and Harriman, the government was beseeched to play an enlarged part by establishing labor-capital committees to work in combination with federal and state industrial commissions, all watched over by the secretaries of commerce and labor and union representatives. This plan reflected Commons's so-called Wisconsin Idea of having responsible, publicly minded representatives of capital and labor meet to settle their differences under the government's watchful eye.

A third statement was made by the employer group, which argued that labor held much of the blame for the industrial war, though it recognized that "many sinners" existed "among the ranks of the employers" as well. All three of the groups agreed fully that conflict now characterized industrial relations. Commons went so far as to recognize the "permanent struggle" that had existed since 1877 that "has frequently resulted in civil war." He went on to say, "It is claimed by some that this contest is irrepressible." For Commons, the solution lay less in specific legislation than in a structured bargaining apparatus in which the government would play an enlightened, mediative role.[24]

Following the publication of the report, Frank Walsh immediately formed the Committee on Industrial Relations to press Congress to enact mediative legislation. Of the many bills proposed, only a few passed, including an eight-hour labor act for the railroads. A few years later the U.S. Commission on Industrial Relations's goal of an active, interventionary state would be fully realized. The causal agent in this development would be a world war.

The Great War, the Rhetoric of Mobilization, and the Presence of the State

When Europe plunged headfirst into the most devastating war it had ever known, America struggled to stay out of the conflict. However, the pull of the armaments market and the shock of German attacks on American ships made this task nearly impossible. In April 1917 America joined the Allies. The United States' entry into World War I would provide a new and unforeseen opportunity to connect the "public interest" with the interventionary actions of the state.

This process would begin with an immense mobilization project headed up by the federal government. To foster support for American involvement in the European war, the government enlisted the technologies of mass advertising. From the thousands of "four minute men" employed to lecture crowds on the necessity of war enthusiasm to the federal Committee on Public Information's relentless propaganda, the public would be constantly reminded that it needed to awaken to a new global threat and participate in a new crusade for democracy itself.

For the most part, Americans embraced the martial spirit, participating in a linguistic project that involved the renaming of German-sounding items and a revitalized vernacular of democracy and anti-authoritarianism. "Hamburger" and "sauerkraut" became "American"-sounding "liberty sandwiches" and "liberty cabbage." Material culture supported this co-channeling of patriotism and hatred, as self-explanatory titles such as *The Prussian Cur* and *The Beast of Berlin* played in theaters while American flags hung from countless poles and windows.

Together, a new enemy and a generalized patriotic patois pushed public discourse in a singularly powerful direction. Nationalist mobilization worked so well that in his aptly entitled book *How We Advertised America* (1920), the former head of the government's Committee on Public Information, George Creel, explained that the war couldn't have come at a better time, given the "many voices" that had previously interpreted America "from a class or sectional or selfish standpoint."[25] The war, he suggested, rescued America from social division by diverting the public's attention to a greater threat, uniting it in the process. His committee would bridge class difference with a self-defensive idiom that defined American democracy in some of the most exclusionary ways available. It proved so popular that capital and labor representatives charged their own rhetoric with a patriotic, xenophobic, and otherwise *herrenvolk* style that would, as shall be discussed below, help frame new boundaries of acceptable behavior.

Similarly, to the delight of a great many Progressive reformers, the European war had reinvigorated a flagging American spirit. In the words of the journal *New Republic,* the war provided "access" to the new "spiritual force" of internationalism and democracy.[26] A worldwide battle between democracy and autocracy had highlighted the preciousness of American political institutions and provided a common enemy for all of the elements of the tripartite society. Yet while the new nationalist surge would unite the country behind the war effort, it also provided new ammunition for the warring industrial forces.

In a remarkable effort to encourage labor quiescence during the war, Secretary of Labor William Wilson likened the United States to a "great union" that had "declared a strike against the tyranny of the German government." Secretary Wilson recognized that war rhetoric and the demands of fast mobilization (a tightening labor market coupled with wartime inflation had given workers more impetus to strike) had helped to encourage labor militancy. At this moment of unity, the class war might escalate due to increased labor power. To avoid this, the secretary warned that to strike now would be to "scab" oneself against the U.S. government. Although such calls might have proven ineffective—in 1917 there were 4,450 strikes, more than in any year previous—in back of them rested a renewed effort by the federal government to intervene in labor conflict.[27]

The National War Labor Board, founded on April 8, 1918, to help coordinate the wartime economy, embodied a new approach to handling the tripartite order evident in federal mediation since the turn of the century. Capital, labor, and public groups were all given a say in shaping a labor policy for the duration of the conflict. This was especially significant in the degree to which the government, acting through the "public" body, helped bring employers and employees to the bargaining table. In a few instances, such as when Western Union summarily fired eight hundred unionists during an organizing drive, the board actually nationalized intransigent corporations, placing its role as mediator for the public blatantly above the interests of capital.[28]

The National War Labor Board served as a concrete manifestation of a growing reform spirit that linked the government with the popular desire for industrial peace. In many ways, it exemplified an intensified version of the Commission of Industrial Relations of 1913–1915 (in fact, it was headed by the man that had run the commission, pro-labor attorney Frank Walsh). Resolving some five hundred labor disputes using primarily its voluntarist moral power of agreed-upon influence, the board exuded the sense that a new era of industrial democracy was afoot. Gompers's vocal support of the war effort supplemented the sense that state cooperation spelled a permanent advancement in the relative position of organized labor. AFL membership grew from 2 million to 4 million during the course of the war.[29]

The price of labor's gains would be an exchange of militant independence for public approval. This included a self-conscious drive by union leadership to realize what John Mitchell had understood in 1902: that working with and through the state meant a shift toward respectability and a step away from a popular image of isolation and belligerency. Gompers recognized that an alliance with the government's war effort constituted an alliance with the majority of Americans, and his role as civilian advisor for the war-preparedness Council of National Defense, along with his virtual no-strike pledge, provided new and permanent links to the federal government's agenda. Unionist rhetoric, filled with nationalist invective and critiques of "un-American" radicalism, gave labor the sense of new responsibility and belonging.

The paradox of socially divisive labor militancy at a time when most workers embraced American unity further reveals labor's own interpretation of the war. For workers, the war foretold a new industrial era in which the "democracy" of union bargaining could replace the "autocracy" of the open shop. Workers criticized "autocracy in industry," using phrases like "American Hohenzollern," "Prussian," and "hun" to describe their managerial opponents.[30] Speaking to the United Mine Workers in 1918, union organizer Mother Jones expressed the new militancy in no uncertain terms. She explained that, as American soldiers fought the Kaiser abroad, they would return to fight American Kaisers at home. "We will have the guns Uncle Sam paid for and we will use them on the pirates and put a stop to slavery."[31]

If advocacy of an alliance with the state was not an unprecedented move for labor (in 1903 United Mine Workers leader John Mitchell had written: "The trade union movement in this country can make progress only by identifying itself with the state"[32]), the Great War did provide a new basis for such identification. The state might even provide the way for labor's ultimate public acceptance and a permanent social role. Underlying the new effort at effecting change at the federal level was a sense that America's government was ultimately democratic and responsive, and that its actions reflected the people's will.

WARTIME NATIONALISM had far-reaching consequences for popular perceptions concerning the dangers of industrial war. During the war, the binary between autocracy and democracy encoded in mobilization rhetoric had cemented links between the state and the public by aligning the interests of the populace at large with the actions taken by the federal government. For labor leaders, this meant that gaining permanent concessions from capital would require an alliance with the state and its mobilization project. A further consequence, perhaps unanticipated by federal authorities, would be that wartime nationalism would excite union rank-and-filers in their ongoing efforts to wrest power from management at the workplace. Lumping the Kaisers abroad with those at home, laborites exposed ongoing working-class frustrations with managerial authority. With phrases ripped from reports and experiences of the European front, labor leaders filled their speeches with vivid references to the Great War. The expression "over the top," appropriated from the experience of trench warfare in which troops charged up and out of their trenches and onto the field, captured a renewed fighting spirit. The phrase would be used again and again in the years to come.

Business leaders used the tense wartime climate, and the coincident Russian Revolution in October 1917, to condemn union militancy as un-American. Labor leaders too could be portrayed as "autocratic" men who forced their membership to join and follow or be barred from employment. When U.S. Steel president Judge Elbert H. Gary explained that the war had created an "unfortunate situation" in which the "vicious element" was trying to bring about revolutions worldwide via "labor unionism," he capitalized on managerial fears lurking beneath the pervasive nationalist sentiment.[33] The war with Germany and the new Bolshevik menace allowed employers to persuasively argue that strikes were instigated and led by radicals who aimed to install a revolutionary, undemocratic government.

Business also benefited from a new assault on traditional bastions of pro-worker reportage. As John Nerone explains in *Violence against the Press*, "the World War I years saw the destruction of a large chunk of the radical network that had been built over the past two decades." In all, about one quarter of all socialist locals were eliminated, and with them numerous small-town radical publications. Further, Woodrow Wilson's postmaster-general denied second-class postal rates to most radical periodicals, barring the national distribution of papers such as *The Masses* and *Appeal to Reason*.[34] The dramatic curtailment of the left press both reinforced business anti-unionism and narrowed the spectrum of pro-labor discourse.

For the general public, the war had made "Americanism" the great totem of civic identity. George Creel's efforts in this case proved successful, as his government agency both capitalized on the patriotic spirit and smothered vocal resistance by way of a successful censorship of radical periodicals. Despite a significant undercurrent of dissent, the war instilled a sense that the public had now become a more unified body than ever before. Although this pulling together did create a strong rhetorical basis for "democratic" union solidarity, it also forced labor to side itself with a nationalistic vision of American democracy. The benefits, and contradictions, of this project would become apparent in the strike year of 1919.

The Steel Strike of 1919

After the armistice, employers quickly set about dismantling or modifying many of the federal industrial agencies that they perceived as hindering them. Although many reformers tried vainly to maintain such institutions as the National War Labor Board, their efforts foundered on a Republican-sponsored backlash to labor's wartime gains. The strike wave of 1919 proved a moment when labor's new position would be tested and soundly defeated. The largest and most significant strike of this period, the steel strike of 1919, illustrates not only the weaknesses inherent in labor's new and ostensibly publicly sponsored position, but also the strengths of the new bonds. While the strike was an utter defeat for the CIO-led Steel Workers Organizing Committee, newspaper coverage reveals how new trends of understanding—namely the notion that the "public" now required concrete representation by the state during major strikes—were becoming entrenched in strike analysis and even in union rhetoric.

To get at the ways in which the Great War cemented this new state role, my analysis of the steel strike of 1919 consists of two parts. The first part will situate the strike historically and review the ways in which the war and global events in its wake (namely the Bolshevik Revolution) affected older themes of strike analysis. Following this, I will evaluate the ways in which the state now played a prominent, if ultimately limited, part in forging a truce between the disputants and claiming the "public" mantle of authority for its actions.

The Steel Strike and the Older Themes of Analysis

The causes of the steel strike involved the nature of the steel industry at the time and the volatile militancy of the wartime labor movement. Long the bane of union organizers, U.S. Steel stood in 1919 as the most conspicuous bastion of corporate open-shop resistance to unions. The National Committee for Organizing the Iron and Steel Workers, a body of laborites intent on creating an industrial steel union, had begun its drive in 1918 under the auspices of the AFL. Led by John Fitzpatrick of the Chicago Federation of Labor and union organizer William Z. Foster, the Organizing Committee proved quite successful. Carrying on the syndicalist tactic of rejecting politics in favor of direct action in a militaristic style, the committee enlisted "Flying Squadrons" of organizers to carry out its industry-wide "campaign." In a short period of time, the Organizing Committee had recruited thousands of workers. Recognizing the threat, major steel corporations refused to talk with them. As U.S. Steel president Judge Gary explained, "we do not confer, negotiate with, or combat labor unions as such." A national steel strike was set to begin Monday, September 22, 1919.[35]

The media quickly captured the momentous nature of such a strike. Steel was essential to the economy, a necessary ingredient in the vital auto, rail, and construction industries. To interfere with these industries, newspapers explained, would be to put the brakes on the process of postwar industrial recovery. On September 21, the day before the strike began, newspapers expressed anxiety and a certain sense of inevitability that this walkout would be a mammoth affair. The *Washington Post* found "both sides in the contest apparently prepared for the battle." It explained that now there was "nothing to do but wait for the test of strength on Monday," which would constitute an "attack of labor" on U.S. Steel.[36]

The same day, the *New York Times* published an editorial entitled "Road toward Industrial Peace" by Dr. Charles Eliot, president emeritus of Harvard University and a participant in President Wilson's upcoming labor conference. In the article, Dr. Eliot explained that the Great War had taught the nation the importance of extending democracy to industry. Given the great victory over despotism recently obtained, it made little sense for corporate managers to behave like autocrats, carrying on their industrial objectives "like aggressive campaigns in war." The solution to industrial war lay in industrial democracy, in which capital and labor would play cooperative roles in determining workplace conditions. Unfortunately, he offered little in the way of concrete proposals.[37]

The timing of the steel strike made its consequences even more dramatic. Wartime nationalism had helped to create a backlash against all forms of radicalism, increasing the perceived need to curb the flow of "dangerous" foreign immigrants. A new Red Scare helped reduce syndicalism and socialism to the appearance of criminal activity, as evident in countless "criminal syndicalism" laws and in the media's numerous refrains against those who threatened the nation with misleading "doctrines of class struggle."[38] Even as it persisted in guiding popular understandings of work stoppages, class war slowly became associated with the foreign agenda of subversive revolution. According to pro-business elements in much of the press, the seeds of revolution were being planted within the labor movement, an allegation reflected in the current wave of labor militancy. Although the IWW had been effectively driven from the scene with state-endorsed violence during the war, the fear that the Wobblies now sought to "bore from within" the labor movement in an effort to create a Russian-style revolution gripped the nation.

AFL leadership bolstered popular fears by warning its membership publicly of the threat of subversive radical elements. This, in turn, supplied media observers with all they needed to accuse the labor movement as a whole of unwittingly incubating revolutionary elements. During talks regarding an impending railroad shopmen's strike in August 1919, the *New York Times* drew attention to the "battle" going on in the AFL over "who shall control the labor situation." As mass strikes became the order of the day (general strikes in Seattle and Winnipeg had recently resulted in entire cities shutting down), many perceived a larger struggle looming in the background. Could all of these strikes be connected to an insidious revolutionary plot? When steel workers voted to walk out on September 22, such a worry could not have seemed entirely unfounded.[39]

On the first day of the steel strike, several hundred thousand steel workers refused to work (a number that constituted nearly half of all steel factory employees). Mills went ominously silent in Chicago, Milwaukee, Cleveland, and numerous smaller cities. For the press, war metaphor unsurprisingly provided the most common mode of analysis for this event. Although serious violence did not immediately ensue, small clashes in Pennsylvania between strikers and corporation-recruited soldiers gave the media its first evidence of battle. Labor, now "marshaling [its] forces" to maintain the strike, faced "charging" state troopers outside of Pittsburgh.[40] The next day, strikers "assaulted" non-union workers in New Castle, Pennsylvania, as mill guards received a "volley" of "missiles" from angry laborers. An Associated Press article acknowledged on September 22 that this was a "preliminary skirmish in the great industrial struggle which opened today between labor unions and the United States Steel Corporation." Several major papers immediately referred to the strike as an "industrial war."[41]

As with previous national strikes, in the weeks to come the walkout took on the appearance of a great battle between two organized forces (despite the truly unorganized reality of the Steel Workers Organizing Committee). Union "ranks" remained solid. Newspapers explained that the "generals on both sides" of the "steel war" remained confident in their efforts, as union leaders and managers touted the gains made from their respective "headquarters." Both the employers and the union "Waged Strike Campaigns," as manifested in walkouts and solidarity parades choreographed by labor leaders, as well as movements by imported strikebreakers and hired armed guards sent in by capital's commanders. When workers left the Bethlehem Steel Works in Pennsylvania, for instance, the media explained that the steel works had been "crippled" by a labor "offensive." This was but a single maneuver "commanded by union leaders" to get new workers to "join the ranks of the strikers."[42]

Pictures showing the "Defensive System of the Gary Steel Mills" or the larger region that was "The Center of the Steel Fight" provided readers with data needed to assess the movements of the soldiers. While Pittsburgh and Chicago represented the primary "strategic points" on the "industrial front," the strike was pointed out to be threatening to both national commerce and regional stability. When strikers from Steubenville, Ohio, threatened to "march" on Wierton, West Virginia, the *Pittsburgh Leader* expressed fear that a "pitched battle" would result, as the steel company had "heavily guarded" its works. Although state troopers would foil the plans of the Steubenville strikers, it was apparent that the boundaries of this battle stretched across state lines and legal jurisdictions.[43]

The war metaphor so apparent in the strike coverage was given an added boost by the fresh memory of the Great War. While the number of Americans involved in combat in Europe was comparatively low, the experience had revivified the industrial war trope with new expressions and references. Labor organizer William Foster constantly employed military language to exhort strikers, telling his workers (and through the press, America) to watch for the next capital "offensive" and join him "over the top." Mother Jones of the United Mine Workers pleaded to returning soldiers, "You went abroad to clean up the Kaiser . . . ain't you men enough to come over and help us get the Kaisers at home? We'll have an army as big as yours and you'll be with us and we'll lick hell out of 'em."[44] Some returning soldier–steel workers even marched in full uniform for the strike effort, an act that earned them jail time for insubordination.

The radical press enthusiastically seconded the "war" assessment of the strike. With typical revolutionary aplomb, headlines like the *Socialist News*'s "Half Million Workers in Open Class War" exuded a jubilant, hopeful air. IWW periodicals like *One Big Union Monthly* and the Chicago *Solidarity* agreed that this strike held revolutionary possibilities. The *Socialist Review* acknowledged that this strike was being fought with "all the forces which the steel corporations could possibly command." While the strike demands themselves might not be "revolutionary," explained the *Review,* "the fact of a strike in the steel industry is most revolutionary and the profound changes which may result from this steel strike may touch the heart of the whole American labor movement." Unfortunately for the strikers, the press had already connected the strike to the revolutionary left, and this resulted in a profoundly anti-union tenor of coverage.[45]

A PRIVATE WAR AT PUBLIC EXPENSE

FROM ONE WHO KNOWS

FIGURES 13 & 14 These cartoons depict the ways in which the public was shown to be injured by the "private war" between capital and labor and the influence of World War I memory on labor conflict representations.

Source: *Outlook*, October 29, 1919.

William Z. Foster, the labor organizer most responsible for organizing the steel strike, was himself a former Wobbly who had terminated his membership in 1911 and gone on to form the Syndicalist League of America before becoming a railroad car inspector and joining a local of the American Federation of Labor. In 1917 he allied with others in a campaign to unionize the meatpacking industry. His efforts at uniting workers across the industry under the AFL umbrella proved highly successful in this instance. His attempts to do the same in the steel industry appeared to be similarly auspicious, but as the steel strike became a national event, his radical past came back to haunt him. A pamphlet he had written in 1911 entitled "Syndicalism" would be quoted freely in the mainstream newspapers and journals. In the tract, Foster had argued that the syndicalist, in "fighting the everyday battles of the working class, intends to overthrow capitalism." In the midst of a Red Scare and a massive steel strike, Foster's exultation of class war confirmed the public's worst fears about labor's ambitions.[46]

While in agreement as to the dangerously revolutionary aspect of the steel strike, large East Coast media outlets typically did not present as one-sided a version of events as did the Pittsburgh papers. The *New York Times* and the *Washington Post,* for example, regularly accused U.S. Steel president Judge Gary of having helped to bring about the strike. Progressive journals like the *New Republic, Nation, Outlook,* and *Survey* often blamed Gary for his role in instigating employee resistance via his tyrannous disregard for legitimate union organization. Even more considerate to the strikers was the *Chicago Herald and Examiner* and to a lesser extent the *New York World.* William Randolph Hearst owned the *Examiner,* and now Frank I. Cobb (having replaced Joseph Pulitzer in 1911) edited the *World.* Cobb was a pro-Wilson Democrat, a man a who once described Democrats as men "[s]ympathetic with labor, but as firmly set against socialism and predatory poverty as against predatory plutocracy."[47]

A self-proclaimed labor sympathizer who regularly advertised his papers in the *American Federationist,* Hearst himself had regularly been criticized as a fomenter of labor violence due to his pro-union, pro-striker proclivities. According to Ambrose Bierce, "in matters of 'industrial discontent' it has always been a standing order in the editorial offices of the Hearst newspapers to 'take the side of strikers' without inquiry or delay."[48] Like Cobb, Hearst recognized the spending power of the blue-collar workforce, and he did not intend to alienate such a substantial market. While the *Herald Examiner* covered the strike as an "industrial battle" with all the frightful war language that went with it, its editorials regularly excoriated Judge Gary's role in exacerbating the situation and defended the AFL's decision to support Foster, who it claimed had been unfairly singled out for a past he no longer owned.

Within the newly charged war trope evident in the coverage, older analytical themes also remained present. Familiar republican refrains abounded.

The cries on both sides of the strike lines against "tyranny," "autocracy," and "despotism" recalled much older Revolutionary language. Although the term "revolution" was by this point freighted with the negative implications of European tyranny, the language of freedom and popular rights continued to supply employers, laborites, and journalists with an explanatory vocabulary. During the war it had been easy to demonize the Germans because their form of government so neatly opposed America's self-image of democracy. Finding similar elements among strike leaders or corporation heads proved a simple, and compelling, task.[49]

The traditional fear of foreignness, which was heightened during and right after the war, especially following the Russian Revolution of 1917, took on new life as the media connected the strike with global events. In an editorial entitled "The Industrial Outlook," a *Washington Post* commentator explained that "Americans are fearful that a series of strikes might result in well-nigh universal disorders and possibly a revolution" just as in Europe.[50] Coincident front-page stories of battles in Russia between the "Reds" and the insurgent forces of democracy added to this feeling.

The newest "foreign" term, "Bolshevism," cropped up again and again in the coverage. Bolshevism, explained one *New York Times* editorial, lay just under the surface of the union movement, and if "class" rather than "universal" interests continued to be stressed, the Red menace would surely make itself apparent. Mill owners explained that the "real test of strength" was not between steel and the unions, but between "the radical and conservative elements in the labor ranks." Immigrant strikers (many of whom were southern and eastern European in origin) were regularly reported to be ignorant pawns of "imported organizers," men whose limited experience with American democracy made them unaware of the subversive evils of radicalism. Advertisements in steel town papers implored immigrant laborers (in a variety of languages) to "Be a 100% American," presenting images of Uncle Sam, smiling with a hand over the shoulder of a workman, pointing toward an American flag.[51] Importantly, during the strike the expression "un-American" would be used by *both* sides to describe the true nature of their opponent.[52]

Following riots in Gary, Indiana, federal troops occupied the town and uncovered weapons, literature, and evidence of subversion, fueling further press accounts of the true "radical" nature of the strike. The *Chicago Tribune* now explained that the strikers aimed for a "Sovietized Mill." The *New York Times* published a tract found at Gary addressed to workmen that explained that capitalists manipulated the government, and would use federal power "against you when you dare strike against the enslavement which they force upon you."[53]

Samuel Gompers himself used the popular fear of communism to consolidate his influence and convince the public of the necessity of responsible unions. He warned that if responsible unions were not recognized, radicals would have more appeal to workers. Further, he accused steel company managers of having brought in violent "gangs from Europe" to labor for them, thus setting the stage for this very strike.[54] Gompers's connection of conservative organized labor with national interest would have far-reaching consequences. Many major newspapers and middle-class journals supported the AFL president's efforts to make organized labor a partner in industrial growth, one sanctioned by the public for its own best interest. Responsible industrial armies, ensured by mass approval to have a right to exist and bargain with one another, might craft the kind of durable peace that comes when two mature forces see eye to eye at last. As the *Washington Post* put it, "Many industrial wars have sprung out of the fact that one side was better organized than the other. If both were fully organized, would they not be compelled to cooperate?"[55]

Most significant in terms of previously established themes of strike analysis, the "public" had become the center of the struggle as never before. In an article published first in the *Philadelphia North American* and reprinted elsewhere during the strike, the writer explained that while justified in its militancy before the war, labor had now alienated the public with its incessant promotion of "union ideas" and its putting "class interest above the safety and welfare of the community." Just as the "force of public sentiment" had previously reduced the power of capital to run roughshod over national interest, now labor had to learn that it was not the supreme power of the land. In a recapitulation of the significance of the "public" in the tripartite society, in which the state was an extension of public interest, the writer explained, "the public is a thing apart from and superior to either capital or labor. In a democracy the public *is* the government" (italics mine).[56]

When Foster's revolutionary text was brought to light, newspapers justified their condemnation of the strike as foreign and radical because the "public . . . believed that the strike was dictated by radical leaders bent on gaining power rather than correcting conditions." Another newspaper explained at the beginning of the strike, correctly, that if violence ensued, "the balance of public opinion would swing against the employes." Both capital and labor recognized the importance of popular appeal during the strike. Indeed, the union published its demands of Judge Gary in the newspapers, and the steel company similarly promoted its public role by constantly reiterating its generous wage rates.[57]

Throughout the steel strike coverage, the "public" found itself positioned at the center of the contest. Politicians appealed to its sense of justice; laborites appealed for its support; employers appealed to its intolerance for foreign ideologies. Most significantly, the "great third class" was beginning to consume the other participants in the industrial war. The *Wall*

Street Journal, reflecting on the failure of the walkout to paralyze the steel industry, noted, "there is a growing realization of the superiority of society's claim upon an individual to that of any private organization."[58] Put another way, workers returning to their jobs had wised up, realizing that they were members first and foremost of a larger, classless public rather than pawns of union organizers. Speaking to the American Legion during the strike, ex-president Theodore Roosevelt argued that labor leaders sought to artificially separate labor and capital into "class groups" alien to America's naturally synchronic nature.[59]

The Public's Federal Guardian during the Steel Strike

Importantly, the coverage of the steel strike revealed more than just the ways in which the First World War and the Bolshevik Revolution added new life to the war frame and traditional fears of foreignness. The war had effected more than a "ratcheting" process (in which existing state structures are intensified). With the advent of such institutions as the National War Labor Board and the Council of National Defense, the war had significantly altered the relationship of the state to society. During the steel strike, millions of faces looked to the federal government for a solution to labor conflict.

Shortly after the strike began, a Senate strike investigation took a prominent place on the front pages. Urging an immediate inquiry into the strike, one senator demanded an investigation "not on behalf of either side" but "in the interest of the great third party to every strike that is not represented, namely, the public at large." The inquirers drew their power from the sense that they now had a responsibility to the electorate to ensure industrial peace. To make their point, they emphasized the especially dire nature of this particular strike. A Democratic senator from Colorado likened it to "a civil war." A Republican senator explained to Congress, "this strike seems to be the first skirmish in industrial warfare." The secretary of the interior warned that "class warfare is here, and it is here to stay and grow" unless efforts to educate both aliens and "the ominous mass of our own unlettered whites and blacks" were made a top priority.[60]

While the Senate investigation went on, the state played an even more prominent role in President Wilson's First Industrial Conference of October 1919. Although the conference had been scheduled before the strike had been planned, it soon became apparent that the strike and the conference would be indelibly interconnected. Regularly referred to as the "industrial peace conference" by the press, major newspapers and journals immediately approved of it and hoped that it would resolve the steel strike before the violence escalated or it became "general." Keeping the world war in mind, the conference was commonly compared to the European peace proceedings at Versailles. Just as Versailles was aimed to prevent a royal elite from selfishly initiating war at the expense of their people, the Industrial Conference would ensure the prevention of "small groups of irresponsible men acting temporarily for capital or labor from inflicting upon the public the loss and suffering inseparable from industrial war."[61]

The coincidence of the Versailles accords and the Industrial Conference was not accidental. According to President Wilson, the purpose of the Industrial Conference was to remake the industrial scene just as he currently sought to remake world relations. At one point during the conference, he pleaded, "At a time nations are endeavoring to find a way of avoiding international war, are we to confess that no method can be found for carrying on industry except in the spirit and with the very method of war?"[62] A new world order and a new industrial order, both based on popular democratic ideals and a responsible, active government, went hand in hand.

The conference participants were divided up into labor, capital, and public groups. While the composition of the labor and capital groups drew no major criticism, the public group, having wealthy business leaders in it, did. The *United Mine Workers' Journal,* at first optimistic about the conference, raged that putting business moguls like John D. Rockefeller and (it could hardly be imagined) Judge Gary himself in the "public" category had reduced the proceedings to "a ridiculous joke."[63] Up-and-coming union leader John L. Lewis actually resigned in protest before the conference convened for this very reason.

While the public representatives at the Industrial Conference by no stretch of the imagination represented the American people at large, they did identify themselves as embodying the third, and potentially most significant, element in the industrial order. As the conference began, Bernard Baruch, chair of the "public" group and former head of the federal War Industries Board, gave "the authoritative intimation that the members representing the innocent bystanders in the war between capital and labor were prepared to abandon the attitude of watchful waiting and benevolent neutrality." The public group would offer several strike-preventing proposals, and even agree with the labor group as to the necessity of union recognition across the board.[64]

The group representing capitalists proved too obstinate in its position on union recognition. After it vetoed Gompers's proposal that unions be recognized as the legitimate and most responsible advocates of workers, the labor group left, soon followed by the capital group itself. While the representatives of the public vainly tried to continue the conference, it was apparent to all that the experiment had failed. Explaining the conference's collapse, a popular journal noted that because strikes ran rampant over the land, holding the conference now was akin to having a European peace conference in 1917 (during the height of the hostilities). An editorial in the *Pittsburgh Leader* lamented that because the capital side had refused to recognize labor's right to organize, and because "surrender" would be impossible for either side, the "alternative" now was something that "no sane mind likes to contemplate. It is filled with horror, horrors that many do not realize." The final hope, explained the author, was that "the great mass which stands between them [capital and labor], which like the civilian population in time of all war suffers most, will decide between them."[65]

The steel strike ended January 8, 1920, when the Steel Workers Organizing Committee finally recognized the futility of continuing an unwinnable strike. The journal *Outlook* conceded that it would be "extremely unlikely" that any conference would ever "end the class war between labor and capital which is now going on or prevent the intensification of that struggle which seems impending." Indeed, it recognized that "the American people are living today in a condition of class warfare. Skirmishes and pitched battles are being fought all over the country in this war, the two parties to which are organized capital and organized labor."[66]

Yet elsewhere in the *Outlook* article there was a glimmer of hope, even at this dark hour. While neither side of the industrial war could be "destroyed" without "destroying the very structure of American society," both could be *made* to live harmoniously together. The Industrial Conference, despite its failure, augured an optimistic future by providing "encouraging evidence of the existence in this country of a great body of fair-minded men and women who are bound by hard and fast obligations to neither capital nor labor, and who can be depended on in any crisis when the broader interests of the country are threatened by the narrow ambitions of any class."[67] By situating the industrial war as being a thing apart from the moderate many, it became something that could be theoretically controlled.

Americanisms

Following the strike wave of 1919, the employer backlash intensified and unions shrank in size and influence. The years to come would be lean ones for labor, as strike rates declined and union membership dwindled.[68] By the end of the 1920s, the annual strike rate fell to levels not seen in over fifty years.[69] In terms of the ongoing process of understanding class war, however, the 1920s meant more than a sad footnote to failed Progressive aspirations or a quiet preface to the dynamism of union militancy to come. A few features of this interwar decade stand out to suggest that the eventual shift away from the "industrial war" frame proceeded along a path reaffirmed by the Great War experience.

The postwar years were not simply a return to *status quo ante;* the First World War experience had set new terms for the meaning of state presence in the industrial world. The federal government had cemented its role as public guardian of industrial order, and labor and capital had recognized that future gains would require public sanction and political attentiveness. Although the National War Labor Board withered away, institutionalized union representation processes and the sense that, in the words of the commissioner of the Bureau of Labor Statistics, "We cannot turn back," meant that class war would take place in a more closely monitored terrain now.[70] Further, as will be seen, the engineers of the New Deal drew much direct experience from the Wilson administration.

The popularity of the term "reconstruction" in this period, evident in numerous book titles (such as *Reconstructing America* and *Reconstruction: A Herald of the New Time*) and essays by influential reformers, reflected a sense that the state needed to have a hand in shaping postwar industrial relations. In a manner harkening back to the post–Civil War era, the public was shown to be unwilling to stand back and watch labor battle with capital. Reconstructing industrial relations would require a watchful, responsive state and an attentive public.

The new role of the state in the industrial realm would not be particularly beneficial for labor, however. Legislation such as the Transportation Act of 1920 created tripartite mediative bodies that worked specifically to prevent the influence of unions in industry. In the nationalist postwar climate, politically chosen "public" and "labor" members were more likely to be anti-union than impartial.[71] Further, the definition of "public" itself received an overhaul in the 1920s, as the Americanization project initiated during the war extended into the following decade and worked to limit labor's range of offensive possibilities.

Government-sponsored Americanization programs, the Immigrant Restriction Acts of 1921 and 1924, and the conspicuous adoption by capitalists of patriotic terminology (that is, "The American Plan") in describing their open-shop offensive, all illustrate the saturation of public discourse with a vernacular of exclusionary citizenship. Coupled with the lingering effects of the wartime alliance between the state and labor and the AFL's carefully choreographed conservatism in the years ahead, the sense that industrial conflict was a foreign product grew and grew.

The "public," a rhetorical designation used to rationalize state intervention during the war, became distinctly more Waspish, conservative, and xenophobic afterward. For labor organizers, the idiom of "Americanism" inspired (or forced) them to situate their objectives as mainstream, publicly minded, anti-radical, and patriotic. The new president of the American Federation of Labor, William Green, who succeeded Gompers in 1924, asserted at every possible convenience his belief that the labor movement was above all a thoroughly American institution with only accommodationist ambitions. His words dripping with the argot of citizenship, Green explained on one occasion, "every good citizen must have a reverential regard for our form of Government." He consistently rejected the inevitability of what he derisively termed "the so-called 'irrepressible conflict'" of capital and labor.[72]

As the public found new definition as an exclusionary group characterized by anti-radicalism and a revamped European wariness, a new category of academic study came into its own, *industrial relations*.[73] In 1920, courses in "industrial relations" first entered universities (appropriately, initially at the University of Wisconsin), and the field took off. Simply stated, industrial relations set itself up as a field aimed at promoting a permanent, harmonious order between capital and labor. Having found a new influence with the federal government during the war, many labor economists fashioned themselves as "industrial relations experts" and sought to find a middle ground between employer demand and employee interest.[74]

The varied practitioners of industrial relations came to very different conclusions and embodied a range of disciplinary approaches, from economics and sociology to psychology and even physiology. One common phrase that appears throughout these early writings is "industrial democracy," a term embodying the hopes for an equitable settlement between the opposing forces.[75] As industrial relations expert Morris Llewellyn Cooke explained in a series of articles published as a pamphlet in 1919 entitled "An All-American Basis for Industry," a new opportunity for democratic peace in the industrial war was at hand. He began, "There appears to be an exact parallel between the situation which confronted the great Lincoln in the second year of the Civil War and the situation as we find it today." The "industrial struggle" had come to an impasse. Shifting analogies, he likened society to a car speeding toward the edge of a precipice. "Unless we somehow reverse the course," disaster was imminent. The solution to the problems created by the industrial "battlefront" was simple: "democracy in industry." The ideal of "peace and cooperation," he articulated, rested on a sharing of power between capital and labor.[76]

Cooke was not alone. "Industrial democracy" bloomed as an ideal solution, not unlike Wilson's ideal of warring nations forming a great league to establish a more democratic balance of power. Oftentimes, the foundation of their arguments rested on an acknowledgment of divining and acting on behalf of the "public interest." In a piece written in the journal *Industrial Management* in 1920, one writer explained that the "industrial engineer" now had the responsibility of bringing agreement "between these two forces [capital and labor]" by allowing "the pleas of the third party, namely, the public, to be heard." In another article published in 1923, a Chicago lawyer explained that because "[t]he master is the public" and because "[t]he strike is war, and war is the poorest method of obtaining justice," responsible new laws would be necessary to disarm, and ultimately integrate, uncooperative industrial "soldiers."[77]

Integrating these "soldiers" into the greater public was a process that operated along numerous fronts in the 1920s. For employers, Americanization programs, the "American Plan" of the open shop, and the implementation of various welfare capitalism initiatives such as employee health plans were all means to the end of the social integration of labor under an ostensibly publicly minded course of action. Similarly, labor leaders argued that their own behavior was guided by a singular public mindedness, and that defending national citizenship motivated their concern that workers be fairly treated. Even rank-and-filers spoke in warm tones about their role in the larger citizenry, as unions such as the immigrant-rich United Textile Workers pledged themselves as organizations for "God and Country."[78]

For its part, the federal government, though dramatically curtailing its interventionist policies after the war, did not fully retreat to its older, hands-off position. It had demonstrated that as public representative, its new role involved ensuring that major strikes did not interfere with the safety of American citizens. In practice, what this meant was a precipitous erosion of organized labor's power, as evident in hostile Supreme Court decisions, the interpretation of the Transportation Act, and politicians inveighing against labor "monopolies." In 1921, bloody conflict erupted in West Virginia between striking miners (some wearing their old army uniforms) and a succession of company soldiers, state militiamen, and federal troops. The press handled the conflict in its accustomed manner, for the most part. The recent war, the Civil War, and the American Revolution all added color to the war frame. The *United Mine Workers' Journal* inveighed on the miners to "sacrifice and hold unfalteringly until the final victory sounds forever the doom of autocracy." Anti-union minister Dr. J. W. Carpenter used the Great War as a different reference, saying, "It is just as much a patriotic duty to clean up Mingo County as it was France." Neil Burkinshaw, writing for the *Nation,* was remarkably sympathetic. His article "Labor's Valley Forge" explained that "[t]he miners of Mingo County are fighting one of the gamest fights in the history of industrial war, fighting for a principle—the emancipation of themselves and their children from the worst economic serfdom in America." What all this discourse had in common was the familiar theme of "industrial war."[79]

As labor retreated in the 1920s, the supposedly "neutral" definition of state responsibility served business well. The most telling example of this new relationship would be in 1922, when the government-sponsored Railroad Labor Board decided to cut shop-craft wages to a point that inspired a massive shopmen's strike. Consisting of some 400,000 men and women, the strike was promptly declared "illegal," as it violated the binding decision of a board that ostensibly recognized both "labor" and "public" groups. Government repression of the strike received little criticism from a public who felt that the government was now acting on behalf of its interest.[80]

By the eve of the Great Depression, the industrial war had been muted by the power of a central and measurably stronger "public" and by a growing federal government supposedly embodying its interests. While this new configuration would be used to justify the suppression of unions in the 1920s (as evident in the 1922 shopmen's strike), in the years ahead labor would find itself in a position to use it to its own advantage. The very components used to justify anti-union tactics in the 1920s—the federal government's acquiescence in the implementation of the open shop, the use of court injunctions to hinder strikes, the patriotism that made union organizing suspect—would be employed to challenge the power of capital in the 1930s.

Regardless, having been concretely linked with state authority, the public could begin to be viewed as a robust entity both exclusive in its righteously narrow self-definition and inclusive in its ability to draft capital and labor into its ranks. Indeed, in the writings and actions of a small cadre of industrial relations experts, Progressive politicians, and "new unionists," one gets an early glimpse at a new industrial order. It would be an order marked by government-enforced peace, with the state standing in as "public" and the armies of capital and labor institutionalized and kept in check as part of a permanent tripartite balance. As Steve Fraser notes, this group dreamed of what the head of the Bureau of Industrial Research called a "new order in the industrial and social world of America." For example, Morris Llewellyn Cooke, the industrial relations expert who demanded that capital and labor accept a "democratic" peace, regularly shared his thoughts with trade unionist Sidney Hillman, who would become instrumental in founding the CIO in later years. Their vision—which would eventually be captured by the idea of "industrial pluralism"—remained marginal in the 1920s. But in the crushing economic catastrophe to come, it would finally find its moment.[81]

6

Co-opting the Combatants

Pluralism on the Front Lines

Like Frankenstein's monster, "industrial war" would not go away, hulking into the twentieth century to frighten Americans with a foreboding message of capital-labor conflict. As strikes raged on and corporations and unions consolidated their power, industrial "battles" continued to occupy a central place in the popular imagination of social disorder. Then, in a development that has puzzled many since, class war slipped quietly from view, even as strike rates showed little evidence of decline.

The causes of this disappearance are connected with the compelling fear generated by the war frame itself: grand battle inspired a demand for peace, and peace required careful diplomacy carried out by the people's representatives. This process was intimately tied with the ascent of the "public" itself, a body first delineated in appeals for industrial peace in the 1880s. Having gradually gained prominence with the expansion of the federal government (embodying the "will" of the people) into workplace relations in the opening decades of the twentieth century, the public became formidable enough to inspire laborites to reevaluate their position in relation to it. Many union leaders, such as AFL presidents Samuel Gompers and William Green, understood keenly the advantages of associating their organizations with the democratic many.

The public proved to be an effective placeholder for the common interests of all, undermining the two-sided social framework that war language facilitated. As capital and labor were reconfigured as organizations within a greater public (rather than as antagonistic classes), a new industrial pluralist discourse replaced war talk. Helped along by the creative power of the federal government in accommodating popular desires for industrial peace in the 1930s, observers began to depict America less as a battlefield occupied by warring industrial armies than as an arena for competing interests. By 1950, industrial war language had been largely replaced by the more inclusive vernacular of citizenship and rights.

Documenting the beginning of the demise of the industrial war frame is the subject of chapter 6, which will begin with an examination of the emergence of a discourse of capital-labor inclusion within a larger public in the New Deal era. I will then turn to the media's evaluations of labor disputes in the 1930s, examining the ways in which mainstream news sources connected the federal government's agenda with the public's desire for industrial peace. Finally, I'll explore the emergence of the word "management" and the pluralist implications of its use as the replacement term for "capital."

Battling the Depression, Fighting for Rights: The Incorporation of Industrial Soldiers in the 1930s

The paradox of the decline of the idea of class war in the midst of Depression-era labor conflicts can be resolved when understood as part of a longer rhetorical transition already under way. The imagined war between capital and labor had created a climate in which public-enforced mediation was seen as the only way of defending cherished democratic institutions from the effects of intense, national labor conflicts. Highly publicized industrial commissions in 1898 and 1911–1915 gave this "great third class" concrete representation; what these federal agencies lacked in influence they made up for in widely publicizing the brutal extent of the class war. When World War I broke out, advocates of federal intervention took advantage of the demands of mobilization, informing a national policy that placed the government at the center of industrial relations. Though the government cut back afterward, the apparatus of federal mediation remained in place.[1]

When hard times struck in 1929, the power of the state to ensure the public interest in social harmony was again dramatically put to the test. As jobs dwindled and working-class radicalism rose, many looked to the national government for stability. Having played a leading role in guaranteeing class harmony during the First World War, government officials sought to recapture their old position using the experience of that war as a primary point of reference. Fighting a new war against an external opponent (not the tyrannous Prussians but the equally despicable Depression), the government integrated employers and employees into a single unit of defense.

According to one contemporary, President Herbert Hoover "repeatedly used the figures of speech of war in his description of the depression."

He constantly referred back to Great War battles in describing his agenda for economic recovery, at one point likening the economic downturn to the "battle of Soissons." At the urging of many within his party as well as economists outside of it, Hoover arranged to enter this new battle with what limited resources the government could deploy given his party's current laissez-faire policy. The Reconstruction Finance Corporation, Hoover's biggest effort at restoring the economy, was, in the words of Federal Reserve governor Eugene Meyer, "a revival of the War Finance Corporation, that's all, but with extended powers."[2]

Hoover's efforts did not extend far enough, complained millions of Americans. The problem was not in his understanding of the economic downturn as an "enemy" to be fought by the government; he simply had not utilized federal power to the degree that this foe required. Having established its ability to intervene in labor relations in the name of public interest, the national government stood poised to deliver a new industrial peace in the cause of national survival. Franklin Delano Roosevelt, the Democratic candidate running against Hoover in 1932, understood this clearly. In a speech delivered on the campaign trail, Roosevelt (like Hoover) explicitly connected the Depression to the Great War, declaring that the nation now faced "a more grave emergency than in 1917."[3] Once in office, he increased the federal presence in industrial life to an unprecedented degree.

Roosevelt's dramatic interventionary efforts captured the imagination of millions of workers. He tapped into languages of republicanism (he critiqued the "economic royalists"), Christian moralism (he proclaimed in his first inaugural address that the "money changers have fled . . . from the temple. . . . We must now restore that temple to the ancient truths"), and war with such ease that workers eventually associated his persona with the government's battle against the Depression. With the passage of Section 7(a) of the National Industrial Recovery Act in 1933, which recognized labor's right to organize, coupled with the popular phrase "the President wants you to join the union," many believed that joining a union could actually be a patriotic act.[4]

Yet the story is not as simple as this. The president did not immediately have the full support of organized labor, nor were his early decisions viewed as being entirely pro-worker. The AFL did not approve of FDR's secretary of labor, Frances Perkins. Firmly entrenched in their own biases and political experiences, the AFL leadership likely believed that a woman could not be capable of dealing effectively in the rough, masculine world of labor relations. Despite all of the advances made by laboring women, despite the distance traveled since the successful campaigns of the suffragists, women in the 1930s remained, in the words of Elizabeth Faue, "in a marginal and subordinated position in the [labor] movement." More openly, the AFL leadership worried that Perkins, who was not firmly linked with the labor movement, would not empathize with their position. A few months after the election, AFL president William Green warned a congressional committee that if appropriate legislation were not passed, labor would conduct a "universal strike." Roosevelt, in return, seemed unwilling to bend toward labor, quailing at Senator Hugo Black's AFL-backed bill that would mandate a compulsory thirty-hour workweek (with no decrease in salary).[5]

Facing an active, energized labor movement, FDR pushed for a recovery bill that reflected a more industry-friendly, "collaborative" effort. The National Industrial Recovery Act (NIRA), passed June 16, 1933, and hailed by the president as "the most important and far-reaching legislation ever enacted by the American Congress," attempted to put in place a tripartite industrial body not unlike the National War Labor Board during World War I.[6] Essentially, the act aimed to find common agreement between capitalists and labor leaders on the grounds of rationalized industrial recovery. The bill's relaxation of antitrust laws pleased the National Association of Manufacturers, while the famous Section 7(a) that guaranteed the right to unionize met the approval of union leaders Sidney Hillman and John L. Lewis. Roosevelt saw this as part of what would be "a great cooperative movement throughout all industry."[7]

Under cover of Section 7(a), workers unionized in droves, assured by the government that they were enlisting in what Roosevelt called "the infantry of our economic army."[8] Secure in their sense that the government was finally listening, they addressed themselves as beneficiaries to the federal government's program of industrial recovery. Many believed Roosevelt's assessment that it was the government's duty to provide for the economic and social rights that its citizens deserved. Speaking of their newfound "rights," workers revealed the power of the imagined connection between their own interests and those of the nation as a whole.[9]

The strike waves of 1933 and 1934 tested the new legislation, and millions of workers soon discovered that despite the friendly talk, the federal government did not in fact "want" them all to unionize. As Hugh Johnson, the government's administrator for the National Recovery Administration (the body created to implement the NIRA), explained in 1933, "it is not the duty of the Administration to act as an agent to unionize labor in any industry." Further, the National Labor Board, created in August 1933 to mediate labor disputes under the NIRA umbrella and designed as a tripartite board with three labor, three capital, and one presiding public representative, found itself stymied by a lack of any legal mandate to enforce its rulings. In short, the outcome of a bill intended to "prevent industrial strife and class conflicts" (in the words of Hugh Johnson) seemed to be exactly the opposite.[10] The failure of the era's largest strike—the General Textile Strike of 1934—epitomized the NRA's shortcomings.[11]

Strikes in steel production, automobile manufacturing, meatpacking, and numerous other areas continued to buffet the industrial core of the United States into 1935. At the same time, the Supreme Court declared the NIRA unconstitutional. This set the stage for what historians call the Second New Deal, a new set of legislation centered on the National Labor Relations Act, also known as the Wagner Act. Passed in July 1935, the Wagner Act was bitterly resisted by the National Association of Manufacturers, who spent more money than had ever been spent before in a corporate lobbying attempt trying to halt its passage.[12] As written, the act aimed to address the "inequality of bargaining power between employees who do not possess full freedom of association or actual liberty of contract" and the "organized" employers. By guaranteeing "freedom" and "liberty," the Wagner Act would help forestall "strikes and other forms of industrial strife or unrest." In fact, the legislation explicitly guaranteed that "nothing in this Act shall be construed so as to interfere with or impede or diminish in any way *the right to strike*" (italics mine).[13]

The Wagner Act thus supplied the tools necessary for industrial labor to make real organizational gains, and it did so in the context of a rhetoric pregnant with a sense that workers had an investment in the state's social agenda, and vice versa. This in turn grew from the ongoing process of inclusion of labor organizations *within* the greater American public, begun years earlier. Back in the 1920s, mainstream union leaders sought to align their unions with the "public interest" in order to retain the position of authority first granted to them by the state during World War I. During the Depression, popular demands for federally assured social stability helped organized labor gain an even deeper foothold. Not only were unionists working for the public interest, they were part of that body as well. In one indignant article written in 1945, a laborite explained that the three-part breakdown of "Labor, Management, and Public" was but a "world of fantasy." In reality, he explained, the "real Public is the American people, most of whom are working people. . . . Public Opinion is what they think."[14]

The efforts of the most militant union federation of the time, the Committee (later renamed Congress) of Industrial Organizations, illuminate the ways in which labor identified itself with the public interest by the late 1930s. CIO organizers aimed, foremost, to integrate the vast numbers of nonunion "unskilled" labor into the ranks of the labor movement, and proved quite successful in their efforts. Starting as a splinter group of industrial unionists within the AFL, the CIO grew to include 3 million workers by the end of the decade.

The CIO's public language reflected a militancy born of a new sense of entitlement. In its periodicals like the *CIO News* (with a circulation of nearly 750,000) and its radio shows throughout the country, the organization addressed a tremendous audience with engaging testimonials and vivid prose that mimicked, in the words of one historian, the populism of the "big-city tabloids."[15] This massive union was more than an "army" battling against the Depression and corrupt employers. Its literature reflected the idea that the CIO was embarking on a "civil crusade" aimed at correcting anti-labor laws and claiming for the masses the "right" to a decent life inherent in the American democratic promise.[16]

To the extent that the CIO did portray itself as a mighty "labor army," its battle was for the *whole* of the American people. As one writer put it in a 1938 issue of the *CIO News,* "The interests of the people are the interests of labor, and the interests of labor are the interests of the people." At the extreme of this logic, strikes could conceivably be understood as actions taken in behalf of the larger public. During a strike against General Motors in Detroit in 1937, this happened: CIO leaders proclaimed, "it is now war between General Motors and America."[17]

In its battle for the American people, the CIO found its most potent theme in the concept of citizenship. Again, here labor utilized an idea with roots extending back before the economy collapsed. Since as early as the American Revolution, laborites had connected their ambitions with the ideals of a free citizenry. After the turn of the twentieth century, the phrase "industrial democracy" captured this notion in a manner appropriate to the experience of alienation and hopelessness that had accompanied the turn to mass production techniques.[18] The First World War had been something of a proving ground for this discourse, as unionists used the battle against Prussian autocracy as a lever for their own attempts to secure more control over the workplace. While labor's efforts had been largely defeated in 1919, rights talk continued to frame workplace demands, bolstered greatly by new connections between the federal government and the working class.

Once linked with the state's recovery program, the language of liberty became a potent weapon to be used against corporate management. CIO periodicals reprinted songs and poems that celebrated unity and state-mandated justice. In the "Song of the CIO," the writer intoned, "We sing for good / Of Brotherhood / We'll win our cause / With humane laws." The challenge was more aimed at the government, to respond democratically to the new wider public interest, than it was against capitalists as a class. Increasingly, such writers framed their ambitions within a larger discussion of American liberties guaranteed by the state. Strikes were explained to be protests against those employers who sought to "commercialize" away "fundamental rights" guaranteed by the Constitution.[19]

In such a manner the CIO made great strides in integrating itself within the larger framework of American identity. Its motto was "Unionism is Americanism." As it rose to become the nation's most influential labor organization, it maintained that its goal was to ensure the rights of its membership, and by extension, the American people at large. The AFL, which opposed the CIO's statist agenda, found itself drawn in by the new democratic climate of industrial unionism and struggled to reconcile older voluntarist beliefs with the demands of the millions of unskilled and hitherto unheard workers who enrolled in labor unions in the decade. The CIO, which by no means embodied the will of all of labor, nevertheless had located the pulse of the masses and capitalized on its desires for federal guardianship.[20]

The CIO's remarkable ascendancy had much to do with the general appeal of its rhetoric. Organizers tapped into rich veins of republicanism, masculinity, righteous battle, and fears of foreignness and wage slavery to make their points. During a protest in Monroe, Michigan, for example, workers carried signs proclaiming, "Fordism is Fascism and Unionism is Americanism." Union leaders spoke eloquently about their new "battle" for rights. Images of muscular workmen upholding the virtues of the union abounded in CIO literature (working women, it should be noted, found themselves relegated to supporting roles). Organizers spoke of the "march" of labor and its renewed quest for "democracy" in the workplace. They referred to their organization as being the crystallization of the popular will for democracy. As John L. Lewis explained in 1936, the average CIO member wanted "a wage sufficient for him to live as an independent American citizen."[21]

In ensuring that unions had a recognized voice (a process that was by no means straightforward or unimpeded), the state appeared to have sealed its commitment to industrial peace. And structurally, workers *did* have a more personal connection to the state in the 1930s than ever before: building from a tenuous alliance with the Democratic Party dating back to the Wilson administration, organized labor adopted Roosevelt's party as the best representative of its interests.[22] A flurry of laborer-minded legislation, such as the groundbreaking Social Security Act of 1935, which gave workers the sense that the federal government was subsidizing their retirement, made the new connections more concrete.

Watching this process unfold, many influential observers applauded the apparent progress. According to Robert Wagner, author of the most potent piece of pro-labor legislation, guaranteeing labor rights meant the "difference between despotism and democracy." Leading labor economist Sumner Slichter seconded this notion, praising collective bargaining as "a method of introducing civil rights into industry." Slichter argued that as "democratic organizations," unions provided an essential role in integrating workers into a harmonious system of responsible labor relations.[23] Though Slichter was wary of a high degree of government intervention, he recognized the importance of federally protected labor rights.

The state proved to be an audacious supporter of employer-employee conciliation in the 1930s. The La Follette Civil Liberties Committee, organized in

1936 to investigate industrial relations, proved markedly different from earlier industrial committees in that it structured its mission as an effort to ensure "rights" rather than simply to explore the extent of industrial war. In fact, during the committee hearings the expression "industrial war" cropped up not in relation to the dynamic between capital and labor but rather in reference to the unlawful activities of specific, unscrupulous employers. Over the next four years, the committee drew attention to individual capital depredations, at one point alerting the public to the fact that "when the armed forces of the employer are injected into the delicate relations of labor and management, the consequences seriously threaten the civil rights of citizens and the peace and safety of whole communities."[24] By publicizing the repressive tactics employers used to quell the organization drive in industry, the La Follette Committee worked to force corporations to give labor cooperation more attention and helped inspire greater corporate acquiescence to pro-labor legislation. The committee vocally urged government intervention in the name of "public interest," and this time the government seemed eager to respond.

Capital also made a significant, if less dramatic, effort to inculcate (or at least ingratiate) itself within the ranks of the public. Experience taught big employers that an apparent disregard for labor or the public worked against their own commercial interests. In an effort to put forward a new image, corporations began to couch their demands within a discourse of "rights." The "right to manage" would prove a powerful counterpoint to the "right to fair employment" advocated by labor organizers.[25] As both employee and employer groups saw themselves increasingly as interest groups within a greater public, their agendas required similar frameworks of appeal.

Business leaders began to nod to the popular sentiment that increased government presence was now necessary. In a speech at the Fifty-fourth General Meeting of the American Iron and Steel Institute, that organization's president remarked, "there is no question but that public opinion desires a strong Government protecting the general welfare against raids or rapacity of any group." However, this strong government did not need to be an "interfering . . . bureaucracy" that obstructed orderly commercial enterprise.[26] Hedging direct federal intervention while at the same time welcoming an enlarged government put employers in an awkward position. As shall be discussed below, this would require a comprehensive overhaul of employer self-definition.

Viewed under any light, the Great Depression pushed old organizations into new positions just as it supplied new organizations with access to old rhetorical themes. As labor disputes moved once again to the front pages of popular periodicals, such changes seemed part and parcel of a transformation in social relations. A brief look at strike coverage during these years illustrates the ways in which these changes manifested themselves.

The Media in the Decade of Turbulence

Understanding worker unrest in the 1930s must begin with the statistics. The number of strikes went up from 753 per year from 1927 to 1932 to approximately 2,542 per year between 1933 and 1938. Literally millions of workers shut down operations—about 2.5 million in the first year of FDR's presidency alone.[27] Following the 1932 election, and especially the passage of the NIRA, several massive work stoppages clearly qualify as national strikes. The General Textile Strike of 1934 that stretched from Maine to Alabama and involved half a million workers, the Minneapolis Teamsters' Strike and the San Francisco Longshoreman's Strike of that same year that resulted in general tie-ups of entire cities, and several others bear the hallmarks of major national events. With the passage of the Wagner Act and the rise of the CIO, renewed worker insurgency (especially with the General Motors sit-down strike of 1936–1937) inspired reporters, consciously or otherwise, to narrate national strikes within the emerging context of inclusion.[28]

Throughout the coverage of many of the largest struggles, war metaphors mixed with rights talk to form a heady mixture of battle and advocacy of government intervention on behalf of the public. Uneasy with the old dichotomy of capital versus labor, newspapers increasingly referred to "big business" or "industry" when discussing the employers' side. "Labor" remained, but its use suggested that it was more a unit of organization (unions and labor were generally synonymous by this point) than a class unto itself. Importantly, the government's role (especially post-Wagner) had become central to understanding the phenomenon of strikes. The *New York Times,* for instance, paid close attention to Michigan's Governor Frank Murphy and the federal labor bureau in its coverage of the GM sit-down strike of 1936–1937.[29]

A survey of strike-related articles in the *United States News* (later to become *US News and World Report*) in the 1930s offers a glimpse of how the state began to be seen as closely connected with labor relations. A weekly journal offering a comprehensive overview of American politics and economics as well as a survey of editorial opinions nationwide, the *United States News* is a reliable indicator of the direction labor coverage took in mainstream reportage in the 1930s. Connecting the federal government's recovery programs with industrial settlement, *United States News* articles revealed the ways in which the public presence, constituted by an interventionary state, had taken a central position in conceptualizations of industrial unrest and social order.

In a 1933 article entitled "The State of the Union Today," the *United States News* argued that the president's recovery program would only work if "some members of the 'army'—employers" did not violate their peace pledges. It applauded President Roosevelt for appealing to employers and employees for peace during a recent coal strike in Pennsylvania, and hoped that the newly created National Labor Board would see that both groups followed through on their promises. In an article written for the *US News* two months later by National Recovery Administrator General Hugh S. Johnson, Johnson argued that the "vast organizations of industry and labor," which formed a "great team" with the federal government, would now have to permit "government participation and control" in their affairs.[30]

Such federal intervention, the *United States News* consistently reiterated, embodied a justifiable extension of popular demand. The state could guide the nation through the Depression by ushering union and employer groups along a path of cooperation. In 1934 the journal published a piece that argued that because "sporadic labor warfare" dampened industrial recovery, it had become necessary to supervise both management and labor. The government, which "represents the whole public interest," would play the role of watchdog for the common good. In another piece, the writer presumed the role of the government as one that offered "its offices for mediation and for smoothing out the fight as much as possible."[31]

Other mainstream media outlets similarly captured the demand for government protection of the public interest in industrial peace. *Fortune,* a pro-business publication of conservative entrepreneur Republican Henry Luce, printed a number of articles exploring multiple aspects of current labor unrest. In "The Industrial War," one writer attempted to make sense of the current "warfare of the most harrowing character" between unions and employers. To do this, he focused on a set of major strikes and the tactics used on both sides of the picket line to delineate the present course of the labor war. Significantly, the writer noted that the federal government must be viewed as a key player in this wave of unrest, having already "strengthened labor's position" under the Roosevelt regime. Placing an understanding of current labor warfare in the context of federal actions (the current cycle of class war was called the "post-NRA phase"), the author attempted to strike a balance between blanket condemnation of labor's tactics and criticism of employers' intransigence in the face of new legislation.[32]

Other middle-class journals expressed more favorable views of the government's newly expanded role in labor relations. *Harper's Magazine,* for example, wrote that the sit-downs were the result not of union aggression but rather of the promises of the New Deal in ensuring collective bargaining. The government (via the La Follette Committee) had exposed the flagrant injustices perpetuated by business and had offered a solution in the Wagner Act of 1935. It was now up to businesses and politicians to make the New Deal promise a reality. Such change, the writer explained, would reflect on the "widespread belief in this country that the worker deserves a larger share of the fruits of industry."[33]

The damage done during strikes made many liberal-leaning journalists push new views of public interest further. Many argued that the state had not delivered on its promise to support workingmen during strike battles. The *Atlantic Monthly* noted that government officials, whether "biased" or not, needed to give the semblance of fairness in regards to labor relations "lest vast political disturbances occur in the land."[34] The *New Republic* quoted an ACLU report which argued that "public officials aiding one side against the other violate their public function" and infringed on the "civil liberties" of "all sides." The writer of the piece believed that most newspaper readers were deceived into thinking the strikers were to blame for labor violence, when in fact the real bias tilted the other way.[35]

The *United States News* included a helpful weekly section in which it surveyed industrial relations as reported in the nation's editorial pages. It found that newspaper opinion was often wary of both capital and labor, while being impatient and hopeful regarding the government's actions. In one issue, the journal approvingly quoted the *Akron Beacon Journal*, which wrote that strikes themselves were the products of industry's "refusal to deal with Federal officials." In another, it lambasted intransigent employers while imploring the present administration to "bring the warring parties together."[36]

The most dramatic strike of the decade, the CIO-led General Motors sitdown strike of 1936–1937, captured the full attention of the media. The strike involved thousands of workers in several cities and would eventually involve a state governor and the president himself. Although war metaphors filled out the contours of the bulk of reportage, other aspects of coverage hinted at a new model of understanding, one premised on government-based conciliation, a close monitoring of public opinion, and an underlying discussion of rights and responsibilities. Furthermore, the battle frame itself carried a sense of hyperbole not evident in that used to account for previous national strikes, suggesting a shift in emphasis from reference to class division to a less dire conflict of interests.

The strikers in this instance were led by men such as CIO president John L. Lewis, who at one point was referred to as a "general addressing his troops," and UAW leader Homer Martin, another man portrayed as a strike "general." Although space was given to maneuvers and strategies—typical of past national strike analysis—new aspects of state intervention and citizenship worked to undermine the cogency of the war metaphor. As *Harper's Magazine* put it, "Inside the [striker-occupied] plants, for all the warlike paraphernalia, the peacefulness and good spirit of the strikers was such as would have touched the heart of a settlement worker." The CIO, explained the writer, had changed Americans' negative view toward labor.[37]

Other mainstream publications similarly muted the implications of this national strike. While it dedicated much of its coverage to the "battle" between the autoworkers and GM in its coverage of the strike, *Time* magazine,

FIGURES 15 & 16 Photography often depicted strikers as less threatening and more orderly than before.

Sources: *Detroit Free Press*, November 22, 1945; *United States News*, March 14, 1941.

a popular periodical that presented lively commentary on national and world events accompanied by photographs, underpinned its analysis with an account of the actions taken by Michigan's governor and FDR's team of strike conciliators. These people were represented as bureaucrats addressing a snag in the system of production, rather than as soldiers facing opposing armies of capital and labor. At one point, *Time* reflected on the shift of the battle "front" from the strike lines of Detroit to the halls of Washington.[38]

Throughout the General Motors strike coverage, labor's position was made clear: this was a battle for American rights. As one journal explained, John L. Lewis was effectively "linking up the success of this movement with the welfare of the nation" in his radio speeches. Lewis connected his ambitions with those stated by the president in his fireside chats, explaining that labor was "on the march toward those better things and better days so eloquently described from time to time by the President of the United States." Similarly, United Auto Workers president Homer Martin published an open letter to the president of GM stating that the present strike affected not only the "corporation and its employees, but also the public."[39] This strategy would be used to even greater effect in the decade to come.

After Governor Murphy and President Roosevelt made it clear that they would not brook standard employer strikebreaking strategies, the strike ended favorably for the union, whose members exulted in the continuation of a "glorious crusade for a better life." The strikers appeared confident that the American public supported their cause, and framed their victory in a manner that reflected their new sense of social integration. One photograph depicted a ragtag but proud line of marching strikers leaving the factory at last, American flags in hand.

Advances in Reporting Technologies

If strike coverage such as that which surrounded the GM sit-downs diluted the terrifying implications of national strikes, developments in the area of journalistic reporting further lessened the impact of the industrial war. In 1937, newspapers began to employ a new technique to correlate public opinion with federal action. Using the novel technique of random sampling, George Gallup demonstrated that popular opinion could be mathematically accounted for. This method first proved viable in 1936, when he demonstrated that a *Literary Digest* prediction that Alf Landon would defeat Roosevelt in the presidential election was incorrect, based as it was on the unscientific "straw polling" technique in use since the 1800s. Gallup's new method, vindicated in his accurate projection of the 1936 election, quickly replaced older methods. Soon newspapers would authoritatively quote "Gallup Polls" to chart the current climate of public opinion.[40]

For the first time, national public opinion had become reliably quan-
tifiable. A Gallup Poll during the early days of the General Motors sit-down
strike of 1936–1937 found that 53 percent of those who had an opinion on the
subject favored the "employers," whereas 47 percent favored the "striking
employees."[41] Hardly reflecting the resounding condemnation stated in *United
States News* reports that upward of 89 percent of editors disapproved of the
strike, this measurement foretold the replacement of traditional editorial
conjecture with precise, brief judgments on the public outlook as it pertained
to different events in the industrial scene.[42] The coming of the Gallup Poll
helped to curtail colorful anti-labor exhortations in the name of "popular
opinion" and forced editorialists to remind readers that they only expressed
their own perspective. It also made the inquiry into labor relations appear to
be a more specific and scientific process. As New Deal legislation transformed
the climate of industrial relations, new forms of analysis buttressed a new
perspective that made older notions of grand social struggle seem increasingly inadequate.

Quantification took other forms in the 1930s as well. Analysis often
included pieces that placed strikes within larger economic developments
using statistics. In one *US News* piece, the 1934 national strikes were shown
to be part of a longer trend in which labor unrest increased as prosperity
increased. In other words, the current strikes were actually a *positive* indicator.[43] Explaining strikes in this manner helped many people to see them
less as incipient revolutions and more as mere hiccups that accompanied
the regular pattern of economic climb and fall in the nation's life. The rise
of labor news specialists, such as the *New York Times*'s "dean of American
labor reporters" Louis Stark, whose main role was to report on strikes and
labor-related gatherings, also demystified labor relations by providing more
in-depth analysis than had previously been seen.[44]

The maturation of photography as a form of journalistic reportage also
made labor conflicts appear less damaging than they had once seemed.
Replacing drawings that clearly borrowed from nineteenth-century war
illustrations, the widespread use of photographs in newspapers had, by the
1930s, denuded strikers of their "army" aspect. Shown calmly lining up outside closed factories, marching happily in parades, and even crowded around
angry policemen, strikers did not appear to be the amassed, combat-ready
shock troops of the proletariat that previous illustrators had often painted
them to be. Even the most violent photographs—a boss clubbing a worker,
a canister of tear gas fired into a crowd, an overturned car surrounded by
enraged workers—never matched the sense of battle summoned by the military-style strike drawings of the 1880s and 1890s. Strikers now seemed like
regular folk, dressed like everyone else and without the gleam of anarchy in
their eyes. And there may have been another, hidden, reason for the overall

paucity of violent labor images in the media. Writes Linda Gordon, "the Popular Front and the New Deal emphasized unity, not conflict, albeit for different reasons: the former to create the largest possible coalition against Nazism, the latter to get its agenda through Congress." For pro-labor photographers like Dorothea Lange, "soft pedaling conflicts of interest" might have reflected their ideal of a government-sponsored "industrial peace."[45] The public interest filtered right into the lens.

In 1936 the magazine *Life* made its first appearance on the shelves. Filled out with large photographs that, in the words of *Life* editor Ralph Ingersoll, would appeal to the "gum chewers" (the masses), the magazine did not impart a sense of social classes at odds. Rather, it gave its audience images of well-off whites participating in various leisure activities, along with pictures of hard-working, "all-American" laborers and farmers. Despite the ongoing waves of labor unrest, *Life* rarely depicted images of toiling blue-collar workers, or union activity. When shown, unions were not portrayed as negative and strike coverage was, in the words of media scholar Sheila Webb, "fair, even positive" (owner Henry Luce, it should be noted, despite being a wealthy Republican, did not oppose the New Deal). Unions in *Life* were not armies marching to battle. In fact, they were entirely marginalized in its pages; *Life* magazine spent only 1 percent of its photo space on labor in the late 1930s. By focusing on middle-class ideals of consumption, opportunity, and success, *Life* played its part in the shifting media narrative aimed at a "greater public." As Ingersoll explained to Luce, the photos in *Life* "are for rich or poor, without regard for race, class, creed or prejudice . . . you use one vernacular to a truck driver, another to a bank president, but bank president and truck driver will stand shoulder-to-shoulder to watch a parade." The parade of photographs in *Life*, without alienating the working class, guided popular attention toward an idealized, harmonious world. Its astounding success spoke to the power of its message.[46]

Like photography, film and radio also offered new, more "realistic" evidence of striker behavior. Radio messages broadcast by union leaders hit a wide range of markets. Occasionally movie stars would support the labor movement in radio interviews that furthered a sense that unions were not abstractly amassed forces but organizations of citizens interested in salvaging the American dream in the Depression years. Films of strikes, while not common in the 1930s, depicted strikers less as organized ranks mobilizing against employer forces than as smaller collections of average-looking working people. Technology had begun to make possible a more accurate, or at least less offensive, view of the labor movement.[47] Another new development that worked to contain and dull labor conflict perception could be seen in the rise of the expression "management."

From "Capital" to "Management"

"Management," a term that began appearing with great regularity in the 1940s, originated in the nineteenth century.[48] Managing labor meant finding ways of monitoring workers, thus neutralizing union control of the shop floor and the attendant problems of wasted time and resources. By the early twentieth century, societies for labor management began to spring up.[49] Frederick Taylor's idea of "scientific management," aimed at circumventing labor's "soldiering" efforts, captured the sense that enlightened managers could contain labor unrest.[50] As the workplace became a more contested space and the federal government became more active in ensuring peace, the expression "management" changed from being primarily used to describe the act of overseeing labor to being the signifier of a new category of capitalist, a transition that signaled a deeper shift in social perception.

The rhetorical transformation of this "specifically American" word began with the rise of personnel managers and the institutionalization of labor relations as an area of scientific study.[51] Since the turn of the century, a small cohort of analysts had celebrated the idea of managerial control as a solution to labor discord. When *industrial relations* and the associated field of *personnel management* came fully into their own in the 1920s, scholars focused on the role of managers in establishing industrial harmony. Titles like *Labor Management, The New Leadership in Industry,* and *The Causes of Industrial Unrest,* a few notable works among a slew of monographs and articles published in this decade, argued that the day of employer autocracy and labor resistance was long gone. It would now be up to a new group, the managers (a term expansive enough to include personnel managers, foremen, and even owners), to act as a "buffer between capital and labor."[52]

In the 1930s, the function of managing workers took on new immediacy. Declining profit margins and industrial unrest inspired employers to develop new approaches to managing their charges. Combined with the rising demand that the federal government intervene more dramatically in an industrial system deemed "sick," managerial exponents intensified their efforts to centralize and formalize control over their workplaces. Between 1929 and 1935 alone, the percentage of large employers with personnel departments nearly doubled. Major corporations looked to new programs of employee representation (such as company unions), refinements and centralization in hiring procedures, and newly regimented internal promotion frameworks.[53]

By this point, monitoring one's workers meant reevaluating traditional capitalist philosophies of laissez-faire and arbitrary control over the workplace. According to Chester Barnard, the most influential management philosopher of the age, the new perspective would require both "genuine restraint of self" and "genuine subjugation of destructive personal interests to social interest."[54] In other words, managers would have to take seriously their self-promoted role of handmaidens of industrial peace and place the "social interest" above all others.

In an address made to the National Association of Manufacturers, E. T. Weir argued that employers needed to recognize their responsibility to show the public that their intentions were to uplift society rather than simply to make an immediate profit. It was "paradoxical," he found, that advertisers had made the masses "accepting" of products while at the same time making consumers skeptical of industry's intentions. Commenting on this problem, an *Atlantic Monthly* writer found that "management" must reassume its "leadership in American industry" by bringing about a "sound economic readjustment." What this readjustment entailed received less space in the article. It apparently included management spurring the production of "more and better things" to "an increasingly large part of the population."[55]

In the subtext to such exhortations there also lurked a warning—the activist state would determine the social interest for them if they would not do it themselves. As managers rose to prominence, critics believed that their presence threatened to subvert the open market and the blessings for the masses that it might bestow. In their influential 1933 book *The Modern Corporation and Private Property*, Adolf A. Berle and Gardiner C. Means argued that "public interest would be held hostage to the private cupidity of managers" if the government did not impose itself. As government intervention became a reality, management proponents were forced to work harder to define a productive role for their group. Men such as Adolf Berle, who was also an advisor to Roosevelt, presented management with a very real threat.[56]

At the same time, economic analysts outside of the corporate world worked to establish close links between industry and the federal government in an effort to facilitate the incorporation of responsible management into the larger public. The March 1935 issue of the *Annals of the American Academy of Political and Social Science* (a national forum of academics, editors, professional analysts, and government officials) tackled the theme "Increasing Government Control in Economic Life." The contributors addressed a number of issues, including the nature of capitalism and the role of the government in regulating the labor market. Some, like former chairman of the board of directors of the National Bureau of Economic Research Harry W. Laidler, argued that "socialized" labor relations, in which workers and government played a more collusive role in regulating the workplace, was best. Others suggested less radical but no less permanent changes in federal-labor-employer relations. Common to all of the respondents was a sense that the government could no longer stand by and watch industrial disputes go on. A new, permanent protocol needed to be established that allowed both managers and their workers to coexist in peace.[57]

Part of this new line of argument stood in flat contradiction to the government's traditional role in labor disputes. As was often pointed out, the state had rarely been favorable to labor in the past. Recognizing this, industrial relations experts explained that the government now had the new function of social guardian, one that should stretch deeply into the realm of capital-labor relations. The "general public," explained Commons student Edwin E. Witte in his landmark 1932 book, *The Government in Labor Disputes,* advocated federal intervention in order to maintain the "public peace." Changes in strike policy were "demanded" by this group, changes that would require a more fair and equitable system of employer-employee relations. It would be up to the government, he explained, to play dual roles of "referee and police-man." Enforcing the "rules of the game" made the government both an active participant and, more importantly, public standard bearer in regulating labor unrest. This new federal presence also required management to behave differently if it were to continue to succeed in stifling labor protest. It would have to address the public audience explicitly during national strikes, rather than merely acting as enforcer of capital's immediate interests.[58]

In a slim volume aimed at public consumption, industrial relations expert William Leiserson presented a clear argument for how the new interventionary state would handle the old problem of class war. In *Right and Wrong in Labor Relations,* Leiserson argued for a pluralistic view of the industrial world. He found "Capital" and "Labor" to be oversimplified "econo-mists' abstractions" that did not address the complex, "intricate" reality of the "human relationships of managers and workers." While there was "no absolute guarantee against industrial wars," a thoughtful federal policy, one that safeguarded both the rights of workers and "the public interest in the maintenance of peace, order and the production of goods and services" would reduce the "problems of democracy in industry" down to a "minimum of strife." While highly critical of employers who refused to deal squarely with workers and obey the emerging New Deal order, Leiserson ended by warning that the "new status" accorded unions "will in time make it necessary for the government to see to it that they perform their duties properly."[59] All of the participants needed to fall in line. Leiserson, who was appointed by FDR in 1939 as a member of the NLRB, clearly represented the emerging pluralist vision. It behooved managers to take notice.

As America took on a war footing in 1939–1945, management became more aggressive in endorsing its new role as industrial peacekeeper. One group of managers formed the Committee for Economic Development in an effort to give business a leading role in establishing a better system of labor relations. In an address given to the National Association of Manufacturers, a businessman explained that employers could "capture the leadership of public opinion only if it makes, and dramatizes, a conscientious and determined effort to solve the nation's economic problems."[60] This would entail close attention to business's self-image in regard to employee relations.

The federal National War Labor Board further facilitated the new managerial role of capital by giving business leaders a say in national wage and work conditions. Soon the issue of management became closely tied with the smooth working of the wartime economy. Helped along by an advertising blitz that associated democracy with products supplied by friendly faced companies, managers eagerly assumed the position of caretaker of public welfare just as the government and organized labor had worked to do in the 1930s.[61] The expression "management" soon took on such importance that the act of managing labor, already associated with the employers' prerogative, became the guiding metaphor for all capitalists.

By 1945 "management" had fully become a stand-in for "capital" itself. Indeed, as early as 1943 commentators were calling for a revision of the "old and familiar phrase" of capital and labor, asking that it be replaced by one in which "management" be included in any meaningful social calculus.[62] This was more than a replacement of nomenclature; it implied a new framework of analysis. Employers had become more responsible for the containment of militant laborers. Their methods would have to be more conspicuous. They would have to "play to the [public] gallery."[63]

The rise of the "public" and the inclusion of capital and labor within its shell ushered in a shift of self-understanding among capitalists. The noun "management" did not imply a discrete social unit the same way that "capital" did. It represented a group *within* the public, fulfilling the specific purpose of managing the labor process, and could include personnel managers, foremen, and even owners. It fit comfortably within the framework of a society broken up by interests rather than one divided by classes.

The adoption of this new expression further defused the binary of capital/labor by facilitating a new role for capital. Rather than a class whose purpose was primarily the accumulation of wealth, "management" was an interest group whose responsible supervision and care of its employees ensured social harmony. Pressured by the state and by an increased awareness of public opinion, many managers found it worthwhile to accept labor legislation (or at least to pay lip service to it) and to advocate a new role of capitalist coordination that promoted current legislative guidelines.[64] The world war that helped solidify this new role for capital, however, would also offer labor new opportunities to claim the "public interest" mantle for itself.

7

A Kind of Peace

The Advent of Taft-Hartley

Addressing a CIO convention on December 4, 1952, in Atlantic City to accept his new role as president of the organization, Walter Reuther spoke of a great war that was currently being waged on a global level. It was the "struggle in the world between freedom and tyranny." Organized labor needed to be unified in this war, a struggle not against capital but rather against "hunger" and exploitation, against the "reactionaries in Wall Street" who used fear to their advantage. To "mobilize" itself for "victory" was the great challenge for organized labor in this postwar era, explained Reuther. That a labor leader framed his language in battle terms was, as has been seen, nothing special. The title of the speech was "We Shall March Together." What is different and new here is the social model contained within. Reuther advocated for a victory that "cannot be won on battlefields. It can only be won on the economic and social field in the struggle for social justice."[1]

Claiming the mantle of representative of the greater public, Reuther offered a vision of labor unity that struck a chord with a working class growing accustomed to seeing itself portrayed as guardian of the public interest. By the early 1950s the labor movement was strong and fully immersed in federal policy-making and national public relations efforts. The experiences of the 1930s and in the Second World War had transformed the very structure of class language. The new rhetoric of class would be predicated on a model of industrial pluralism, in which organized labor had a necessary, countervailing role to play in establishing a responsible, mutually beneficial social equilibrium with management and the state. This chapter will trace the embedding of this new

framing mechanism at mid-century, from the General Motors strike of 1945–
1946, in which the new terms of social understanding expressed themselves in
the midst of a massive postwar strike, to the advent of the Labor-Management
Relations Act of 1947 (also known as the Taft-Hartley Act) and the perceived
"labor-management accord" that followed.

A People's Strike: The Good War and the
General Motors Strike of 1945–1946

The American experience in World War II intensified the ongoing process
of incorporation and created new prospects for the public personas of both
management and labor. Just as during the First World War, labor leaders
joined federal bureaucrats in devising a system of economic harmony. President Franklin D. Roosevelt appointed CIO luminary Sidney Hillman to the
National Defense Advisory Commission and sold the body (formed in 1940)
in such a way so as to give the impression that labor, management, and the
state were all on the same team. Later in the war, other agencies designed to
ensure the smooth and continuous production of war-related materials and
to placate a public anxious for industrial peace also took shape.[2]

During the war the state acted conspicuously to project the appearance of
public defender of industrial peace. To this end, agencies such as the National
Defense Mediation Board (formed in 1941) established tripartite councils consisting of equal numbers of capital (commonly referred to as "industry" or
"management" by this point) and labor representatives, with always at least
one "public" representative in the form of a government-appointed official.
Such federal agencies worked to facilitate a wartime labor truce by enforcing a No Strike Pledge, a system of grievance procedures, and a guarantee of
membership for unions. This last step was an unprecedented state-enforced
closed shop measure, which business leaders found themselves in no position
to dispute.

The hardened links between the state's and labor's objectives presented
an opportunity for those in the labor movement who envisioned a strong
union presence in shaping national policy. United Automobile Workers vice
president Walter Reuther, for example, suggested a factory conversion program in which auto factories would make airplanes in order to help the war
effort. While this proposal was not fulfilled and labor's influence was greatly
curtailed by the far more powerful business interests involved in war production, the heady promise of labor inclusion under the government's guidance combined with a tightened labor market to help the CIO (and the AFL,
it must be noted) gain hundreds of thousands of new members and see its
influence expand on a national level.[3] Though its disciplinary powers would
be tested (as war-related inflation set in, workers struck in record numbers,

often in direct opposition of national union command), the CIO made great strides toward establishing national unions as an integral element in the public-state domain.

AFTER THE ALLIED VICTORY, the nation anxiously watched to see how the postwar system of industrial relations would take shape. The cancellation of defense industry orders, the ending of wartime wage and overtime policies, the end of the No Strike Pledge (a promise increasingly violated since 1943), and deep fears of another depression had created an explosive industrial climate. When a strike wave of unmatched proportions rocked the nation, all of the apprehensions seemed to be realized. Stoppages in rubber, oil, appliance, construction, coal, and transportation industries occurred at the same time. General strikes erupted in a number of cities. In all, some 5 million workers would go on strike in the year following V-J Day.

In the midst of all this turmoil, workers struck General Motors in an episode that highlighted the effects of the New Deal-era promise of civic inclusion. Strongly influenced by Walter Reuther, the United Automobile Workers now took the bold position that it was striking *for* the public interest, not against it. On the heels of a "Labor-Management Charter" in which labor leaders offered a public resolution advocating the virtues of continued union influence, collective bargaining, and free enterprise, the GM strike would be a conspicuous proving ground for labor's newfound vision of public solidarity.

The walkout that began on November 21, 1945, originated in the simple idea that wartime gains needed to carry through to the postwar period. According to Walter Reuther, a wage increase in the auto industry, one not tied to a rise in car prices, would offset the expected income decline due to the projected loss of overtime pay. This would, he believed, act as a powerful counter-lever to the postwar inflation that many feared might precede a new depression. Labor reporter Patricia Bronte explained that this move had "lifted the whole matter of collective bargaining to a new high level by insisting that advancement of labor interests shall not be made at the expense of the public." By securing continued working-class spending power, Reuther offered a union-led role in maintaining the economic upswing. He asked in a union press release, "which party is truly concerned with the public welfare—the Union or the Corporation?"[4]

The labor press happily answered Reuther's rhetorical question in the weeks to come. The *CIO News Service* exulted that the UAW was "fighting not only their own but the people's battle—against profiteering and price increases, and for increased mass purchasing power to promote prosperity and avert depression."[5] Again and again, union leaders stressed the connection between the public and the strikers. Radio addresses, open letters to President Harry Truman (in office since the death of Roosevelt in April 1945), speeches, and numerous press releases embodied the union's all-out effort to craft an amenable public opinion.

Having learned the necessity of appealing to the public, organized labor framed its actions as both self-defensive and patriotic. Veteran autoworkers were encouraged to protest in full uniform—the UAW even held a "Veterans' Day" march in Detroit on January 12, 1946. R. J. Thomas, president of the UAW, told the press that General Motors had "forced" the strike on his union by not complying with the request that it prove to the public its inability to pay. Walter Reuther even went so far as to accuse GM president C. E. Wilson of conducting a "sit-down strike" against the union, and the country as a whole, by not arbitrating with the UAW and thus threatening reconversion! He accused the corporation of fomenting "industrial war" and forcing disastrous inflation upon the public.[6] He boldly demanded that GM "open its books" and prove that it could not afford to give a raise without raising prices.[7]

Key to this argument was establishing the essential "public"-ness of organized labor itself. Reuther explained that as consuming and producing members of society, workers had more to do with economic progress than any other group. The *Nation* quickly observed that Reuther's "workers are consumers" argument gave uncommon force to his position. His assertion that he was fighting "the government's battle" further helped his cause by linking his actions to those of the public-supported interventionist state evident in the recent war. By making high wages a part of public security, he entered the territory recently gained by the federal government in forcing "public interest" into labor relations. Such connections between the UAW and the federal agenda helped make the union appear an essential partner in establishing postwar prosperity. In an article in the *Nation* written by Reuther himself, he declared that "the strike of the G.M. workers is the fight of all Americans who want a lasting peace of full production, full consumption, and full employment."[8]

For many conservatives, Reuther's fight seemed a transgression into managerial territory. If unionists praised the challenge to "the concept that an employer is the sole judge as to whether his business could or could not give the workers a living wage," business advocates did not.[9] Corporate press releases accused the union of behaving "irresponsibly" in light of its own public role as employee representative. American Manufacturer's Association general manager George Romney told the press that "the workers cannot win, the country cannot win. Only a power-hungry clique of union leaders, with short-sighted disregard of their members' welfare and the public's interest, stand to gain."[10] Connecting strike unrest to the "commands" of union leaders was a long-standing business stratagem. Now that organized labor had attached itself to the public interest, the new strategy would be to demonstrate that union leaders were working *against* the interests of their own membership and the rest of the public. This tactic would be used to great effect in the years to come.[11]

In the majority of the media coverage of the strike, condemnations of labor and capital received a more balanced treatment under the rubric of the public's interest in peace between the two combatants. At first, reporters mainly sought to capture the strike's enormity and significance. The *New York Times* portended a "'battle of the Titans,' in which the forces of the world's largest union, 1,000,000 strong," were "arrayed against three of the world's largest corporations, with the stakes so high that it would not be an exaggeration to state that every American ultimately would be affected by the outcome." Because the strike threatened economic recovery, the *Times* was not alone in condemning the union's new strategy of higher wages without higher prices. In numerous editorials, papers across the country criticized Reuther's rhetoric as being purposely incendiary. However, as the strike dragged on, the *Times* began to blame both the union and GM "management" for hurting the public interest. Other major papers did the same.[12]

As evident in many editorial sections, offering balanced industrial coverage during this strike meant pointing out the flaws in the arguments of both sides, labor and management. Public opinion, explained editors, demanded a fast end to this standoff and the establishment of a new, harmonious postwar relationship between the corporation and its employees. Magazines such as *Fortune, Time,* and *Life* (these three owned by Republican media mogul and Reuther-respecter Henry Luce) as well as more liberal periodicals such as *Nation* and *New Republic* all gave the cause of the autoworkers serious consideration, criticizing GM for not listening to government arbiters and painting the strikers as regular folk rather than revolutionaries or ignorant followers.[13]

The liberal journal *Nation* published accusations that GM "wanted" the strike in order to destroy the union. In one piece, a writer criticized the mainstream media for publishing anti-Reuther "propaganda." In another, a reporter compared GM's leadership to Germany's during the recent war.[14] The *New Republic,* another liberal journal, presented one of the most forceful anti-corporate opinions on the strike. It accused General Motors of "Plotting a New Depression."[15]

The fear of a new depression hung heavily over the General Motors strike. Due to the new relationship between the federal government and the people, many believed that the state now had a responsibility in crafting a new set of industrial relationships. The much-used expression "reconversion," employed to describe the transition from a war to a peace economy, implied that the state's ambition was not to rebuild but to return the economy to the state of healthy consumption that had been in the works since the first Keynesian policies were implemented in 1939. Unlike after World War I, when society needed to be "reconstructed," the state in this instance had only to navigate management and labor through industrial "reconversion" until both arrived at a comfortable point of equilibrium.

Complementing the sense that new circumstances required careful planning and attentiveness to public interest, images of the 1945–1946 GM strike revealed a much different picture than images used for past national strikes. A largely nonviolent strike, this "battle of the Titans" was portrayed less as a physical "battle" than an across-the-table confrontation between leaders. Photographs juxtaposing GM's President C. E. Wilson and the UAW's President Walter Reuther showed two conservatively dressed men with few physical differences aside from age. Along with other well-dressed union, management, and government representatives, newspapers documented a serious, formal, and decidedly nondescript class of industrial participants.

The use of the term "management" itself during the strike augured a new pattern of strike analysis. Not viewed primarily as "capital" representatives, General Motors employers would be described as a single interest in a wider field of business interests (albeit the largest one). Being "managers" of a single business rather than "generals" of capital, men like Wilson and Alfred P. Sloan appeared less threatening. They dealt with their company's employee dispute using a process of careful negotiation rather than armed confrontation. Given the orderly appearance of this strike, "management" seemed not just a replacement term for capital but a new category altogether, one stripped of the dangerous implications of industrial war.

Some journalists immediately recognized important differences between this strike and earlier ones. Comparing it with the sit-downs of 1937, which also involved the United Automobile Workers and General Motors, one writer for the *Detroit Free Press* noted that the local community viewed the current strike with "the resignation of people who have been snowed in" rather than with "the fierce antagonism of property's myrmidons beating back the proletarian horde."[16] While the 1937 strike had been more dramatic, the new strike did not herald as wide a gulf from the past as the author implied. Indeed, epochal strike events in the 1930s often appealed as much to abstracted "rights" as they did to the audience's sense of social upheaval. The 1937 sit-down strike itself had been monitored closely by cameras, given clear treatment by scientific pollsters, and packaged as an event that involved mainly degrees of managerial or worker "rights." The 1945–1946 strike contained all of those elements, but with less of the accompanying war jargon employed in the 1930s.

Change was also evident in the media's overall coverage of this event, as older modes of analysis seemed quainter and less pertinent than ever. War metaphor, for instance, remained a cogent descriptive method, yet it clearly was taken less literally than before. At first glance, it appears as though it was alive and well. Phrases like "strategy," "battle," "industrial front," "conflict," "invade," "mobilize," "labor blockade," and even the occasional "industrial war" glittered on front pages of major news sources. And as in 1919, the recent world war bled through into coverage to add an extra element of drama. "D-Day in Detroit" and union-made comparisons of GM to the Nazis were only a few of many World War II–specific allusions applied during the strike.[17]

However, the war metaphor had a more innocuous meaning this time around.[18] This "war," explained journalists, threatened the nation mainly with "inflation," with slowing "reconversion," or with the unfortunate continued use of less "safe" old cars. While all of these things were unpleasant, they hardly deserved the use of war language evident in the column headings. Rather than being on the cusp of social disintegration (as in 1886), on the "ragged edge of anarchy" (as during the Pullman Strike of 1894), or facing the looming prospect of social revolution (as in 1919), this national strike threatened Americans with slower economic recovery and less access to new cars. Even Reuther's much publicized "divide-and-conquer" strategy related to making competing car companies more profitable, not to destroying those firms.[19]

No longer tied to the notion of a divided society, war references had simply become less consequential. As was evident in the coverage of the General Motors sit-down strike, the field of industrial battle had shifted from the factories to the corridors of organizational power. More than this, the nature of the battle itself had changed. Union objectives were phrased in terms of rights rather than disassociated economic demands dependent on a clash of entrenched class groups. Their interests were those of the people at large—a better life ensured by federal guardianship of rights and incomes. Although the GM strike was very large, and was clearly linked to other massive strikes in other industries by the press, it did not receive the classification of "social war" used as recently as 1919. With abundant evidence being offered for this episode's being yet another massive industrial battle, the media did not seem comfortable in framing this strike as one.

In another reflection of the ascendant pluralist vision of social relations, condemnation of the strikers did not include longstanding themes of foreignness or slavery. The foreign designation, in fact, was remarkably muted throughout the coverage. The downplaying of ethnicity during this strike reflected the flattening process that had accompanied the move of labor into the public's ranks. Several other factors had pushed this process along in the Depression. For instance, economic hardship had helped crush older institutions such as ethnic banks, charities, parochial schools, and mutual aid societies under its weight. The CIO had welcomed first- and second-generation immigrants into its folds as partners in its project to fulfill the American dream for all. By 1945, editors found it very difficult to separate such individuals from the public as a whole.[20]

One article in *Life* magazine entitled "G.M. Striker Has a Very Busy Life" sympathetically depicted a day in the life of a typical auto striker. Painting a very human portrait of striker Andrew Nabozny, *Life* explained how "a man who goes out on strike today still does a hard day's work." In a series of photographs accompanied by text, Nabozny is shown giving relief money to his wife, punching-in a strike time card at the union office, standing in a picket line, and huddled around a fire with other strikers. In all of the pictures, his averageness is stressed; at no point are any racial or ethnic references made about him, despite his obviously "ethnic- sounding" name. Nor is he portrayed as a "soldier."[21] The apparently egalitarian nature of coverage implied a different reading of strikers. No longer portrayed as products of un-American ideologies, as dregs cast from Europe, as incipient revolutionaries awaiting their demagogue, what we now call "white ethnic" strikers were depicted as being "just like the rest of us."[22] While the divisive theme of "wage slavery" still cropped up in union condemnations of General Motors and the anti-labor legislation being offered to Congress, this term too seemed drained of its original racial meaning.

As the Nabozny article suggests, the incorporative vision of society undermined the power of the national strike itself. The new world of social relations was an arena for "interests" rather than warring classes, closely monitored by polls (at one point 60 percent of Americans favored a 15 percent autoworker pay raise[23]) and guarded by government officials. A writer for the *New York Times* expressed the distance traveled since the battles of the Depression, saying that this strike "assumed the aspects of a battle of experts rather than the essentially violent character of the big strikes in 1937." Another litmus test of difference might also be made: the term "capital," commonly used in leading headlines regarding the strike, referred not to any industrial army but instead to Washington, D.C.[24]

As self-conscious interest groups, both the UAW and GM intensified their appeals for public support as the struggle dragged on. Walter Reuther boldly connected the goals of the strikers not only with the public interest but also with promises made during the recent war. He used the warm memory of the late President Roosevelt by connecting the strike with the "freedom from want." He blamed General Motors for opposing the "wishes and hopes of the vast majority of the American people, who devoutly want to see realized the promise of a post-war world of peace, freedom and plenty." At one point, Reuther suggested that a corporate victory, and the ensuing economic collapse, might even lead to a third world war.[25]

Corporate leaders vigorously retaliated, accusing the union of trying to undermine America's "competitive system" and replacing it with a

government controlled, union-regulated one. American Manufacturers'
Association manager George Romney charged the union with substituting
"revolutionary economic and political objectives for the legitimate objectives of collective bargaining." To gain more support, General Motors placed
a series of advertisements that explained that if the strike succeeded, higher
wages would usher in a new economic decline. In one ad, a man poured the
contents of an "Abnormal Buying Power" bottle into a mostly empty "Shortage
of Goods" bottle. The caption explained that this would create a "dangerous
mixture." All this is to say that GM made every effort to show how a UAW victory would hurt the public.[26]

With the new, wider public as central player in the strike, the actions of
the federal government received close attention. At the outset, newspaper
editors openly pondered the question of federal intervention in this strike.
The day before it got under way, the *Detroit News* (the more conservative of
the two major Detroit papers) reported that if collective bargaining were to
fail during the upcoming strike, it would be up to the "Government" to intervene on behalf of the "public interest." Once the workers left their posts, the
secretary of labor went to talk to both sides in an act that papers referred to
as "an effort to arrange a truce." When this apparently went nowhere, the
president was roundly criticized for standing by and watching as management
and employees stalled postwar production.[27]

When Truman finally chose to appoint a "fact-finding" commission and
asked that the strike cease while the commission investigated, both the UAW
and GM protested—the union because it knew this would ruin their momentum, GM because it did not trust the government to look out for its interests.
The strike continued unabated. When the commission found that GM could
in fact afford to increase salaries 17.5 percent, the autoworkers celebrated the
decision as just. General Motors, however, refused to abide by Washington's
findings. Over the long weeks ahead, the corporation proved that the federal
government did not have the power to induce management to surrender
its "right" to set wages as it saw fit. The public pressure built, however, and
General Motors finally agreed to pay an amount slightly less than the government's recommendation, thus symbolically proving its sovereignty.

The results of the final decision were mixed. While the UAW exulted its
"victory for the American people," it had not established itself as the savior
of American prosperity as it had hoped and, in the words of one historian,
met the results with "far more relief than exultation." The GM strike had
ended after seemingly taking the lead from a concurrent national strike in
steel that had resulted in higher wages without pricing restraints. Shortly
after the GM decision, the government rescinded its wartime price caps
and the pay raise was eventually passed on to consumers. Reuther's defense
that his union was no "narrow, economic pressure group" now seemed flat

FIGURES 17 & 18 In the first image, the public is shown to be a "policeman" for social order. Note that he is more powerful than the President. In the second, the sports metaphor is evident in this baseball analogy for the reconversion problem.

Sources: *Detroit Free Press*, December 5, 1945 (reprinted by permission of the *Detroit Free Press*); *Detroit News*, January 11, 1946.

and self-serving. A *New York Times* editorial titled "Whose 'Victory'?" summarized popular uncertainty regarding the powerful role of "big labor" in the postwar world.[28]

Whatever role big labor was to have, the state's status as arbitrator clearly needed reexamination. In the weeks leading up to GM's final decision, newspapers depicted the state's role in the negotiations as being a "referee" or "umpire." As a "referee," the government stood in the role of both observer and watchdog, exactly the role that Roosevelt and labor leaders in the 1930s had expected it to have. Democracy and public interest had made industrial peace an extension of responsibly managed interests. As influential economist Sumner Slichter put it, the "best hope" for industrial peace "in a democracy" lay in "real collective bargaining, two-sided, with the government in a mere umpire role." Ominously, the very lengthiness of the arrival of the GM decision suggested that the umpire was not yet taken seriously.[29]

Nevertheless, now that the industrial war metaphor seemed a less-than-true fit, sports analogies proved a contagious and enduring replacement. One editorial cartoon depicted labor strikes as akin to baseball strikes, with labor, management, Congress, and even the president swinging away at a "reconversion problem" ball. Another playfully compared the federal "umpire" to a baseball umpire, telling labor and management team managers that they had "20 seconds to play ball." As a game requiring a referee, labor relations could be depicted less as a struggle and more like a competition for ample resources. As referee, the state had a means of translating popular desires for industrial jurisprudence into a framework of "fair" workplace relations. It could be an indispensable actor without seeming too imposing.[30] To cement its status as referee, a new labor law would be necessary to give the state guidelines for interference in the postwar industrial world.

Taft-Hartley and the End of Unrestrained Labor Warfare

At the height of the 1945–1946 General Motors strike, the issue of codifying a new and more peaceable set of postwar labor relations took center stage at the Labor-Management Conference called by President Truman. Although the meeting was initiated prior to the strike, its coincidence with the walkout made the public attention given to it all the more significant. While this sounded like a good idea to most, the *Wall Street Journal* warned that the conference might actually "encourage industrial warfare because the leaders of the C.I.O. unions will use it to strengthen their position." Despite such fears, the conference only proved that without the visible presence of a strong federal government, neither side would relinquish any ground. When the conference ended in resounding failure and strikes went on unabated, many pressed the federal government for a more comprehensive labor law.[31]

The chief requirement of a new law would be to recognize the new, inclusive vision of society that had surfaced over the past few years. Referred to as "industrial pluralism" by recent scholars, this popular conception of society understood America to consist of a collection of interest groups grounded in an egalitarian political system. With beginnings in the writings of John Commons, and earlier still in the work of William James and John Dewey, the pluralist model of social relations proved widely popular once the antagonistic model of class war finally lost its resonance in the 1940s. Interest groups, unlike armies, had a vested concern in the smooth operation of a fair system of rules.

One of the hallmarks of industrial pluralism was a sense that labor and management were essentially equals, participating together in working out labor conditions. With capital and labor armies now replaced by competing management and labor groups, all operating within a greater American public, it became common sense to expect a labor law that recognized both and that also compelled them to remain true to their contributory purposes.[32] The new interdependent model enmeshed labor and management within a social network held together by the common "public" thread of American identity. In the words of contemporary scholar Wayne Leslie McNaughton, labor and management now found themselves beholden to "society as a whole." An amorphous "force" that contained the two groups within its grasp, this greater public had the right to impose its will on any other group whose "interests" diverged from its own. McNaughton correlated this public interest, in terms of industrial relations, with a desire for high production and social peace.[33]

In a provocative article written by Donald R. Richberg, the former general counsel and chairman of the National Recovery Administration during the 1945–1946 GM strike, the ex-official explained that the best way to foster industrial peace in America's "interdependent" society would be to make laws that did not forbid strikes but instead made them unnecessary. The refusal of the autoworkers and General Motors to obey all of Truman's requests during the strike, Richberg pointed out, only highlighted the inadequacies of current legislation. Phrasing his warning in no uncertain terms, Richberg explained how "unrestrained labor warfare is bringing untold suffering and incalculable losses to the American people." He went on to charge that management-labor struggles were "destroying economic security, undermining Government authority and sowing broadcast the seeds of civil war." To prevent this "unrestrained labor warfare," Richberg proposed that the "labor profiteers and racketeers" (a list which included CIO head Philip Murray, the AFL's William Green, and United Mine Workers' John L. Lewis) be seriously curtailed in their influence.[34]

Richberg's proposal built upon a growing critique of organized labor that claimed that while rank-and-file members were part of the public, union

leaders were not. In fact, this argument held that leadership elements within
unions were primarily responsible for the major strikes that hurt the public
interest. As "public enemies" (Richberg's phrase), they needed to be removed
or restrained to safeguard the common interest. Economist Sumner Slichter
explained in his postwar book *The Challenge of Industrial Relations: Trade Unions,
Management, and the Public Interest* that trade unions, led by parochial leaders,
had arrayed their membership against management, thereby threatening the
"interests which all groups have in common."[35] In settling the issue, new labor
legislation would have to separate the will of labor bosses from that of their
membership. The solution would arrive in the form of a new and high-profile
labor law, the Labor-Management Relations Act of 1947.

The Taft-Hartley Act, as the Labor-Management Relations Act was also
called, was an amendment to the 1935 National Labor Relations (or Wagner)
Act. Couching its protocols in the language of rights, the writers of the act
explained, "industrial strife . . . can be avoided or substantially minimized if
employers, employees, and labor organizations each recognize under law one
another's rights in their relations with each other." Taft-Hartley would "protect the rights of the public" by, among other things, curtailing the still-fear-
ful power of national strikes. This it accomplished by allowing the president
to suspend strikes for sixty days if they threatened the country's welfare, by
outlawing sympathy boycotts, by disqualifying strikers from voting in union
representation elections if their strike violated fair labor practice guidelines,
by curtailing strikes of federal employees, and by establishing firmly the
state's role in setting uniform grievance procedures.[36] The Taft-Hartley Act
passed through Congress over President Truman's veto to become an influential piece of labor legislation for the rest of the century.[37]

Many pundits viewed Taft-Hartley as the midwife to a new era of labor-
management cooperation. One social scientist, for example, noted six months
after its passing that there had been a significant disappearance of strikes "of
national import." Other close observers, typically from within the ranks of
the labor movement, saw a new era of repression taking shape. Taft-Hartley,
they contended, was a "slave labor" act, an unmasked assault on labor's "fundamental rights." According to John L. Lewis, "There is not any reason why
American working men should permit vigilantes [that is, Congress] to trample
down their liberties and the American way of life."[38] Truman had believed that
the act would alienate the labor movement from the Democratic Party, and in
a radio address agreed that the bill "would take fundamental rights away from
our working people." While the act ultimately proved neither a social panacea
nor the death-knell of organized labor, it did stir up a lively public debate over
the nature of "big labor" and "big business" in the pluralist postwar world.[39]

Of all the concrete changes wrought by the Taft-Hartley Act, perhaps the
most important were its public insertion of national politics into employee-

employer relations and its specific targeting of national strikes (as seen in the presidential "cooling-off" measure). In establishing the federal government as a permanent participant in resolving major labor disputes, the act linked the interventionary promise of the original Wagner Act with the conservatism of Cold War America. The public had finally gained a permanent position in the settlement of industrial disputes. Federally appointed arbitrators now saw themselves as referees to a contest of fundamentally equal interest groups, an interpretation that would seriously curtail the power of unions to wage strikes on their own terms. No longer an army, labor had become a mere bargaining unit, a counterweight in appearance but not in power to capital's new "management" role.

Significantly, the intrusive aspect of a permanent government presence did not set business at ease. *Business Week*'s editor later declared that the act had actually made unions stronger by committing them "to political activity on a scale and pace never before approached."[40] One manager warned, "Any management satisfaction derived from immediate setbacks to organized labor's progress should be tempered by the realization that under present government policy significant terms of the employment relationship are to be determined by the government." Another noted that now management would "hold the spotlight as labor did from 1935 to 1947. Public scrutiny of management's actions . . . will be supplemented, plant by plant, by that of employees." He continued, "The [new] question will be, 'How is management using the new powers it has acquired . . . ?' and not merely 'Are the labor unions obeying the law?'"[41]

The spotlight had done more than shift; it had positively fragmented when cast through the prism of pluralist, interest group analysis. By definition, pluralism presupposed a multiplicity of loci for employer-management disputes. Replaced by a conundrum of interest group politicking, industrial war framing made little sense in the late 1940s. Discerning the nature of this new world occupied the attention of a new wave of well-published social commentators. Some, like historian Arthur Schlesinger Jr., praised the merits of "genuine cultural pluralism." Schlesinger explained in his 1949 book *The Vital Center* that as a social outlet, "widespread and spontaneous group activity" promised to deliver America from the twin evils of fascism and communism that lurked in the wings of industrial expansion. John Kenneth Galbraith in his 1952 classic *American Capitalism* cast unions not as combatants but rather as a "countervailing power" to corporate power. In his pluralist description, strikes are seen not as evidence of class conflict but rather as a "manifestation of the continued health of the system." Others found a depressing enervation in the interest-fractured society. In his landmark 1951 study *White Collar,* sociologist C. Wright Mills found unions to be "pressure group" units of class sedation and the middling masses to be utterly "apathetic" to the larger workings of society.[42]

Either way, the interdependent society and the state that refereed it had taken industrial war from the center of popular concern. Incorporated as interest groups within a broadly defined public, capital and labor ceased to be popularly represented as armies locked in battle. Once this new pluralist model of society became encoded within legal, statutory, and especially popular interpretations of industrial conflict, unrestrained labor warfare would be viewed as a thing of the past.

Conclusion

The End of Class Conflict?

In 1955 *Life* magazine published an article entitled "New Affluence, Unity for Labor." Accompanied by handsome, glossy images of orderly meetings, union leaders in business suits sitting beside comfy fireplaces or in glassy conference rooms, and a handy table of union progress over the decades, this remarkable article asserted that the age of violent class conflict was essentially over. "From its bloody beginnings," the author intoned, "U.S. labor has in less than a century made progress as dramatic as the change of horse and carriage to jet transport." With the help of responsible federal legislation and growing wealth, unionism had reached "new respectability and affluence." Led by a "new breed" of labor leaders, "skilled executives drawing sizeable salaries, living in gracious homes and working in posh offices as impressive as their management counterparts can boast," the labor movement, now unified under the AFL-CIO banner, was no longer a threat to the republic. Its leaders, explained the article, had ceased to be "anticapitalist."[1] These smiling men in suits were more J. P. Morgan than Eugene V. Debs.

This view of organized labor is about as far a cry from the mad-eyed, dynamite-toting anarchists of Remington's Pullman Strike images as one can imagine. What had happened? As my previous analysis suggests, the answer is not as simple as the progressive march of "responsible" legislation and increased union rationality that *Life,* and indeed much industrial-related writing in the postwar period, implied. The transformation toward the new, pluralist frame had begun decades earlier, and while it had been accompanied by both political changes and an actual decline in labor-related violence (but not in strikes, not until much later), it did not simply "match up" with these structural changes. Rather, the new vision of industrial America had emerged in dialectical response to both lived experience and the collapse of a popular interpretive frame.

The new pluralist frame had placed a multiplicity of interest groups at the core of a greater American public. A legion of commentators and theorists strove to adapt the new frame to their social analyses in the postwar decades, and today we still live with the fruits of their labors. In 1954, labor economist Robert Dublin summarized the trend in an essay on labor relations, explaining that "industrial conflict" had finally been "institutionalized" by the democratic processes inherent in interest group bargaining. Class war was no longer a serious concern.[2]

Influential commentators writing in the postwar years agreed that America's newly "interdependent" society mitigated against labor unrest on any significant scale. Due to the mollifying nature of a complex modern industrial society, interest groups (among them, labor unions) had trumped class as a source of identity. Often these writers went a step further, arguing that pluralism's triumph reflected a deeper trait of the American psyche. Reaching back to the insights of John Commons and his protégé Selig Perlman, prominent sociologist Daniel Bell argued that job-consciousness had always been the reigning mind-set of American laborers, and that socialistic ideological currents had finally exhausted themselves as constructive aspects of modern Western culture.[3] In the Cold War years, America's triumph over class-consciousness could be viewed as both a trait of an exceptional identity and an evolutionary fact of industrial progress.

While industrial pluralism supplanted the war frame, like the previous model, its imposition upon popular thought left gaps between rhetoric and reality. Shoring up such gaps became a mission for some scholars. In an essay published in 1966, sociologist Harold Wilensky addressed lingering, problematic references to "class" in both academic periodicals and the larger media. He explained that these class references constituted a false "rhetoric" that "obscures more than it reveals." While he agreed that "sporadic" and limited class-consciousness may have existed in the past (such as during the mid-1880s), any enduring notion of class identity surely had never been the norm. Rather, American workers found their outlet in the political realm. Now that labor had "taken its place in the coalition of interest groups that dominates the Democratic party," class identity meant little.[4]

Political inclusion in the 1930s had worked, argued Wilensky, because it reflected a deeper antipathy to class and a strong pragmatic desire among laborers for a greater share of America's wealth. A "multiplication of occupational worlds" and "advanced specialization" had further made the idea of "two armies massed on an industrial battlefield" irrelevant to modern

America. Wilensky used data to support his hypotheses, quoting a study of Detroit workers published in 1963 that found that "the closer one pushed to a Marxian model . . . the smaller the fraction [of interviewees possessed what] one could call class consciousness." He reached the conclusion that "Few Americans see capital and labor as classes; few see them at war."[5]

In many ways, Wilensky's analysis struck a chord of truth. Class had never been an unambiguous or even a particularly welcome concept in American society. From the Revolutionary days, social hierarchy of any sort seemed an undesirable vestige of privilege and corruption leftover from a European past. United by a common idiom of liberty and popular sovereignty, Americans had detested all forms of "class legislation" since at least the early nineteenth century. Even during the terrible industrial war years at the turn of the century, the reformer Jane Addams could tell a reporter, "I object to the word *class*. It is unAmerican. There are no classes in this country."[6] She said this despite the fact that just a few years prior she had described the Pullman Strike as "open warfare of opposing social forces."[7] Perhaps in Addams's contradiction we get to the very heart of the problem. Class indeed is a "conundrum," to paraphrase a recent history of the subject.[8]

Add to this new "common sense" a number of concrete factors that further empowered the postwar pluralist model. The American standard of living rose dramatically, giving workers a greater sense of material interest in their country's national stability. Since the idea of 'buying off' working-class discontent dated at least to Werner Sombart's early twentieth-century observations on American laborers, industrial pluralists found the argument both familiar and welcome. Another supporting factor could also be found in the bipolar political division of the world between the Soviet Union and the United States. This supported pluralist ideology by situating a "middle class," democratic America against a totalitarian Russia, compelling Americans to stress what they had in common over what divided them. The purges of communists from the ranks of organized labor, at the behest of the Taft-Hartley Act, further disciplined the unions into the position of patriotic upholders of America's economic institutions.[9]

However resonant this classless version of history seemed then and now, it glosses over what is now recognized as an elemental period of social tumult. Kept alive by left-leaning historians like Louis Adamic and Samuel Yellen in the 1930s, by New Left scholars during the 1960s and 1970s, and a number of New Labor historians since, class war remains recognized as an integral part of labor's history. As numerous academic writers have shown, strikes and working-class unrest *never* ceased, despite the "wishful thinking" of industrial pluralists.[10]

I believe it is possible to reconcile pluralist observations that class identity never fully took root with the numerous accounts of the persistence of class war. Though it never congealed into a full-blown working class ideology, as a cultural artifact, "industrial war" was, for a period of about eight decades, a central feature of American life. Supporting a binary model that positioned armies of capital and labor locked in battle, the industrial war frame facilitated a compelling vision of society that required neither ideological coherence nor a commonly agreed-upon course of action. Rather, it lent Americans a common vernacular with which to discuss and understand the uncertain processes of capitalist development.

In a sense, class war *did* end in the late 1940s. By this point, an overwhelming majority of Americans felt comfortable in their belief that an institutionalized network of democratic interest groups, coupled with a referee-style government, had decisively checked republic-threatening industrial upheaval. Perhaps more insidiously, as Elizabeth Fones-Wolf has documented, this coincided with a full-frontal media campaign by big business to discredit class-based unionist analysis and promote a celebration of free enterprise.[11]

Following the 1945–1946 strike wave, corporations and their allies began a concerted publicity campaign to reverse what the periodical *Public Relations News* found to be "incontrovertible" evidence that organized labor had captured "the public's good will—in spite of stopping the public's trains, planes, boats, trolleys, elevators, and even turning off its lights." Indeed the CIO had managed to get both the ABC and CBS radio networks to broadcast their shows nationwide starting in 1945.[12] To counteract this influence, the National Association of Manufacturers, along with a panoply of corporations (from General Electric to General Foods) and corporate-sponsored organizations such as the Chamber of Commerce, plus numerous employer and industrial associations, began a spending spree aimed at promoting free enterprise and associating union leadership with criminality. As early as 1946 sociologist Robert Lynd warned that employers were prepared to "spend unlimited money" to "control public opinion" in order to place the government at their bidding and put "labor behind the eight ball."[13] Through the 1950s, business spent millions in an often creative campaign that impressed upon the public a message that "big labor" needed to be watched and unfettered business offered unlimited benefits.

Clearly, however, business overstated their fears. The public did not really give organized labor *carte blanche*. Rather, unionization (and striking) had become a "right," guaranteed by the government and supported by the public, but a right that did not go without federal supervision. Despite labor's loud protests, Taft-Hartley became a justifiable means of public oversight, one specifically aimed at curtailing the possibility of devastating national strikes. Industrial war was to be contained and neutralized—shop floor struggles bound by grievance procedures, mass strikes forestalled by executive orders, and the wider spectrum of labor's most cherished arsenal (the closed shop, secondary strikes, and so on) considerably narrowed.

This institutionalization of labor relations has weakened organized labor. Writes one historian, "Simply put, the Taft-Hartley Act was designed to reduce labor power dramatically."[14] This rings true, but the legislation was more than a crass employer-backed broadside. Its language and popular understanding disclosed a new social conceptualization, a "rights consciousness" (in the words of David Brody)[15] that evolved out of the exigencies of an emergent industrial pluralism. In fact, the act states: "It is the purpose and policy of this Act . . . to protect the rights of individual employees in their relations with labor organizations."[16] In other words, in a society of interests, each individual's interest must be considered. "Protecting" the rights of the rank-and-file against the depredations of union bosses, as harmful as this was for labor, was fully in line with much pluralist thinking about securing the public welfare.[17] Taft-Hartley cemented the pluralist vision of society into law.

As the industrial pluralist frame took precedence, the mass media, when not giving the public union crooks like those in Elia Kazan's popular 1954 film *On the Waterfront,* or images of smug business-unionists (George Meany sitting by the fire in *Life*), did not give the public *anything.* As early as 1948 packing house workers noted in a strike bulletin that a strike rally twelve thousand people strong got no mention at all in some newspapers. As the *Daily Strike Bulletin* caustically noted, "So if you were at a big meeting the other night, brothers and sisters, just forget it. After all, if the papers didn't report it, it couldn't have taken place."[18]

With organized labor out of mind, locked safely away into the role of political interest group and purged of communist influence, and national strikes tamed by Taft-Hartley, the commentators, politicians, and media outlets turned their attention elsewhere. In the halls of power, "management" of the economy and the establishment of rational social programs took priority.[19] In universities, a theoretically adventurous "postcapitalist vision" replaced the older, more rigid political economics that painted productive forces at odds.[20] Finally, the newspaper itself, once the main source of information about the industrial war, began its steady decline. The triumph of television in the 1950s coincided with a downturn in news consumption generally. Whereas once most adult Americans read a newspaper every day (especially older people), the numbers began to decrease dramatically. Today, neither online nor even TV news has replaced this. And as Christopher Martin has shown, surviving newspapers tended, since the 1970s, to aim for "upscale" audiences. Strike stories came to focus not on the cause of the workers involved but on the impact on the consumer.[21] The fracturing of the industrial war frame helped reinforce and magnify the effect of a new intellectual and media climate.

But class conflict did not end. Not in the classical Marxian sense, or even in less ideological terms of strike rates, worker complaints, and other qualitative studies of social discontent. While union composition has receded and changed, and industrial disputes have become more formal affairs, it takes little effort to unearth ongoing discontent, despair, and a seething sense of class-based inadequacy.[22]

Indeed, today it would behoove us to ask the media to "bring the workers back in." In one of the few studies on the matter, Jonathan Tasini found in 1990 that union activity accounted for little over 1 percent of total airtime.[23] Michael Parenti notes that in the modern media, strikes are unconnected to any sense of class struggle, but rather have "something of a senseless origin." Striking workers appear irrational. On the rare occasions when unions do make the news, they are making "demands." A more sensible management, on the other hand, makes "offers."[24] In light of today's scant labor coverage, it is difficult to imagine a time when class war gripped the nation. It is even hard to trace the steps back to the early years of the industrial pluralist model. Commentators seem to have left Galbraith's classic pluralist vision of "countervailing powers" in the dust. Unions appear to have moved from relevancy to nuisance in much mainstream reporting.

Gramsci's insights are worth returning to at this point. According to Gramsci, the dominant class rules not only by force but also by consent. Writing of "parliamentary" regimes, he explains in *The Prison Notebooks* that "The 'normal' exercise of hegemony . . . is characterised by the combination of force and consent. . . . Indeed, the attempt is always made to ensure that force will appear to be based on the consent of the majority, expressed by the so-called organs of public opinion—newspapers and associations."[25] If anything, the history of the industrial war frame indicates that when administered, force drove its own consent. Put plainly, when mass strikes upended social order—whether or not the capitalists were at fault—the return to order became paramount. Critique of those who reaped massive profits, be they Jay Gould or Judge Gary, quickly took a backseat to the driving, compelling narrative of total war.

Yet the process was anything but smooth. The argument that the media simply served capitalist interest does not get us far enough toward understanding the complexities of the transition to a corporate-capitalist order. As has been seen, the mass media did not blindly support capitalist interests the whole way—there was nothing obvious or straightforward in the establishment of business hegemony in America. However, when viewed through the media's narrative techniques, it is evident that capitalist interests were ultimately served in the process. A master frame of "industrial war," emerging after the Civil War, imparted a terrifying vision of social forces in combat. This frame, undoubtedly supported by a generalized pro-business "policy" in the major press outlets, helped provide context and direction for the push toward industrial peace. Ultimately this peace would come at the hands of a third party, the public, whose representatives would preserve capitalism by exorcizing the specter of the national strike. After incorporating the combatants and reconfiguring them as "interests," a new narrative of "responsible," managed capitalism took root.

As a coda, it is interesting to note that today "class war" is not a term that has completely vanished. Occasionally it will pop up in the media, a quaint turn of phrase deployed in a politically flavored attack on the other side for tax policies or populist utterances.[26] Startlingly, one of America's most popular news hosts (right-wing commentator Lou Dobbs) wrote a bestseller in 2006 titled *The War on the Middle Class.* Yet, if anything, this book reveals the chasm in perception that has opened since the demise of the industrial war frame. Dobbs's war is not the same beast encountered by John Commons and his associates at the turn of the twentieth century. Instead, it is the assault of the "special interests" on the "rights" of the "middle class."[27] This middle class, in his analysis, includes nearly everybody. The public has swallowed the old combatants whole. For all intents and purposes, the "industrial war" has ended.

NOTES

INTRODUCTION   A QUESTION OF THE AGE

1. John Commons et al., "Is Class Conflict in America Growing and Is It Inevitable?" *American Sociological Society, Papers and Proceedings* 2 (December 1907): 138–147, reprinted in the *American Journal of Sociology* 13 (1908): 756–783.

2. Jeremy Atack and Peter Passell, *A New Economic View of American History from Colonial Times to 1940,* 2nd ed. (New York: Norton, 1994), 458.

3. These are the opening words of chapter 1 of Andrew Carnegie's book *Triumphant Democracy; or, Fifty Years' March of the Republic* (New York: Charles Scribner's Sons, 1888), 1.

4. A number of seminal studies explore class language on the other side of the Atlantic, but only a few American histories explicitly examine popular class discourse. Works by Martin J. Burke, Elizabeth Faue, Gary Gerstle, Stephen P. Rice, and a few others have begun to mine the rich territory of class-related rhetoric in print media in the United States. Key European and British studies include Gareth Stedman Jones, *Languages of Class: Studies in English Working Class History, 1832–1982* (Cambridge: Cambridge University Press, 1983); Asa Briggs, "The Language of 'Class' in Early Nineteenth-Century England," in *Essays in Labour History,* ed. Asa Briggs and John Saville (London: Macmillan, 1960); and William Sewell, *Work and Revolution in France: The Language of Labor from the Old Regime to 1848* (New York: Cambridge University Press, 1980). U.S. studies include Stephen P. Rice, *Minding the Machine: Languages of Class in Early Industrial America* (Berkeley: University of California Press, 2004); Martin J. Burke, *The Conundrum of Class: Public Discourse on the Social Order in America* (Chicago: University of Chicago Press, 1995); Gary Gerstle, *Working-Class Americanism: The Politics of Labor in a Textile City, 1914–1960* (Cambridge: Cambridge University Press, 1989); Elizabeth Faue, *Community of Suffering and Struggle: Women, Men, and the Labor Movement in Minneapolis, 1915–1945* (Chapel Hill: University of North Carolina Press, 1991).

5. Karl Marx, *Capital,* vol. 1 (London: Penguin Group, 1976), 344.

6. Antonio Gramsci, *Further Selections from the Prison Notebooks,* ed. and trans. Derek Boothman (London: Lawrence and Wishart, 1995), 155.

7. Antonio Gramsci, *Selections from the Prison Notebooks,* ed. and trans. Quintin Hoare and Geoffrey Nowell Smith (New York: International Publishers, 1971), 12; see also

T. J. Jackson Lears, "The Concept of Cultural Hegemony: Problems and Possibilities," *American Historical Review* 90, no. 3 (June 1985): 568.

8. For a summary analysis of the market imperatives influencing the media (albeit one focused on present conditions), see Alan B. Albarran, *Media Economics: Understanding Markets, Industries and Concepts* (Ames: Iowa State University Press, 1996), especially chapters 1 and 4. For an account of this process in the nineteenth century, see Gerald J. Baldasty, *The Commercialization of News in the Nineteenth Century* (Madison: University of Wisconsin Press, 1992).

9. Sociologist Edward Ross quoted in Robert W. McChesney and Ben Scott, eds., *Our Unfree Press: 100 Years of Radical Media Criticism* (New York: New Press, 2004), 4.

10. Upton Sinclair, *The Brass Check: A Study of American Journalism* (Pasadena: Upton Sinclair, 1920), 150.

11. Warren Breed, "Social Control in the Newsroom: A Functional Analysis," *Social Forces* 33, no. 4 (1955): 326–335.

12. On Hearst's belief in the public's reluctance to swallow pro-corporate journalism, see Alfred McClung Lee, *The Daily Newspaper in America: The Evolution of a Social Instrument* (New York: Octagon, 1973), 195.

13. James K. Hartog and Douglas M. McLeod, "A Multipersective Approach to Framing Analysis: A Field Guide," in *Framing Public Life: Perspectives on Media and Our Understanding of the Social World*, ed. Stephen Reese et al., 147 (Mahwah, N.J.: Lawrence Erlbaum Associates, 2001). For a summary of framing theory, see also Karen S. Johnson-Cartee, *News Narratives and News Framing: Constructing Political Reality* (Lanham, Md.: Rowman and Littlefield, 2004), 24–31.

14. Christopher R. Martin, *Framed!: Labor and the Corporate Media* (Ithaca, N.Y.: Cornell University Press, 2004), 8.

15. Ibid.; Peter Golding and Graham Murdock, "Culture, Communications, and Political Economy," in *Mass Media and Society*, ed. James Curran and Michael Gurevitch, 27 (London: Arnold, 1991).

16. John A. Noakes, "Official Frames in Social Movement Theory: The FBI, HUAC, and the Communist Threat in Hollywood," *Sociological Quarterly* 41, no. 4 (autumn 2000): 660.

17. See Richard A. Gonce, "John R. Commons's 'Five Big Years,' 1899–1904," *American Journal of Economics and Sociology* 61, no. 4 (2002), 755–777.

18. The influence of the Civil War in facilitating national communications systems is discussed in Phillip Shaw Paludin, *A People's Contest: The Union and Civil War, 1861–1865* (Lawrence: University Press of Kansas, 1996), 70. As for the wage-driven nature of American work at this time, see David Montgomery, *Beyond Equality: Labor and the Radical Republicans, 1862–1872* (New York: Knopf, 1967), 30.

19. See the bibliography for the complete list.

20. On news framing, see Reese et al., *Framing Public Life;* Theodore Glasser, ed., *The Idea of Public Journalism* (New York: Guilford Press, 1999), xvi; Erving Goffman, *Frame Analysis: An Essay on the Organization of Experience* (New York: Harper and Row, 1974); Stanley J. Baran, *Mass Communication Theory: Foundations, Ferment, and Future*, 2nd ed. (Belmont, Calif.: Wadsworth, 2000); Lance Bennett, *News: The Politics of Illusion*, 2nd ed. (New York: Longman, 1988). Also see Allan Rachlin, *News as Hegemonic Reality: American Political Culture and the Framing of News Accounts* (New York: Praeger, 1988); Gaye Tuchman, *Making News: A Study in the Construction of Reality* (New York:

Free Press, 1978); and Dan Schiller, *Objectivity and the News* (Philadelphia: University of Pennsylvania Press, 1981).

21. On professionalization and Progressive-era labor legislation, see Benjamin G. Rader, *The Academic Mind and Reform: The Influence of Richard T. Ely in American Life* (Lexington: University of Kentucky Press, 1966).

22. For Commons's views on capital and labor at this time, see his *Labor and Administration* (New York: Macmillan, 1913).

23. Commons, "Is Class Conflict in America Growing and Is It Inevitable?" 756–759, 762, 765–766.

24. Quoted in Graham Adams Jr., *Age of Industrial Violence, 1910–1915: The Activities and Findings of the United States Commission on Industrial Relations* (New York: Columbia University Press, 1966), 218.

25. I introduced this argument in Troy Rondinone, "'History Repeats Itself': The Civil War and the Meaning of Labor Conflict in the Late Nineteenth Century," *American Quarterly* 59, no. 2 (June 2007): 397–419.

26. For the power of the Revolution of 1848 for Germans, see Bruce Levine, *The Spirit of 1848: German Immigrants, Labor Conflict, and the Coming of the Civil War* (Urbana: University of Illinois Press, 1992).

27. Quoted in Priscilla Murolo and A. B. Chitty, *From the Folks Who Brought You the Weekend: A Short, Illustrated History of Labor in the United States* (New York: New Press, 2001), 97–98.

28. Key to my approach is an understanding of metaphors as being essential in the ordering of reality. As George Lakoff and Mark Johnson suggest, metaphors structure how we perceive the world. Understanding certain things by situating them in terms of others, we employ metaphors at the most basic levels of understanding. Seeing time as money, inflation as an entity, and words as containers for ideas, for example, helps bestow meaning on concepts otherwise left unexplained. In this manner, to paraphrase one theorist, metaphors "bring a subject to life" by relating a known quantity to an unknown object. George Lakoff and Mark Johnson, *Metaphors We Live By* (Chicago: University of Chicago Press, 1980). See Douglas Berggren, "The Use and Abuse of Metaphor I," *Review of Metaphysics* 16, no. 2 (December 1962): 242.

CHAPTER 1   WITH COLORS FLYING

1. On Duane and the Cordwainers' Strike, see Ronald Schultz, *The Republic of Labor: Philadelphia Artisans and the Politics of Class, 1720–1830* (New York: Oxford University Press, 1993), 160–164.

2. William Duane, "The Price of Labor," *Aurora*, November 27, 1805, in John R. Commons et al., eds., *A Documentary History of American Industrial Society*, vol. 6 (New York: Russell and Russell, 1958), 77. On the Philadelphia Cordwainers' Strike of 1806, see John R. Commons, "American Shoemakers—A Sketch of Industrial Evolution, 1648–1895," *Quarterly Journal of Economics* 24 (November 1909): 38–84; Commons et al., eds., *A Documentary History*, vol. 3, introduction and chapter 1; Ian M. G. Quimby, "The Cordwainers Protest: A Crisis in Labor Relations," *Winterthur Portfolio* 3 (1967): 83–101; Christopher L. Tomlins, *Law, Labor, and Ideology in the Early American Republic* (Cambridge: Cambridge University Press, 1993), 110, 131–138, 140, 142, 146, 178; Robert J. Steinfeld, "The Philadelphia Cordwainers' Case of 1806:

The Struggle over Alternative Legal Constructions of a Free Market in Labor," in *Labor Law in America: Historical and Critical Essays*, ed. Christopher L. Tomlins and Andrew J. King, 20–43 (Baltimore: Johns Hopkins University Press, 1992); Richard Twomey, "Jacobins and Jeffersonians: Anglo-American Radical Ideology, 1790–1810," in *The Origins of Anglo-American Radicalism*, ed. Margaret C. Jacob and James R. Jacob, 313–328 (Atlantic Highlands, N.J.: Humanities Press International, 1991).

3. Commons et al., eds., *A Documentary History*, 3:220, 228, 229, 230.

4. Ibid., 3:221.

5. Ibid., 3:147, 167.

6. Duane, "The Price of Labor," *Aurora*, November 27, 1805, in Commons et al., eds., *A Documentary History* 6:77.

7. Commons et al., eds., *A Documentary History*, 3:205, 235. In a July 4, 1806, toast printed in the *Aurora*, Rodney was hailed as remaining "honest and true to the principles of '76" (*Aurora*, July 9, 1806).

8. According to the *Oxford English Dictionary*, this was the first recorded use in print of the term "strike," as opposed to "struck," to refer to a work stoppage (though C. R. Dobson's work seems to contradict this). *Oxford English Dictionary*, 2nd ed. (Oxford: Clarendon Press, 1989), s.v. "strike." See Commons et al., eds., *A Documentary History*, 3:371.

9. For the world of working-class street parades, see Susan G. Davis, *Parades and Power: Street Theater in Nineteenth-Century Philadelphia* (Philadelphia: Temple University Press, 1986), chapter 5; Sean Wilentz, "Artisan Republican Festivals and the Rise of Class Conflict in New York City, 1788–1837," in *Working-Class America: Essays on Labor Community and American Society*, ed. Michael H. Frisch and Daniel J. Walkowitz, 37–77 (Urbana: University of Illinois Press, 1983). The antebellum strike is discussed in David Grimsted, "Ante-Bellum Labor: Violence, Strike, and Communal Arbitration," *Journal of Social History* 19 (1985): 5–28. A discussion of the strike "card" is in Philip S. Foner, *History of the Labor Movement in the United States*, vol. 1: *From Colonial Times to the Founding of the American Federation of Labor* (New York: International Publishers, 1962), 118–120. On the fears aimed at "monopolistic" unions, see Daniel Jacoby, *Laboring for Freedom: A New Look at the History of Labor in America* (Armonk, N.Y.: Sharp, 1998), 48.

10. "Turn out" as strike did not make it into Webster's compendium for several more decades. The persistence of the pastoral ideal in nineteenth-century America is discussed in Leo Marx, *The Machine in the Garden: Technology and the Pastoral Ideal in America* (New York: Oxford University Press, 1964).

11. This article is reprinted in John Commons et al., eds., *History of Labour in the United States*, vol. 1 (New York: Macmillan, 1918), 110–111.

12. For example, see C. R. Dobson, *Masters and Journeymen: A Prehistory of Industrial Relations 1717–1800* (London: Helm, 1980), 82. On the revolutionary inclinations of colonial sailors, see Jesse Lemisch, "Jack Tar in the Streets: Merchant Seamen in the Politics of Revolutionary America," *William and Mary Quarterly* 25, no. 3 (1968): 371–407.

13. "Combination of Seamen," *The Spectator*, October 23, 1802, and "Combination of Seamen," *New York Evening Post*, October 22, 1802, reprinted in *Keepers of the Revolution: New Yorkers at Work in the Early Republic*, ed. Paul A. Gilje and Howard B. Rock, 204–205 (Ithaca, N.Y.: Cornell University Press, 1992). Also see Paul A. Gilje, *The*

Road to Mobocracy: Popular Disorder in New York City, 1763–1834 (Chapel Hill: University of North Carolina Press, 1987), 180–183.

14. Commons et al., eds., *A Documentary History,* 3:329. An 1801 bakers' strike in New York even inspired a public dialogue on the nature of "monopoly" and "capitalist" oppression, though this was a truly rare example. See Howard B. Rock, "The Perils of Laissez-Faire: The Aftermath of the New York Bakers' Strike of 1801," *Labor History* 17, no. 3 (1976): 372–387.

15. Sean Wilentz, *Chants Democratic: New York City and the Rise of the American Working Class, 1788–1850* (New York: Oxford University Press, 1984), 100.

16. Frank Luther Mott, *American Journalism, A History: 1690–1960,* 3rd ed. (New York: Macmillan, 1969), 167–180.

17. Commons et al., eds., *History of Labour in the United States,* 1:169.

18. A broad review of the changes wrought by the market in the early nineteenth century is presented in Charles Sellers, *The Market Revolution: Jacksonian America, 1815–1846* (New York: Oxford University Press, 1991). On antebellum strike patterns, see David Montgomery, "Strikes in Nineteenth-Century America," *Social Science Quarterly* 4 (February 1980): 81–103; Sean Wilentz, "The Rise of the American Working Class, 1776–1877: A Survey," in *Perspectives on American Labor History: The Problems of Synthesis,* ed. J. Carroll Moody and Alice Kessler-Harris, 84 (De Kalb: Northern Illinois University Press, 1989). A list of strikes taking place between 1833 and 1837 is in Commons et al., eds., *History of Labour in the United States,* 1:478–484. On deskilling and the changing nature of the workforce, see Wilentz, *Chants Democratic,* 108–112; Bruce Laurie, *Working People of Philadelphia, 1800–1850* (Philadelphia: Temple University Press, 1980), especially chapter 1. Wilentz refers to this period as the era of the "journeymen's revolt" in *Chants Democratic,* as does Kim Voss in *The Making of American Exceptionalism: The Knights of Labor and Class Formation in the Nineteenth Century* (Ithaca, N.Y.: Cornell University Press, 1993).

19. Howard B. Rock, *Artisans of the New Republic: The Tradesmen of New York City in the Age of Jefferson* (New York: New York University Press, 1979), 276.

20. Bruce Laurie, *Artisans into Workers: Labor in Nineteenth-Century America* (Urbana: University of Illinois Press, 1997), 79–85.

21. David Brody, "Time and Work during Early American Industrialism," in *In Labor's Cause: Main Themes on the History of the American Worker* (New York: Oxford University Press, 1993), 34.

22. *Pennsylvania Packet,* April 30, 1776, quoted in Gary Nash, *The Urban Crucible,* abridged ed. (Cambridge, Mass.: Harvard University Press, 1986), 243.

23. It is worth noting, however, as Sean Wilentz points out, artisans continued to struggle with a lingering "stigma against 'meer mechanicks'" (Wilentz, "Artisan Republican Festivals," in Frisch and Walkowitz, eds., *Working-Class America,* 43).

24. William Manning, *The Key of Liberty: Showing the Causes Why a Free Government Has Always Failed and a Remedy Against It,* in *The Key of Liberty: The Life and Democratic Writings of William Manning, a Laborer, 1747–1814,* ed. Michael Merrill and Sean Wilentz, 138 (Cambridge, Mass.: Harvard University Press, 1993). On the deluge of Revolutionary language, see Thomas Gustafson, *Representative Words: Politics, Literature, and the American Language, 1776–1865* (Cambridge: Cambridge University Press, 1992), 195–269. On the importance and uses of Revolutionary memory, see Michael

Kammen, *A Season of Youth: The American Revolution and the Historical Imagination* (Ithaca, N.Y.: Cornell University Press, 1988).

25. Joyce Appleby, *Inheriting the Revolution: The First Generation of Americans* (Cambridge, Mass.: Belknap Press, 2000), 27–28.

26. By *laborites*, I refer to the cohort of trade union activists in the 1820s and later who employed Revolutionary rhetoric to criticize capitalist imperatives. For "equal rights" talk, see Daniel T. Rodgers, *Contested Truths: Keywords in American Politics since Independence* (New York: Basic Books, 1987), 72–79.

27. Robert Townsend, Richardson Ryan, and Benjamin Hoghland, "To the Public," *American Citizen,* April 10, 1809, reprinted in Gilje and Rock, eds., *Keepers of the Revolution,* 101–104.

28. Wilentz, "Artisan Republican Festivals," 47; Wilentz, *Chants Democratic,* 87–89; Richard B. Stott, *Workers in the Metropolis: Class, Ethnicity, and Youth in Antebellum New York City* (Ithaca, N.Y.: Cornell University Press, 1990), 158; Davis, *Parades and Power,* 188–119.

29. *National Trades' Union,* October 17, 1835, reprinted in Commons et al., eds., *A Documentary History,* 5:343–346.

30. *Public Ledger,* June 10, 1836, quoted in Laurie, *Working People of Philadelphia,* 96. The journeymen's metaphorical connection to Independence is discussed in Wilentz, *Chants Democratic,* 61–103.

31. The "Ten-Hour Circular" was printed in *The Man* on May 13, 1835, and the *National Trades' Union* on May 16, 1835, and is reprinted in Commons et al., eds., *A Documentary History* 6:94–99.

32. Foner, *History of the Labor Movement in the United States,* 1:109.

33. See, for example, "Democratic Celebration," *Niles' Weekly Register,* July 15, 1837.

34. "The Approaching Election," *Working Man's Advocate,* October 31, 1829.

35. *United States Gazette,* July 11, 1835, quoted in Davis, *Parades and Power,* 136.

36. Paul Johnson, *A Shopkeeper's Millennium: Society and Revivals in Rochester, New York, 1815–1837* (New York: Hill and Wang, 1978); Anthony F. C. Wallace, *Rockdale: The Growth of an American Village in the Early Industrial Revolution* (New York: Knopf, 1978).

37. E. P. Thompson, *The Making of the English Working Class* (New York: Knopf, 1966), 9.

38. These statements are quoted from an excellent study of religion and labor in antebellum America: Jama Lazerow, *Religion and the Working Class in Antebellum America* (Washington, D.C.: Smithsonian Institution Press, 1995), 30, 31, 210, 211. On the democratization of religion in antebellum America, see Nathan O. Hatch, *The Democratization of American Christianity* (New Haven, Conn.: Yale University Press, 1989). On the connection between the language of evangelical Protestantism and the Revolution, see Rhys Issac, "Preachers and Patriots: Popular Culture and the Revolution in Virginia," in *The American Revolution: Explorations in the History of American Radicalism,* ed. Alfred Young, 125–156 (DeKalb: Northern Illinois University Press, 1976).

39. There is a substantial historiography dealing with the concept of wage slavery. Of special importance here are David Roediger, *The Wages of Whiteness: Race and the Making of the American Working Class,* rev. ed. (London: Verso, 1999), and Marcus

Cunliffe, *Chattel Slavery and Wage Slavery: The Anglo-American Context, 1830–1860* (Athens: University of Georgia Press, 1979).

40. Reprinted in Commons et al., eds., *A Documentary History,* 6:94–99.

41. *The Man,* February 22, 1834, quoted in Roediger, *The Wages of Whiteness,* 69.

42. On free labor ideology, see Eric Foner, *Free Soil, Free Labor, Free Men* (Oxford: Oxford University Press, 1995).

43. Duane, "The Price of Labor," *Aurora,* November 27, 1805, in Commons et al., eds., *A Documentary History,* 6:77.

44. In Foner, *History of the Labor Movement in the United States,* 1:119.

45. Duane, "The Price of Labor," *Aurora,* November 27, 1805, in Commons et al., eds., *A Documentary History* 6:77. On employer "cards," see Foner, *History of the Labor Movement in the United States,* 1:119.

46. Wilentz, *Chants Democratic,* 387.

47. "Glorious!!!" *Working Man's Advocate,* July 25, 1835. This is quoted in Foner, *History of the Labor Movement in the United States,* 1:117.

48. On the influence of metaphor in providing an organizational base for knowledge, see George Lakoff and Mark Johnson, *Metaphors We Live By* (Chicago: University of Chicago Press, 1980).

49. Edward Earle, "War Between Democracy and Aristocracy," *Working Man's Advocate,* March 15, 1834, quoted in Dan Schiller, *Objectivity and the News* (Philadelphia: University of Pennsylvania Press, 1981), 40.

50. See, for example, William Sewell, *Work and Revolution in France: The Language of Labor from the Old Regime to 1848* (New York: Cambridge University Press, 1980); Thompson, *The Making of the English Working Class.* This fact is pointed out in Kim Voss, *The Making of American Exceptionalism,* 44.

51. Frances Wright D'Arusmont, "The People at War," *Free Enquirer,* November 27, 1830, reprinted in Commons et al., eds., *A Documentary History,* 5:178.

52. *Congressional Globe,* 24th Congress, 2nd Session, App., 168, January 14, 1837, quoted in Allan Kulikoff, *The Agrarian Origins of Capitalism* (Charlottesville: University Press of Virginia, 1992), 85.

53. Priscilla Murolo and A. B. Chitty, *From the Folks Who Brought You the Weekend: A Short, Illustrated History of Labor in the United States* (New York: New Press, 2001), 46.

54. Commons et al., eds., *A Documentary History,* 6:39.

55. Quoted in Laurie, *Working People of Philadelphia,* 90.

56. "Coffin handbill" quoted in Daniel Jacoby, *Laboring for Freedom,* 44.

57. David M. Gordon, Richard Edwards, and Michael Reich, *Segmented Work, Divided Workers: The Historical Transformation of Labor in the United States* (Cambridge: Cambridge University Press, 1982), 56–78; Wilentz, *Chants Democratic,* 108–110.

58. For an analysis of public space and social regulation, see Mary P. Ryan, *Civic Wars: Democracy and Public Life in the American City during the Nineteenth Century* (Berkeley: University of California Press, 1997), 54–55. Antebellum riots are discussed in Paul A. Gilje, *Rioting in America* (Bloomington: Indiana University Press, 1996), 60–86; David Grimstead, "Rioting in Its Jacksonian Setting," *American Historical Review* 77 (April 1972): 361–397; Michael Feldberg, *The Turbulent Era: Riot and Disorder in Jacksonian America* (New York: Oxford University Press, 1980).

59. By way of comparison, ethnic- and slavery-related social disturbances were far more violent and feared by elites. See Feldberg, *The Turbulent Era.*

60. Although exceptionally radical, Seth Luther's comments were widely printed. In the May 7, 1835, edition of the *Boston Morning Post,* for example, a speech of Luther's is published on page 1 in which he warns "if our opponents obstinately resist the arguments of the soundest political economy, we must obtain our rights by other means."

61. Martin J. Burke, *The Conundrum of Class: Public Discourse on the Social Order in America* (Chicago: University of Chicago Press, 1995), 83.

62. *Pennsylvanian,* June 12, 1835, quoted in Davis, *Parades and Power,* 136.

63. The *Gazette* noted on June 12, 1835, that "the turning out for wages is sanctioned by custom, but the turning out for rum will not due in these temperance times."

64. *The Herald,* February 24, 1836.

65. "Riots—State of the City," *The Herald,* February 25, 1836.

66. *Niles' Weekly Register,* June 20, 1835 (page 273); March 19, 1836 (J. L. Wendell, "Trades Unions—Legal Opinion," pages 45–46), April 2, 1836 (page 74), April 23, 1836 (pages 130–131). On Niles's approach and personal history, see Norval Neil Luxon, *Niles' Weekly Register: News Magazine of the Nineteenth Century* (Baton Rouge: Louisiana State University Press, 1947).

67. On these examples and the increasing tendency to connect strikes to the Trades Union movement in order to condemn them both, see Walter Hugins, *Jacksonian Democracy and the Working Class: A Study of the New York Workingmen's Movement 1829–1837* (Stanford, Calif.: Stanford University Press, 1960), 59–62.

68. Alexis de Tocqueville, *Democracy in America,* vol. 2 (New York: Vintage Books, 1945), 202–205.

69. By the Jacksonian period, America was a nation of readers. See Lee Soltow and Edward Stevens, *The Rise of Literacy and the Common School in the United States: A Socio- Economic Analysis to 1870* (Chicago: University of Chicago Press, 1981). Regarding the influence of evangelical Christianity on media and literacy, see David Paul Nord, "The Evangelical Origins of Mass Media in America, 1815–1835," *Journalism Monographs* 88 (1984): 1–30.

70. By 1850 there was one newspaper copy circulated daily per 4.5 inhabitants in the growing city of New York, as compared with one copy for each 16 New Yorkers in 1830. Nationwide, daily newspaper circulation rose from 1,200 news outlets in 1830 to 3,000 in 1860. See Mott, *American Journalism,* 225–226; Alexander Saxton, "Problems of Class and Race in the Origins of the Mass Circulation Press," *American Quarterly* 36 (1984): 212. A different measurement of the growth of the newspaper—per capita delivery of newspapers went from 0.7 in 1820 to 2.7 in 1840—is presented in Richard R. John, *Spreading the News: The American Postal System from Franklin to Morse* (Cambridge, Mass.: Harvard University Press, 1995), 4.

71. Michael Schudson, *The Power of News* (Cambridge, Mass.: Harvard University Press, 1995), 43–48; Gaye Tuchman, *Making News: A Study in the Construction of Reality* (New York: Free Press, 1978), chapter 1; Schiller, *Objectivity and the News,* chapters 1–2.

72. Schiller, *Objectivity and the News,* 10, 55–56.

73. Jon Bekken, "The Working-Class Press at the Turn of the Century," in *Ruthless Criticism: New Perspectives in U.S. Communication History,* ed. William S. Solomon and Robert W. McChesney, 153 (Minneapolis: University of Minnesota Press, 1993).

74. C. K. McFarland and Robert L. Thistlewaite, "20 Years of a Successful Labor Paper: *The Working Man's Advocate*, 1829–1849," *Journalism Quarterly* 60, no. 1 (1983): 37.

75. On political economy in the Jacksonian period, see Paul K. Conkin, *Prophets of Prosperity: America's First Political Economists* (Bloomington: Indiana University Press, 1980). Leggett's editorials are collected in William Leggett, *Democratick Editorials: Essays in Jacksonian Political Economy*, ed. Lawrence White (Indianapolis: Liberty Press, 1984).

76. For the new language of "classes," see Burke, *The Conundrum of Class*, especially chapters 2 and 3. On the transformation of American political rhetoric and style, see Andrew W. Robertson, *The Language of Democracy: Political Rhetoric in the United States and Britain, 1790–1900* (Ithaca, N.Y.: Cornell University Press, 1995), 53, 68–95.

77. Quoted in William Cahn, *A Pictorial History of American Labor* (New York: Crown, 1972), 70.

78. "Unequal Taxation," *Working Man's Advocate*, March 27, 1830.

79. Orestes Brownson, *The Laboring Classes*, 3rd ed. (Boston: Greene, 1840), 9. On Mike Walsh, see Wilentz, *Chants Democratic*, 326–335. For an earlier, influential expression of anticapitalist rhetoric, see Thomas Skidmore, *The Rights of Man to Property!* (New York: Ming, 1829).

80. On Henry C. Carey and the "harmony of interests," see his *Principles of Social Science* (Philadelphia: Lippincott, 1858–1859). A more mainstream series of articles on the harmony of interests appeared in *Merchant's Magazine*, vols. 41 and 42, 1859–1860, by Thomas Prentice Kettell. Boynton's remarks are printed in Joseph H. Moore, "Social Reform," *Herald of Truth* (November 1, 1847): 365

81. The distaste of the wages system is discussed in Jonathan A. Glickstein, *Concepts of Free Labor in Antebellum America* (New Haven, Conn.: Yale University Press, 1991). Greeley's editorial on strikes appears in the *New York Tribune*, July 24, 1850. The address to the New York Typographical Society is quoted in Norman Ware, *The Industrial Worker, 1840–1860: The Reaction of American Industrial Society to the Advance of the Industrial Revolution*, (Chicago: Quadrangle Books, 1964), 58.

82. Brownson, *The Laboring Classes*; Walsh in *Subterranean*, November 8, 1845, quoted in Wilentz, *Chants Democratic*, 332; Robert Rantoul Jr., "The Education of a Free People," *Christian Register and Boston Observer*, June 27, 1840.

83. "Labor and Laborers," *Mechanic's Advocate* (Albany), April 15, 1847.

84. "Capital and Labor," *Hunt's Merchant Magazine and Commercial Review* 12 (April 1845): 396.

85. Ibid.

86. "The Labor Movement," *Scientific American* 8, no. 31 (April 16, 1853): 246; "Trade Strikes," *Scientific American* 2, no. 12 (March 17, 1860): 185.

87. This editorial theme dates back at least to 1835, when *Hazard's Register of Pennsylvania* explained on January 4th that "Strikes are dangerous expedients. They never yet have been of any advantage to those concerned in them, but in the end generally prove highly injurious."

88. "Riot at Allegany City," *Mechanic's Advocate* (Albany), August 12, 1848; "Strikes and Their Effects," *Mechanic's Advocate* (Albany), September 30, 1848; and "The Slop Shop Strike," *Mechanic's Advocate* (Albany), October 28, 1848.

89. See *Herald* and *Tribune*, August 5, 1850. The influence of German political émigrés on the American labor movement is discussed in Bruce Levine, *The Spirit of 1848:*

German Immigrants, Labor Conflict, and the Coming of the Civil War (Urbana: University of Illinois Press, 1992).

90. Arthur Bestor, "The Evolution of the Socialist Vocabulary," *Journal of the History of Ideas* 9 (1948): 259.

91. Labor responses to the *New York Herald*'s treatment of their cause as "socialistic" are an excellent example of this. See *Tribune* and *Herald* strike analyses and editorials, July 1850.

92. Jack P. Greene, *Intellectual Construction of America: Exceptionalism and Identity from 1492–1800* (Chapel Hill: University of North Carolina Press, 1993), 107, points out that fears of wealthy manipulation originated in eighteenth-century observations of Europe, where severe inequality and aristocratic power seemed to go hand in hand. See also James L. Huston, *Securing the Fruits of Labor: The American Concept of Wealth Distribution 1765–1900* (Baton Rouge: Louisiana State University Press, 1998), chapter 2.

93. "Wages and Living in Cities," *New York Tribune,* April 20, 1854. Occasionally as many as twenty-five strikes would be reported in a single issue of the *Tribune* or *Times.* See Commons et al., eds., *History of Labour in the United States,* 1:607.

94. On the subject of hardening class lines at this time, see Susan E. Hirsch, *Roots of the American Working Class: The Industrialization of the Crafts in Newark, 1800–1860* (Philadelphia: University of Pennsylvania Press, 1978), 79.

95. On the origins of the Associated Press and its implications for news reportage, see Oliver Gramling, *AP: The Story of News* (Port Washington, N.Y.: Kennikat Press, 1969); Michael Schudson, *Discovering the News: A Social History of American Newspapers* (New York: Basic Books, 1978), 4.

96. See "The Song of the Shoemakers' Strike" and verses in "The Women's Meeting in Behalf of Labor" in *Frank Leslie's Illustrated Newspaper,* March 17, 1860.

97. Ibid.

98. Analysis of media strike coverage is in James L. Huston, "Facing an Angry Labor: The American Public Interprets the Shoemakers' Strike of 1860," *Civil War History* 28, no. 3 (1982): 197–212.

99. *New York Herald,* April 3, 1860, quoted in Huston, "Facing an Angry Labor," 210.

100. Lincoln's speech is reprinted in Roy P. Basler, ed., *The Collected Works of Abraham Lincoln,* vol. 4 (New Brunswick, N.J.: Rutgers University Press, 1953–1954), 13–30. Although the Republican Party used anticorporate sentiment to threaten wealthy northern business interests to eschew an alliance of "the lords of the loom and the lords of the lash," it counted on businessmen's support and a broader coalition of northern voters who could believe that a nascent capitalist existed in each working-man. For that matter, the egalitarianism of the Democrats never led them to the barricades; the object was never to actually kill the aristocrats (whoever they were) but instead to modify the system of laws that permitted wealth to subvert democracy.

101. "The Labor Question," *Scientific American* 1, no. 10 (September 3, 1859): 153; "The Evils of Trades' Strikes," *Scientific American* 2, no. 4 (January 21, 1860): 54.

CHAPTER 2   DRIFTING TOWARD INDUSTRIAL WAR

1. William Sylvis, "Address Delivered at Buffalo, N.Y., January, 1864," in James C. Sylvis, *The Life, Speeches, Labors, and Essays of William H. Sylvis* (Philadelphia: Claxton, Remsen, and Haffelfinger, 1872), 96–127. Sylvis's suggestions for labor included

cooperation among workers, the continuance of the labor press, and a denial of the theory of supply and demand that dictated wage rates. See Jonathan P. Grossman, *William Sylvis: Pioneer of American Labor* (New York: Columbia University Press, 1945). The phrase "irrepressible conflict" itself originates in a speech made by William Seward in the 1850s in reference to growing sectional differences.

2. This relates to Price and Tewksbury's argument of the "applicability affect," in which media frames "activate certain ideas" in the public. In this case, total war language activated Civil War ideas. See Vincent Price and David Tewksbury, "Switching Trains of Thought: The Impact of News Frames on Readers' Cognitive Responses," *Communication Research* 24 (1997): 486; Karen S. Johnson-Cartee, *News Narratives and News Framing: Constructing Political Reality* (Lanham, Md.: Rowman and Littlefield, 2004), 28.

3. See David Montgomery, *Beyond Equality: Labor and the Radical Republicans, 1862–1872* (New York: Knopf, 1967); Nancy Cohen, *The Reconstruction of American Liberalism, 1865–1914* (Chapel Hill: University of North Carolina Press, 2002).

4. The best study of the influence of the war on labor is Montgomery, *Beyond Equality*. While Montgomery recognizes the politicization of the war experience, I am looking at the broader discourse of class in relation to the war.

5. Typical examples of this standard periodization include Robert V. Bruce, *1877: Year of Violence* (Chicago: Dee, 1989); Shelton Stromquist, *A Generation of Boomers: The Pattern of Railroad Labor Conflict in Nineteenth-Century America* (Urbana: University of Illinois Press, 1987); Sidney Lens, *The Labor Wars: From the Molly Maguires to the Sitdowns* (New York: Doubleday, 1973); and Walter Licht, *Industrializing America: The Nineteenth Century* (Baltimore: Johns Hopkins University Press, 1995), 166.

6. Henry James, *Hawthorne* (New York: Harper and Brothers, 1901), 139, quoted in George M. Frederickson, *The Inner Civil War: Northern Intellectuals and the Crisis of the Union* (New York: Harper and Row, 1965), 1.

7. There are numerous excellent studies on the ways in which the Civil War affected Americans. These include Frederickson, *The Inner Civil War;* Anne C. Rose, *Victorian America and the Civil War* (New York: Cambridge University Press, 1992); Stuart McConnell, *Glorious Contentment: The Grand Army of the Republic, 1865–1900* (Chapel Hill: University of North Carolina Press, 1992); T. J. Jackson Lears, *No Place of Grace: Antimodernism and the Transformation of American Culture, 1880–1920* (Chicago: University of Chicago Press, 1994); and Louis Menand, *The Metaphysical Club* (New York: Farrar, Strauss, and Giroux, 2001). On the impact of war experience in veterans' lives, see Glen H. Elder Jr., "Military Times and Turning Points in Men's Lives," *Developmental Psychology* 22, no. 2 (1986), 233–245; Thomas C. Leonard, *Above the Battle: War-Making in America from Appomattox to Versailles* (New York: Oxford University Press, 1978); Drew Gilpin Faust, *This Republic of Suffering: Death and the American Civil War* (New York: Knopf, 2008); and Russell L. Johnson, *Warriors into Workers: The Civil War and the Formation of Urban-Industrial Society in a Northern City* (New York: Fordham University Press, 2003).

8. Walt Whitman, "Specimen Days," quoted in Leonard, *Above the Battle, 17.*

9. James A. Ward, *Railroads and the Character of America, 1820–1887* (Knoxville: University of Tennessee Press, 1986), 153. According to Ward, "The Civil War, with its four long years of bloody news from various fronts, with its glorification of the manly virtues of force and fury, only served to gild the language of corporate executives with strong, vivid, and often gory metaphors."

10. Andrew W. Robertson, *The Language of Democracy: Political Rhetoric in the United States and Britain, 1790–1900* (Ithaca, N.Y.: Cornell University Press, 1995), 124–125; Richard Jensen, *The Winning of the Midwest: Social and Political Conflict* (Chicago: University of Chicago Press, 1971), 7–8.

11. Mark Philip Katz, *From Appomattox to Montmartre: Americans and the Paris Commune* (Cambridge, Mass.: Harvard University Press, 1998), 98; Frederickson, *The Inner Civil War.*

12. Edwin Emery and Michael Emery, *The Press and America: An Interpretive History of Mass Media,* 4th ed. (Englewood Cliffs, N.J.: Prentice Hall, 1978), 206, 222. Total numbers of newspapers rose from 3,000 in 1860 to 4,500 in 1870, and 7,000 in 1880.

13. Katz, *From Appomattox to Montmartre,* 139. Also see Havilah Babcock, "The Press and the Civil War," *Journalism Quarterly* 6 (March 1929): 1–5. The war also injected new life into the telegraph.

14. "Capital and Labor," *Old Guard* 5, no. 2 (1867): 119–121; "Trades Unions and Strikes," *Hours at Home; A Popular Monthly of Instruction and Recreation* 9, no. 6 (October 1869): 485–491; "The Eight Hour Strikes," *The Merchants' Magazine and Commercial Review* (August 1, 1868): 91. These works and others here are taken from a close survey of the *American Periodical Series.* See the bibliography.

15. Importantly, Walker, Carey, and Bolles all went on in their discussions to reiterate theories of the harmony of interests. See Amasa Walker, *The Science of Wealth: A Manual of Political Economy* (Boston: Little, Brown, 1866); Henry C. Carey, *Capital and Labor* (Philadelphia: Collins, 1873); Albert S. Bolles, *The Conflict between Labor and Capital* (Philadelphia: Lippincott, 1876). These works are treated in Martin J. Burke, *The Conundrum of Class: Public Discourse on the Social Order in America* (Chicago: University of Chicago Press, 1995), 134–140.

16. Veterans, for example, were instrumental in the building of the transcontinental railroad. For Ira Steward on labor after 1865, see John R. Commons et al., eds., *A Documentary History of American Industrial Society,* vol. 9 (New York: Russell and Russell, 1958).

17. Quoted in Page Smith, *The Rise of Industrial America: A People's History of the Post-Reconstruction Era* (New York: Penguin Books, 1984), 167. On the postwar discontent among laborers, see Steven J. Ross, *Workers on the Edge: Work, Leisure, and Politics in Industrializing Cincinnati, 1788–1890* (New York: Columbia University Press, 1985), chapter 8.

18. Philip S. Foner, *History of the Labor Movement in the United States,* vol. 1: *From Colonial Times to the Founding of the American Federation of Labor* (New York: International Publishers, 1962), 328; Grace Palladino, *Another Civil War: Labor, Capital, and the State in the Anthracite Regions of Pennsylvania, 1840–68* (Urbana: University of Illinois Press, 1990), 121–165.

19. Foner, *History of the Labor Movement in the United States,* 1:358.

20. For example, during a city railroad strike during the war, the *New York Times* conceded "it is a very empty sort of consolation to tell them [workers] that their sufferings can all be traced to the working of natural laws" (*New York Times,* February 21, 1863).

21. A group of union leaders at the first National Labor Congress in 1865 declared that "strikes . . . have been productive of great injury to the laboring classes" (quoted in Montgomery, *Beyond Equality,* 151).

22. *Boston Daily Evening Voice*, November 3, 1865, quoted in Montgomery, *Beyond Equality*, 90–91.

23. Montgomery, *Beyond Equality*, 140–141.

24. "The Labor Cause—Report of Committee on Cooperation," in *American Workman* (Boston) (June 26, 1869).

25. Henry George, *Progress and Poverty: An Inquiry into the Cause of Industrial Depressions and of Increase of Want with Increase of Wealth* (New York: Doubleday and McClure, 1900), 5. According to James L. Huston, when George wrote of inequality as an "inescapable fact of contemporary economic life," the "public accepted the statement as true." See James L. Huston, *Securing the Fruits of Labor: The American Concept of Wealth Distribution, 1765–1900* (Baton Rouge: Louisiana State University Press, 1998), 345.

26. David M. Gordon, Richard Edwards, and Michael Reich, *Segmented Work, Divided Workers: The Historical Transformation of Labor in the United States* (Cambridge: Cambridge University Press, 1982), 79–99; David Montgomery, "Strikes in Nineteenth-Century America," *Social Science Quarterly* 4 (February 1980): 88; Mike Davis, *Prisoners of the American Dream: Politics and Economy in the History of the U.S. Working Class* (London: Verso, 1986), 18–19.

27. William G. Roy, *Socializing Capital: The Rise of the Large Industrial Corporation in America* (Princeton, N.J.: Princeton University Press, 1997), 78.

28. Leo Marx, *The Machine in the Garden: Technology and the Pastoral Ideal in America* (New York: Oxford University Press, 1964).

29. Walter Licht, *Working for the Railroad: The Organization of Work in the Nineteenth Century* (Princeton, N.J.: Princeton University Press, 1983), chapters 3 and 5.

30. On conflicting attitudes toward the railroads, see John Lauritz Larson, *Bonds of Enterprise: John Murray Forbes and Western Development in America's Railway Age* (Cambridge, Mass.: Harvard University Press, 1984), 171–195; David O. Stowell, *Streets, Railroads, and the Great Strike of 1877* (Chicago: University of Chicago Press, 1999), 13–35. Railroad magnate Cornelius Vanderbilt even proclaimed "What do I care about the law? Hain't I got the power?" (quoted in Matthew Josephson, *The Robber Barons: The Great American Capitalists, 1861–1901* [New York: Harcourt Brace Jovanovich, 1962], 15).

31. On newspaper coverage of the 1873 strike, see Herbert G. Gutman, "Trouble on the Railroads in 1873–74," in *Work, Culture, and Society in Industrializing America: Essays in American Working-Class and Social History* (New York: Knopf, 1976), 295–320.

32. *Philadelphia Inquirer*, December 29, 30, 31, 1873; *Chicago Tribune*, December 31, 1873; *New York Times*, December 28–31, 1873; Gutman, "Trouble on the Railroads," in *Work, Culture, and Society in Industrializing America*, 302–306.

33. J. A. Dacus, *Annals of the Great Strikes in the United States* (St. Louis: Scammell, 1877), iv. Variations of this phrase would crop up repeatedly in later works on the strike.

34. Press sources analyzed for the 1877 strike include the *Baltimore Sun, Boston Evening Transcript, Chicago Times, Chicago Daily Tribune, Chicago Daily News, Cincinnati Commercial Tribune, Harrisburg Independent, New Orleans Times, New Orleans Daily Picayune, New York Sun, New York Times, Pittsburgh Commercial and Gazette, San Francisco Chronicle, The Irish World, Leslie's Illustrated Weekly, Nation, National Labor Tribune*, and assorted periodicals in the American Periodicals Series.

35. "Railroad Employes on Strike," *New York Times*, July 17, 1877; "Riotous Strikers," *Chicago Tribune*, July 18, 1877; "The Season for Strikes," *New Orleans Times*, July 18, 1877.

36. "The Railroad Men's War," *New York Times,* July 19, 1877; "Riotous Strikers," *Chicago Tribune,* July 18, 1877; *Pittsburgh Commercial and Gazette,* July 25 to 30, 1877.

37. *Cincinnati Commercial Tribune,* July 18–21, 1877. Similarly, the *New Orleans Picayune* traveled from "Railroad Troubles" on the 20th to "Railroad War" by the 23rd.

38. "Trouble Anticipated at Chicago," *San Francisco Chronicle,* July 23, 1877.

39. *Pittsburgh Commercial and Gazette,* July 20, 1877; "The South Is Solid," *New Orleans Times,* July 26, 1877.

40. This is testimony not only to national memory but also to the power of the Associated Press and the network of telegraphs already in place.

41. "Pitched Battles," *Chicago Tribune,* July 27, 1877; *New York Times,* July 27, 1877; *Cincinnati Commercial Gazette,* July 27, 1877.

42. John Donaghy, "Robert M. Ammon, the Leader of the Pittsburgh and Fort Wayne Railroad Strike, at His Post, Directing the Movements of the Strikers," *Frank Leslie's Illustrated Newspaper,* August 11, 1877.

43. "The Great Strike," *New Orleans Times,* July 24, 1877. Examples of this martial style go on and on. There would be a "gallant charge" of militiamen, or if the police and military had not routed the mob, rioters might have "complete control of the city." Strikers would "capture" certain points of strategic interest such as telegraph offices and roundhouses. Beneath the headline "PITCHED BATTLES," the July 27, 1877, *Chicago Tribune* promised to provide details on the "Steady War on the Southwest Side of the City." In a special dispatch early in the strike entitled "Midnight News from the Seat of War," the *Baltimore Sun* noted that after controlling the trains, the strikers still "remain at their posts" (July 18, 1877).

44. *Chicago Tribune,* July 20, 1877.

45. *New Orleans Picayune,* July 25, 1877.

46. Philip S. Foner, *The Great Labor Uprising of 1877* (New York: Monad Press, 1977), 42.

47. "The Strike," *San Francisco Chronicle,* July 23, 1877.

48. See Stowell, *Streets, Railroads, and the Great Strike of 1877.*

49. On the makeup of rioters in one urban setting, see Stowell, *Streets, Railroads, and the Great Strike of 1877.*

50. Jon Bekken, "The Working-Class Press at the Turn of the Century," in *Ruthless Criticism: New Perspectives in U.S. Communication History,* ed. William S. Solomon and Robert W. McChesney, 153 (Minneapolis: University of Minnesota Press, 1993).

51. "The First Cause of the Strike," *National Labor Tribune,* July 28, 1877.

52. "What We Should Fight," *National Labor Tribune,* April 18, 1876.

53. Other labor organs were a bit more enthusiastic and dramatic in war representation than the *National Labor Tribune.* See *The Irish World, The Labor Standard,* and the *Workingman's Advocate* in July and August of 1877.

54. "The War for Bread," *The Irish World,* July 28, 1877.

55. "Politicians and Brigands," *New York Times,* July 26, 1877. Here the reporter associated the mob with Thomas Carlyle's history of the French Revolution (*New Orleans Picayune,* July 26, 1877). On African Americans and white women in the strike, see Foner, *The Great Labor Uprising of 1877.* On the West Coast, the Chinese served the bill even more dramatically as the target of both the press and the strikers, uniting opinion makers and white workers behind race hatred.

56. "Thoughts on the Riots," *San Francisco Chronicle,* July 24, 1877.

57. "The Cause and Remedy," *The Brotherhood of Locomotive Firemen and Engineers*, September 1877.

58. Bruce, *1877: Year of Violence*, 276.

59. Ross, *Workers on the Edge*, 250.

60. *Chicago Tribune*, July 24, 1877. Portions of this speech are also quoted in Foner, *The Great Labor Uprising of 1877*, 143–44. Also quoted in *Chicago Times*, July 24 1877; *Chicago Daily News*, July 24, 1877. By making reference to the veteran organization the Grand Army of the Republic, Parsons further welded historical remembrance to the mood of discontent and public sympathy for the plight of the "wage slave."

61. James Moorhead, *American Apocalypse: Yankee Protestants and the Civil War 1860–1869* (New Haven, Conn.: Yale University Press, 1978).

62. "The Prayer Meeting—The Riot from a Religious Standpoint," *Pittsburgh Commercial and Gazette*, July 26, 1877.

63. Quoted in Katz, *From Appomattox to Montmartre*, 157.

64. "The Rule of the Mob," *Chicago Tribune*, July 25, 1877.

65. *Niles' Weekly Register*, 1835. See Louis Adamic, *Dynamite: The Story of Class Violence in America*, rev. ed. (New York: Viking, 1934), 7–8, for a discussion of antebellum foreigner fears.

66. Quoted in Milton Meltzer, *Bread and Roses: The Struggle for American Labor, 1865–1915* (New York: Vintage Sundial Books, 1967), 90. Tom Scott, president of the Pennsylvania Railroad, similarly called for a "rifle diet" for the strikers.

67. Quoted in Ward, *Railroads and the Character of America*, 163.

68. See David Paul Nord, "The Business Values of American Newspapers: The 19th Century Watershed in Chicago," *Journalism Quarterly* 61 (1984): 267, for the convergence of opinion toward the end of the strike in ideologically different Chicago newspapers.

69. Robert P. Porter, "The Truth about the Strike," *The Galaxy* 24, no. 6 (December 1877): 725–732.

70. *New York Bulletin*, "The Causes of the Strike," reprinted in *The Cincinnati Tribune*, July 27, 1877.

71. Dacus, *Annals of the Great Strikes in the United States*; Allan Pinkerton, *Strikers, Communists, Tramps and Detectives* (New York: Carleton, 1878). The strike also inspired Henry George to write *Progress and Poverty* and inspired numerous novelists as well. See Nell Irvin Painter, *Standing at Armageddon: The United States, 1877–1919* (London: Norton, 1987), 26.

72. *National Labor Tribune*, August 4, 1877.

73. See for example Bruce, *1877: Year of Violence*; Stromquist, *A Generation of Boomers*; Lens, *The Labor Wars*; Licht, *Industrializing America*, 166.

74. Indeed, the image of the 1877 strike as being a "curtain-opener" prevails to this day in American histories. See, for instance, Steve Babson, *The Unfinished Struggle: Turning Points in American Labor, 1877–Present* (Lanham, Md.: Rowman and Littlefield, 1999).

75. "The Late Riots," *The Nation* 25, no. 631 (August 2, 1877): 68–69.

76. Quoted in Bruce, *1877: Year of Violence*, 314.

77. Dacus, *Annals of the Great Strikes in the United States*, iii.

78. As early as 1878, *Appletons' Annual Cyclopaedia* noted "1877 [had] witnessed the culmination of many important events" (quoted in Katz, *From Appomattox to Montmartre*, 192). The continued power of this will be discussed below.

79. Robert M. Fogelson, *America's Armories: Architecture, Society, and Public Order* (Cambridge, Mass.: Harvard University Press, 1989), 52–54.

80. See Charles H. Page, *Class and American Sociology: From Ward to Ross* (New York: Schocken Books, 1969); Benjamin G. Rader, *The Academic Mind and Reform: The Influence of Richard T. Ely in American Life* (Lexington: University of Kentucky Press, 1966); John A. DeBrizzi, *Ideology and the Rise of Labor Theory in America* (Westport, Conn.: Greenwood Press, 1983).

81. John Bates Clark, "Profits Under Modern Conditions," in John B. Clark and Franklin S. Giddings, *The Distributive Process* (Boston: Ginn, 1888), 35.

CHAPTER 3   THE MARCH OF ORGANIZED FORCES

1. "Fresh Aspects of the Labor Question," *Unitarian Review* 28, no. 1 (July 1887): 73–74.

2. "Losses by the Strike," *New York Times*, March 18, 1882; *New York Times*, March 7, 1880. This analysis is based on my survey of labor-related articles in the *New York Times* conducted for the period 1880–1889.

3. C. H. Reeve, "The Ethics of Strikes and Lockouts," *American Journal of Politics* 2 (January 1893), 75.

4. On the press during the 1880s, see Edwin Emery and Michael Emery, *The Press and America: An Interpretive History of Mass Media*, 4th ed. (Englewood Cliffs, N.J.: Prentice-Hall, 1978), especially chapter 16.

5. Between 1870 and 1900, the number of daily newspapers quadrupled.

6. Denis Brian, *Pulitzer: A Life* (New York: Wiley and Sons, 2001), 79.

7. Michael Schudson, *Origins of the Ideal of Objectivity in the Professions: Studies in the History of American Journalism and American Law, 1830–1940* (New York: Garland, 1990), 212.

8. Ibid., 222, 206.

9. Emery and Emery, *The Press and America*, 244–247.

10. Alfred McClung Lee, *The Daily Newspaper in America: The Evolution of a Social Instrument* (New York: Octagon, 1937), 83. New York published 22.8 percent of all daily sheets in 1880, though that figure declined steadily as more newspapers circulated throughout the nation. See ibid., 84.

11. Lee, *The Daily Newspaper in America*, 26, 261–266; Samuel Gompers, *Seventy Years of Life and Labor: An Autobiography*, ed. Nick Salvatore (Ithaca, N.Y.: ILR Press, 1984), 17.

12. This is taken from my analysis of newspapers during the Telegraphers' Strike of July–August 1883, which includes the *Washington Post, San Francisco Chronicle, Los Angeles Daily Times, Chicago Tribune, St. Louis Post-Dispatch, Boston Evening Transcript, Cleveland Plain Dealer, New York Times, Leslie's Illustrated*, and *New Orleans Daily Picayune*.

13. "An Engine Killed," *Waco Daily Examiner*, March 9, 1886.

14. "Strikers and Non-Combatants," *Chicago Tribune*, July 18, 1883.

15. Christopher P. Wilson, *The Labor of Words: Literary Professionalism in the Progressive Era* (Athens: University of Georgia Press, 1985), 17–39.

16. Journals examined during the 1880s include *Puck, Nation, Harper's Weekly, Andover Review, Unitarian Review, Quarterly Journal of Economics, Baptist Quarterly Review, Overland Monthly, The Century Magazine, International Review, Our Continent,* and *The Chautauquan.*

17. "Fresh Aspects of the Labor Question," *Unitarian Review* 28, no. 1 (July 1887): 71; "The New Monopolists," *The Chautauquan* 16 (1885), 541; George E. McNeill, "Democracy of Labor Organization," *The Arena* 1, no. 1 (December 1889): 69–82.

18. Lyman Abbot, "Danger Ahead," *Century Magazine* 31 (1885–1886): 51–59. This piece is analyzed in Carl Smith, *Urban Disorder and the Shape of Belief: The Great Chicago Fire, the Haymarket Bomb, and the Model Town of Pullman* (Chicago: University of Chicago Press, 1995), 118–119.

19. While Martin J. Burke has argued that there "was no single language of class . . . [but] instead a variety of terms . . . that Americans used, and a number of interpretive frameworks in which they used them," I have found that the divided society seems to have offered the most popular, and likely most politically expedient, social model. See Martin J. Burke, *The Conundrum of Class: Public Discourse on the Social Order in America* (Chicago: University of Chicago Press, 1995), 160–161.

20. R. Heber Newton, "Communism," *Unitarian Review* (December 1881): 505. The Populists, another popular mass movement of the late nineteenth century, also relied on social division in their rhetoric. See Norman Pollack, ed., *The Populist Mind* (Indianapolis: Bobbs-Merrill, 1967).

21. James L. Huston, *Securing the Fruits of Labor: The American Concept of Wealth Distribution, 1765–1900* (Baton Rouge: Louisiana State University Press, 1998), chapter 10.

22. See, for example, William Graham Sumner, "Industrial War," *Forum* 2 (1886): 1–6.

23. See Leo Marx, *The Machine in the Garden: Technology and the Pastoral Ideal in America* (New York: Oxford University Press, 1964).

24. *Pittsburgh Telegraph,* quoted in Philip Foner, *History of the Labor Movement in the United States,* vol. 1: *From Colonial Times to the Founding of the American Federation of Labor* (New York: International Publishers, 1962), 521.

25. According to Mother Jones, the Knights originally were Civil War veterans who recognized a new "war" afoot between capital and labor. The *National Labor Tribune* enthused that the KOL "makes every man in it purer and better" (*National Labor Tribune,* April 24, 1875, 2, reprinted in Commons et al., eds., *A Documentary History of American Industrial Society,* vol. 10). Less ecstatic was Allan Pinkerton, who explained to the public that the Knights were "probably an amalgamation of the Mollie Maguires and the Commune" (Allan Pinkerton, *Strikers, Communists, Tramps and Detectives* [New York: Carleton, 1878], 88).

26. Labor held no monopoly on knighthood, of course. There were numerous other organizations that found "knights" to be a handy moniker.

27. Initiation Ritual reprinted in *American Labor: A Documentary Collection,* ed. Melvyn Dubofsky and Joseph A. McCartin, 116 (New York: Palgrave Macmillan, 2004).

28. Leon Fink, *Workingmen's Democracy: The Knights of Labor and American Politics* (Urbana: University of Illinois Press, 1985), 9; Robert E. Weir, *Beyond Labor's Veil: The Culture of the Knights of Labor* (University Park: Pennsylvania State University Press, 1996).

29. Quoted in Fink, *Workingmen's Democracy,* 4.

30. For a full discussion on the Knights and strikes, see Norman J. Ware, *The Labor Movement in the United States, 1860–1895: A Study in Democracy* (Gloucester, Mass.: Smith, 1959), chapter 7.

31. Terence Powderly noted incredulously, "Just think of it! Opposing strikes and always striking!" (quoted in Richard O. Boyer and Herbert M. Morais, *Labor's Untold Story* [New York: United Electrical, Radio and Machine Workers of America, 1970], 89). After the Knights-backed telegrapher's strike of 1883 failed, Powderly recognized that a more substantial strike fund would be necessary. Nevertheless, the strike fund continued to reflect organizational resistance to establish a deep reservoir of striker support, providing a paltry $7,000 in relief in the tumultuous years to come. Not that this lack of funds affected the incidence of spontaneous walkouts. As economist Richard T. Ely noted in 1886, countless everyday strikes formed crucibles of alliance for the union. The numbers bear out this assessment—the success of the massive KOL-led Wabash Railroad Strike of 1885, to give the most dramatic example, helped increase membership sevenfold from about 100,000 to over 700,000 members.

32. See Stuart Bruce Kaufman, *Samuel Gompers and the Origins of the American Federation of Labor, 1848–1896* (Westport, Conn.: Greenwood Press, 1973).

33. David Montgomery, "Strikes in Nineteenth-Century America," *Social Science Quarterly* 4 (February 1980): 89.

34. Montgomery, "Strikes in Nineteenth-Century America"; David M. Gordon, Richard Edwards, and Michael Reich, *Segmented Work, Divided Workers: The Historical Transformation of Labor in the United States* (Cambridge: Cambridge University Press, 1982); David Montgomery, "Workers' Control of Machine Production in the Nineteenth Century," in *Workers' Control in America: Studies in the History of Work, Technology, and Labor Struggles* (Cambridge: Cambridge University Press, 1979), 9–31.

35. According to David Montgomery: "A quiver full of epithets awaited the deviant: 'hog,' 'hogger-in,' 'leader,' 'rooter,' 'rusher,' 'runner,' 'swift,' 'boss's pet,' to mention some politer versions" (Montgomery, "Workers' Control of Machine Production in the Nineteenth Century," in *Workers' Control in America,* 13).

36. "Harmony of interests" is elaborated in Huston, *Securing the Fruits of Labor.*

37. Clark quoted in Burke, *The Conundrum of Class,* 163.

38. Henry Carter Adams, "An Interpretation of the Social Movements of Our Time," *International Journal of Ethics* 2 (October 1891): 45, quoted in John A. DeBrizzi, *Ideology and the Rise of Labor Theory in America* (Westport, Conn.: Greenwood Press, 1983), 77.

39. Stephen Skowronek, *Building a New American State: The Expansion of National Administrative Capacities, 1877–1920* (Cambridge: Cambridge University Press, 1982); Nancy Cohen, *The Reconstruction of American Liberalism, 1865–1914* (Chapel Hill: University of North Carolina Press, 2002).

40. Richard T. Ely, *The Labor Movement in America* (1886; reprint, New York: Arno, 1969), 2–6, 149; Benjamin G. Rader, *The Academic Mind and Reform: The Influence of Richard T. Ely in American Life* (Lexington: University of Kentucky Press, 1966).

41. Adams, "An Interpretation of the Social Movements of Our Time," 45; DeBrizzi, *Ideology and the Rise of Labor Theory in America,* chapter 6; Thomas L. Haskell, *The Emergence of Professional Social Science: The American Social Science Association and the Nineteenth-Century Crisis of Authority* (Urbana: University of Illinois Press, 1977).

42. Ely quoted in DeBrizzi, *Ideology and the Rise of Labor Theory in America,* 46.

43. John Bates Clark, *The Philosophy of Wealth: Economic Principles Newly Formulated* (New York: Kelley, 1967), 66.

44. In numerical terms, the strike rate escalated to an unheard-of level—in 1886 alone there were some 1,432 strikes, more than triple the number of any year between 1881 and 1884. See Montgomery, "Strikes in Nineteenth-Century America," 92, 98; Selig Perlman, "Chapter IX: The Great Upheaval, 1884–86," in John Commons et al., *History of Labour in the United States,* vol. 2 (New York: Macmillan, 1918), 366–394. These strikes are surveyed in Ronald Filippelli, ed., *Labor Conflict in the United States: An Encyclopedia* (New York: Garland, 1990).

45. "The Situation," *San Antonio Daily Light,* March 11, 1886.

46. Ruth A. Allen, *The Great Southwest Strike* (Austin: University of Texas Press, 1942), 11–12; William G. Robbins, *Colony and Empire: The Capitalist Transformation of the American West* (Lawrence: University Press of Kansas, 1994), 31–32.

47. This is quoted in Commons et al., *History of Labour in the United States,* 2:371.

48. See, for example, the cover of *Puck,* March 29, 1882. Fagin was a sinister Jewish criminal in Charles Dickens's *Oliver Twist.* On antisemitism in America in this period, see Leonard Dinnerstein, *Antisemitism in America* (New York: Oxford University Press, 1995), chapter 3.

49. Matthew Josephson, *The Robber Barons: The Great American Capitalists, 1861–1901* (New York: Harcourt Brace Jovanovich, 1962), chapter 9.

50. Hall attended a KOL District Assembly meeting, and although he was granted permission to attend, he was fired by the same foreman who let him leave. The strike that followed is recounted and analyzed in several works, among them F. W. Taussig, "The Southwest Strike of 1886," *Quarterly Journal of Economics* 1 (January 1887): 185–216; Allen, *The Great Southwest Strike;* Theresa Ann Case, "Free Labor on the Southwestern Railroads: The 1885–1886 Gould System Strikes" (Ph.D. diss., University of Texas at Austin, 2002); Gerald G. Eggert, *Railroad Labor Disputes: The Beginnings of Federal Strike Policy* (Ann Arbor: University of Michigan Press, 1967), 61–80; Filippelli, ed., *Labor Conflict in the United States,* 491–495, Philip S. Foner, *History of the Labor Movement in the United States,* vol. 2: *From the Founding of the A.F. of L. to the Emergence of American Imperialism,* 2nd ed. (New York: International Publishers, 1975), 83–86.

51. As Theresa Ann Case points out, at least two newspapers, the *Missouri Republican* and the *St. Louis Post-Dispatch,* "urged railroads to settle the strikers' grievances" at the start of the strike. See Case, "Free Labor on the Southwestern Railroads," 295.

52. Cover of *Puck,* March 31, 1886.

53. "Plain Talk," *Waco Daily Examiner,* March 7, 1886.

54. Periodicals reviewed during the Great Southwest Strike of 1886 include the *New York Times, Washington Post, Waco Daily Examiner, San Antonio Daily Light, St. Louis Post-Dispatch, Los Angeles Daily Times, San Francisco Chronicle, National Labor Tribune, Quarterly Journal of Economics, Journal of United Labor, Harper's Weekly, Puck, Andover Review,* and assorted journals from the American Periodicals Series.

55. Compare, for example, strike coverage in the *Waco Daily Examiner,* the *Los Angeles Daily Times,* and the *New York Times* from March 12, 1886, on. The "battle of two giants" quote is taken from "Commencing to Weaken," *Washington Post,* March 19, 1886.

56. "The Situation," *San Antonio Daily Light,* March 11, 1886; *San Antonio Daily Light,* [March] 22, 1886.

57. *San Francisco Chronicle,* March 13, 14, 17, 1886; "The Root of the Evil," *St. Louis Post-Dispatch,* March 22, 1886; "The Labor Revolution," *National Labor Tribune,* March 20, 1886; "Labor Troubles and Citizenship," *National Labor Tribune,* April 3, 1886.

58. *Nation,* April 8, 1886; *Waco Daily Examiner,* March 19, 21, 24, 1886; "Struggles of Labor," *St. Louis Post-Dispatch,* April 7, 1886; "The Strikers Losing Ground," *New York Times,* March 16, 1886; "Losses By the Strike," *New York Times,* March 18, 1886; *New York Times,* March 19, 1886; "The Knights' Mistake," *New York Times,* March 21, 1886.

59. "One Thousand Men Rush to Capture the Stronghold of the 'Scabs,'" *St. Louis Post-Dispatch,* March 24, 1886; "Baptism of Blood," *St. Louis Post-Dispatch,* April 3, 1886; "Pastor Smith on Strikes," *New York Times,* April 5, 1886; Allen, *Great Southwest Strike,* 79.

60. "Warring Workers," *Los Angeles Daily Times,* March 23, 1886; "The Wage War," *Los Angeles Daily Times,* April 6, 1886; "Commencing to Weaken," *Washington Post,* March 19, 1886; Allen, *Great Southwest Strike,* chapter 4.

61. "Impending Anarchy," *Waco Daily Examiner,* March 24, 1886.

62. Allen, *Great Southwest Strike,* 134.

63. *Fort Worth Gazette,* April 11, 1886, quoted in Allen, *Great Southwest Strike,* 134–135.

64. "Impending Anarchy," *Waco Daily Examiner,* March 24, 1886.

65. Circular printed in part in numerous newspapers. Complete text reprinted in Allen, *Great Southwest Strike,* 88–89.

66. William Ross, "A Giant Is Rising," *John Swinton's Paper,* April 18, 1886.

67. "The Outlook Not Clear," *New York Times,* April 7, 1886.

68. "The Laboring Man's Rise," *New York Times,* March 29, 1886; Thomas Nast, "Willful Slavery Makes Woeful Suffering," *Harper's Weekly,* April 17, 1886.

69. Quoted and analyzed in Theresa Ann Case, "The Radical Potential of the Knights' Biracialism: The 1885–1886 Gould System Strikes and Their Aftermath," *Labor: Studies in Working-Class History of the Americas* 4, no. 4 (winter 2007): 101–102.

70. Thomas Nast, "What's in a Name?" *Harper's Weekly,* April 10, 1886.

71. J. A. Wales, "The Law of Arbitration, Or the Quarreling Giants," *Puck,* April 7, 1886.

72. Quoted in Allen, *Great Southwest Strike,* 142.

73. Ibid., 130.

74. Fink, *Workingmen's Democracy,* 126.

75. Gerald N. Grob, *Workers and Utopia: A Study of Ideological Conflict in the American Labor Movement, 1865–1900* (Chicago: Quadrangle Books, 1969), 85; Philip Yale Nicholson, *Labor's Story in the United States* (Philadelphia: Temple University Press, 2004), 118.

76. *Farmers' Alliance,* May 7, 1891, quoted in Pollack, *The Populist Mind,* 4; William C. Oates, "The Homestead Strike. A Congressional View," *North American Review* (September 1892): 364; Nelly Booth Simmons, "Battle Hymn of Labor," printed in *Arena* 38 (March 1892): 401–404.

77. Strike data taken from Montgomery, "Strikes in Nineteenth-Century America," 92.

78. According to Richard Edwards, "The list of strikes [during this period] reads like a roster of consolidations." See his *Contested Terrain: The Transformation of the Workplace in the Twentieth Century* (New York: Basic Books, 1979), 50.

79. David Ray Papke, *The Pullman Case: The Clash of Labor and Capital in Industrial America* (Lawrence: University Press of Kansas, 1999), chapter 1.

80. On Debs and the Pullman Strike, see Nick Salvatore, *Eugene V. Debs: Citizen and Socialist* (Urbana: University of Illinois Press, 1982), chapter 5.

81. *New York Times*, June 27, 1894.

82. A survey of the press and the strike is given in Almont Lindsey, *The Pullman Strike: The Story of a Unique Experiment and of a Great Labor Upheaval* (Chicago: University of Chicago Press, 1971), chapter 13; *New York Times*, July 1, 1894; *New York World*, July 12, 1894.

83. Brian, *Pulitzer: A Life*, 178–179.

84. Bly quoted in Brian, *Pulitzer: A Life*, 179.

85. David Paul Nord, "The Business Values of American Newspapers: The 19th Century Watershed in Chicago," *Journalism Quarterly* 61 (1984). For an historical account of pro-business bias in Chicago's press, see Zonita Jeffrys, "The Attitude of the Chicago Press toward the Labor Movement, 1873 to 1879" (Master's thesis, University of Chicago, 1936). Also see Jon Bekken, "The Working-Class Press at the Turn of the Century," in *Ruthless Criticism: New Perspectives in U.S. Communication History*, ed. William S. Solomon and Robert W. McChesney, 152 (Minneapolis: University of Minnesota Press, 1993).

86. "Roads Tied Up Tight," *New York World*, July 4, 1894; "Attacked the Regulars," *New York World*, July 5, 1894.

87. The *New York Times* wrote simply that Debs had "declared war" on the GMA.

88. I have examined the *New York Times, New York World, Chicago Tribune, Chicago Times, San Francisco Chronicle, Baltimore Sun, Los Angeles Times, New Orleans Picayune, The Railway Times, The Arena, Harper's Weekly, Railroad Trainmen's Journal, American Federationist*, and *Nation*.

89. "Strike Is Now War" and "Debs versus the Public," *Chicago Tribune*, July 2, 1894.

90. H. von Holst, "Are We Awakened?" *Journal of Political Economy*, September 1894.

91. Quoted in "Labor's Great Protest," *New York World*, July 13, 1894. At the same meeting reformer Henry George claimed he was against strikes and got hissed by the crowd.

92. On Uncle Sam and his Lincolnesque appearance, see Alton Ketchum, "The Search for Uncle Sam," *History Today*, April 1990, 20–26.

93. "Fourth of July," *Railway Times*, July 2, 1894.

94. "The Railroad Insurrection," *New York Times*, July 7, 1894; Lindsey, *The Pullman Strike*, 191–193.

95. *Chicago Tribune*, July 3, 9, 1894; *Louisville Courier-Journal* quoted in *Chicago Tribune*, July 12, 1894. The *New York World* wondered why the federal government allowed Debs to "sit like a commanding general in his headquarters and wage open warfare against the State?" in its July 9, 1894, edition. The generally moderate journal *Harper's Weekly* feared that "the nation is fighting for its own existence just as truly as in suppressing the great rebellion" ("The Boycott of the Pullman Company," *Harper's Weekly*, July 7, 1894).

96. *Chicago Times*, July 13, 1894; *New York World*, July 8, 1894; *New Orleans Picayune*, July 8, 1894; *Baltimore Sun*, July 9, 1894. Such war descriptives permeate all of the coverage researched here.

97. According to the July 1 edition of the *New York World,* Omaha, Nebraska, was in "Flat Rebellion." A July 9 editorial in the *World* is entitled "It Is Rebellion."

98. "The Boycott of the Pullman Company," *Harper's Weekly,* July 7, 1894; *Chicago Evening Post* quoted in *Chicago Tribune,* July 3, 1894; "Common Sense in the Senate," *Nation,* July 19, 1894; O. F. McJunkin, "The Great Strike," *Railroad Trainmen's Journal,* September 1894.

99. "Let Us Have Peace," *Chicago Times,* July 6, 1894.

100. *American Railway Times,* August 15, 1894.

101. Arthur McEwan, "The Gigantic Struggle between Capital and Labor," *San Francisco Examiner,* July 9, 1894.

102. "The Deadly Riot Gun," *New York World,* July 3, 1894.

103. Larry Peterson, "Photography and the Pullman Strike: Remolding Perceptions of Labor Conflict by New Visual Communication," in *The Pullman Strike and the Crisis of the 1890s: Essays on Labor and Politics,* ed. Richard Schneirov, Shelton Stromquist, and Nick Salvatore, 98 (Urbana: University of Illinois Press, 1999).

104. "Chicago Not Alarmed," *New York World,* July 10, 1894; Frederic Remington, "Chicago under the Mob," *Harper's Weekly,* July 21, 1894; Robin Archer, *Why Is There No Labor Party in the United States?* (Princeton, N.J.: Princeton University Press, 2008), 115; Painter, *Standing at Armageddon,* 123.

105. Quoted in "The Big Strike," *Railroad Trainmen's Journal,* September 1894.

106. "No General Walk-Out," *Washington Post,* July 14, 1894. Citing "complications" around the "present crisis" that were "so grave in nature that we cannot advise a course which would but add to the general confusion," the AFL declined to join the strike.

107. Walter Blackburn Harte, "A Review of the Chicago Strike of 1894," *The Arena,* September 1894; *American Federationist,* September 1894; *The Railway Times,* August, September 1894.

108. Golden Rod, "After the Strike," *Chicago Tribune,* July 14, 1894; "Debs Has Reached His Appomattox," *Chicago Tribune,* July 14, 1894.

109. All quoted in "Governors, Mayors, Millionaires, Labor Leaders, Editors, and Plain Business Men Telegraph about the Strike," *New York World,* July 15, 1894.

CHAPTER 4   THE EMERGENCE OF THE "GREAT THIRD CLASS"

1. Alexander Hamilton, John Jay, and James Madison, *The Federalist* (New York: Random House, 1937); Lincoln used the expression "a People's Contest" in a speech delivered on July 4, 1861. Quoted in Phillip Shaw Paludin, *A People's Contest: The Union and Civil War, 1861–1865* (Lawrence: University Press of Kansas, 1996), ix. On the use of "the people," see Robert Wiebe, *Self-Rule: A Cultural History of Democracy* (Chicago: University of Chicago Press, 1995).

2. The historiography of Progressivism is extensive and filled with debates over the particulars. See Daniel T. Rodgers, "In Search of Progressivism," *Reviews in American History* (December 1982): 113–131; David Kennedy, "Overview: The Progressive Era," *Historian* 37 (May 1975): 453–468; Glenda E. Gilmore, ed., *Who Were the Progressives?* (New York: St. Martin's Press, 2002). For a somewhat recent synthetic work that incorporates the argument of crisis, see Stephen J. Diner, *A Very Different Age: Americans of the Progressive Era* (New York: Hill and Wang, 1998).

3. On the rise of the "public" at the end of the nineteenth century, see Shelton Stromquist, *Reinventing "The People": The Progressive Movement, the Class Problem, and the Origins of Modern Liberalism* (Urbana: University of Illinois Press, 2006); Michael Kazin, *The Populist Persuasion* (New York: Basic Books, 1995), 51. The naming of the People's Party also illustrates the flourishing of this idea in the 1880s and 1890s. On the multiple and contested meanings of the "People" earlier in the nineteenth century, see Daniel T. Rodgers, *Contested Truths: Keywords in American Politics since Independence* (New York: Basic Books, 1987), chapter 3. William Graham Sumner's 1883 lecture "The Forgotten Man" powerfully captured the sense that the average, hard-working American man was beset by a number of challenges, among them trade unions. See William Graham Sumner, "The Forgotten Man," in *William Graham Sumner: The Forgotten Man and Other Essays,* ed. Albert Galloway Keller, 465–495 (New Haven, Conn.: Yale University Press, 1918).

4. "The Strike in the Southwest," *Harper's Weekly,* April 13, 1886; "The Real Trouble," *National Labor Tribune,* April 3, 1886. On the rise of the "public," see Kazin, *The Populist Persuasion,* 51.

5. "The Pullman Strike," *Baltimore Sun,* June 27, 1894; "The Railroad Tie-Up," *New York World,* June 29, 1894, 6.

6. *Chicago Tribune,* June 24–July 16, 1894.

7. William Graham Sumner, "The Philosophy of Strikes," reprinted in Keller, ed., *The Forgotten Man and Other Essays,* 240.

8. Louis Galambos, *The Public Image of Big Business in America, 1880–1840: A Quantitative Study in Social Change* (Baltimore: Johns Hopkins University Press, 1975), chapter 3.

9. Adolph S. Ochs, "Business Announcement," *New York Times,* August 19, 1896; Michael Schudson, *Origins of the Ideal of Objectivity in the Professions: Studies in the History of American Journalism and American Law, 1830–1940* (New York: Garland, 1990), 213–230; Edwin Emery and Michael Emery, *The Press and America: An Interpretive History of Mass Media,* 4th ed. (Englewood Cliffs, N.J.: Prentice Hall, 1978), 279–285.

10. John R. Commons et al., "Is Class Conflict in America Growing and Is It Inevitable?" *American Journal of Sociology* 13 (1908), 756–783. Importantly, Commons was far from the first to think in such terms. In his congressional testimony on the Pullman Strike in 1894, scholar Edward Bemis referred to the public as "the great third party." See Testimony of Edward W. Bemis, United States Strike Commission, *Report on the Chicago Strike of June–July, 1894,* 53rd Congress, 3rd sess., Senate Executive Document No. 7 (Washington, D.C.: Government Printing Office, 1895), 644.

11. Stephen Skowronek, *Building a New American State: The Expansion of National Administrative Capacities, 1877–1920* (Cambridge: Cambridge University Press, 1982).

12. This was not the first time the government spent time looking at the labor situation. As early as 1877 state governments examined mass strikes. In the 1880s, the federal government began systematically investigating the conditions that gave rise to strikes in Senate hearings and various commissions. See Bruno Cartosio, "Strikes and Economics: Working-Class Insurgency and the Birth of Labor Historiography in the 1880s," in *American Labor and Immigration History, 1877–1920s: Recent European Research,* ed. Dirk Hoerder (Urbana: University of Illinois Press, 1983), and John Arthur Garraty, ed., *Labor and Capital in the Gilded Age: Testimony Taken by the Senate Committee upon the Relations between Labor and Capital, 1883* (Boston: Little, Brown, 1968).

13. Reprinted in the *NCF Review* 1, no. 10 (January 1, 1905): 6; quoted in James Weinstein, *The Corporate Ideal in the Liberal State, 1900–1918* (Boston: Beacon Press, 1968), 9. On the National Civic Federation, see Marguerite Green, *The National Civic Federation and the American Labor Movement, 1900–1925* (Washington, D.C.: Catholic University of America Press, 1956); Bruno Ramirez, *When Workers Fight: The Politics of Industrial Relations in the Progressive Era, 1898–1916* (Westport, Conn.: Greenwood Press, 1978); David Montgomery, *The Fall of the House of Labor: The Workplace, the State, and American Labor Activism, 1865–1925* (New York: Cambridge University Press, 1987), chapter 6; Christopher L. Tomlins, *The State and the Unions: Labor Relations, Law, and the Organized Labor Movement in America, 1880–1960* (Cambridge: Cambridge University Press, 1985), 73–74. Mitchell quoted in Weinstein, *The Corporate Ideal in the Liberal State,* 9.

14. Green, *The National Civic Federation,* 5–6; John R. Commons, *Myself: The Autobiography of John R. Commons* (Madison: University of Wisconsin Press, 1964), 82.

15. Importantly, industrial relations constituted a major, but not the singular focus of the NCF. See Craig Phelan, *Divided Loyalties: The Public and Private Life of Labor Leader John Mitchell* (Albany: State University of New York Press, 1994), 124.

16. *Chicago Tribune,* December 20, 1900, quoted in Green, *The National Civic Federation,* 11.

17. Unfinished letter to John R. Kirby, quoted in Green, *National Civic Federation,* 13.

18. Commons, *Myself,* 73.

19. Phelan, *Divided Loyalties,* ix.

20. The book contained Mitchell's own ideas despite being largely ghostwritten by Walter Weyl. See Phelan, *Divided Loyalties,* 205.

21. John Mitchell, *Organized Labor: Its Problems, Purposes and Ideals and the Present and Future of American Wage Earners* (Philadelphia: American Book and Bible House, 1903), 420.

22. Ibid., 306.

23. Samuel Gompers, *Seventy Years of Life and Labor: An Autobiography,* ed. Nick Salvatore (Ithaca, N.Y.: ILR Press, 1984), 148.

24. The NCF membership was often anything but partial to organized labor. See Andrew Wender Cohen, *The Racketeer's Progress: Chicago and the Struggle for the Modern American Economy, 1900–1940* (Cambridge: Cambridge University Press, 2004), 34; Sidney Fine, *"Without Blare of Trumpets": Walter Drew, the National Erectors' Association, and the Open Shop Movement, 1903–1957* (Ann Arbor: University of Michigan Press, 1995); Montgomery, *The Fall of the House of Labor,* chapter 6. In his autobiography, Commons would state emphatically, however, that "The Civic Federation was not packed against labor. For the time being I was the Civic Federation. I know I was not packed" (Commons, *Myself,* 85).

25. See, for example, Henry Carter Adams, "An Interpretation of the Social Movements of Our Time," *International Journal of Ethics* 2 (October 1891): 40–45, and "Economics and Jurisprudence," *Economic Studies* 2 (February 1897): 24–33. Adams's theories are discussed in John A. DeBrizzi, *Ideology and the Rise of Labor Theory in America* (Westport, Conn.: Greenwood Press, 1983), chapter 6.

26. As historian Melvyn Dubofsky has pointed out, class conflict "dominated the hidden agenda of Progressivism." See Melvyn Dubofsky, *The State and Labor in Modern America* (Chapel Hill: University of North Carolina Press, 1994), 37.

27. War language suffuses all of the periodicals examined.

28. "The Great Anthracite Strike Situation Remains Unchanged," *Weekly Miners' Journal,* June 16, 1902; "An Impossible Situation," *New York Times,* July 10, 1902.

29. On real and mythical aspects of UMWA unity, see John H. M. Laslett, ed., *The United Mine Workers of America: A Model of Industrial Solidarity?* (University Park: Pennsylvania State University Press, 1996), 4–9.

30. *New York Times,* June 17, September 27, 1902; *Lancaster Examiner* opinion reprinted in the *Weekly Miners' Journal,* September 26, 1902.

31. *United Mine Workers' Journal* quoted in Robert J. Cornell, *The Anthracite Coal Strike of 1902* (New York: Russell and Russell, 1971), 161; "The Issues of the Strike," *New York Times,* September 4, 1902; Philip S. Foner, *History of the Labor Movement in the United States,* vol. 3: *The Policies and Practices of the American Federation of Labor, 1900–1909* (New York: International Publishers, 1973), 96.

32. F.M.F. Cazin, "Mr. Hewett and the Strike," *New York Times,* September 7, 1902.

33. "Strikes," *New York Times,* June 2, 1902.

34. "Mitchell Speaks to Miners," *New York Times,* August 2, 1902; "President Mitchell Issues a Statement," *New York Times,* June 24, 1902.

35. The *Toledo Blade,* for example, wrote that the decision not to support a general coal strike was "wise . . . the sympathies of the public will [now] be more generally directed to the miners of Pennsylvania" (quoted in Cornell, *The Anthracite Coals Strike,* 163).

36. For the period May–October 1902, I have looked at the *New York Times, Weekly Miners' Journal, Mauch Chunk Coal Gazette, Washington Post, Arena, United Mine Workers' Journal, Wilkes-Barre Times,* and *New York World.*

37. Quoted in Cornell, *The Anthracite Coal Strike,* 96.

38. On anticorporate sentiment at the time, see James L. Huston, *Securing the Fruits of Labor: The American Concept of Wealth Distribution, 1765–1900* (Baton Rouge: Louisiana State University Press, 1998).

39. Cornell, *The Anthracite Coal Strike,* 96.

40. Theodore Roosevelt to Murray Crane, October 22, 1902, quoted in Henry Pringle, *Theodore Roosevelt: A Biography* (New York: Cornwall Press, 1931), 270.

41. Roosevelt recalled his strike experience in his autobiography. See Theodore Roosevelt, *Theodore Roosevelt: An Autobiography* (New York: Macmillan, 1913), 511–516.

42. "The Position of the Anthracite Operators," *New York Times,* June 12, 1902; "Politicians Soon May End the Coal Strike," *New York Times,* September 13, 1902.

43. "Preacher Scores Operators," *New York Times,* September 8, 1902; "Coal Crisis Pulpit Topic," *New York Times,* October 13, 1902; "Arbitration," *Wilkes-Barre Times,* May 22, 1902; "A. S. Hewett Discusses Wages of Miners," *New York Times,* September 2, 1902; "Thinks Miners Will Win," *New York Times,* October 11, 1902.

44. "No Decision Was Reached," *Weekly Miners' Journal,* October 11, 1902; *New York World,* October 15, 1902.

45. The symbolic makeup of this body was of utmost importance: the operators refused to have a "labor" representative involved, but when the title was changed to "eminent sociologist," they relented.

46. Cornell, *Anthracite Strike of 1902,* 209. This innovation was tenuous in the extreme. In his autobiography Roosevelt reported that he had readied Major-General

198 NOTES TO PAGES 104-108

Schofield to go to Pennsylvania, telling him that "the crisis was only less serious than that of the Civil War, [and] that the action taken would be practically a war measure" (Roosevelt, *Theodore Roosevelt: An Autobiography*, 514).

47. Susan E. Wilson, "Theodore Roosevelt's Role in the Anthracite Coal Strike of 1902," *Labor's Heritage* 3, no. 1 (1991): 4–23.

48. "The Great Coal Strike and Its Lessons," *The Arena* 29, no. 1 (January 1903): 1–25; "A Pitiful Case," *Mauch Chunk Coal Gazette*, July 24, 1902.

49. William E. Forbath, *Law and the Shaping of the American Labor Movement* (Cambridge, Mass.: Harvard University Press, 1991), chapter 3.

50. Samuel Gompers distrusted legislation because it subjected unions to the "tyranny" of the courts. See Forbath, *Law and the Shaping of the American Labor Movement*, 96.

CHAPTER 5   THE FIST OF THE STATE IN THE PUBLIC GLOVE

1. Theodore Roosevelt, "The New Nationalism," in Michael Waldman, *My Fellow Americans: The Most Important Speeches of America's Presidents, from George Washington to George W. Bush* (New York: Sourcebooks, 2003), 70. On Theodore Roosevelt's reflections on class conflict, see his *Theodore Roosevelt: An Autobiography* (New York: Macmillan, 1913), chapter 13.

2. Roosevelt, "The New Nationalism," in Waldman, *My Fellow Americans*, 70–76.

3. See David Montgomery, *Workers' Control in America: Studies in the History of Work, Technology, and Labor Struggles* (Cambridge: Cambridge University Press, 1979), 97. Strikes also increasingly took on the character of "assaults" on managerial authority.

4. Frederick Winslow Taylor, *The Principles of Scientific Management* (New York: Harper and Brothers, 1919), 10–15, 100–104.

5. Until recently, syndicalism has been considered an aberration, a pocket of extreme resistance to capitalism carried on by only a small portion of the workforce. A shift in understanding, inaugurated by the New Labor Historians, has shown us a different picture. From David Montgomery's assertion that union radicalism stood at the center of industrial unrest to Howard Kimeldorf's monograph revealing the syndicalist core of much union agitation, the notion that union militancy was central to labor's project is now difficult to dispute. Although there were many types of syndicalism, from the revolutionary variety that urged the overthrow of the state to the conservative "business syndicalism" of the AFL, strikes and boycotts typically were substituted direct political action in these years. On the mainstream nature of IWW rhetoric, see Donald E. Winters Jr., *The Soul of the Wobblies: The I.W.W., Religion, and American Culture in the Progressive Era, 1905–1917* (Westport, Conn.: Greenwood Press, 1985); Melvyn Dubofsky, *We Shall Be All: A History of the Industrial Workers of the World* (Chicago: Quadrangle Books, 1969).

6. This membership figure, which could be a bit dubious, is in Howard Kimeldorf, *Battling for American Labor: Wobblies, Craft Workers, and the Making of the Union Movement* (Berkeley: University of California Press, 1999), 3.

7. The phrase "Fighting Front" comes from the IWW pamphlet "What Is the I.W.W.?—A Candid Statement of Its Principles, Objects, and Methods," reprinted in *Industrial Workers of the World Pamphlets* (Chicago: Industrial Workers of the World, n.d.), 22.

8. On strike strategy, see *Industrial Workers of the World Pamphlets*. On the tactics and culture of the IWW, see Winters, *The Soul of the Wobblies*.

9. Kimeldorf explains that "Despite the vast ideological chasm at the top of both organizations, at the bottom their local affiliates often came together on many of the same demands." See his *Battling for American Labor*, 154.

10. See, for example, Samuel Gompers, "The I.W.W. Strikes," in *American Federationist* 20, no. 8 (August 1913): 622–624, or his "Hold Yourselves Well in Hand," in *American Federationist* 23, no. 11 (November 1916): 1074–1075. Gompers's attitude on strikes is discussed in Florence Calvert Thorne, *Samuel Gompers—American Statesman* (New York: Philosophical Library, 1957), chapter 11.

11. See also the *United Mine Workers' Journal*, which consistently discussed the "war against organized labor" in its "News Notes from the Field" and later "Rank and File" departments. Of course, the term "syndicalism" connoted violent radicalism in the press. See, for example, James Conway Davies, "Review of J. G. Brooks' American Syndicalism: The I.W.W.," *Economic Journal* 24, no. 96 (December 1914): 584–586.

12. Eugene Debs, "Homestead and Ludlow," *International Socialist Review* (August 1914). This and other key speeches recognizing class war are reprinted in Jean Y. Tussey, ed., *Eugene V. Debs Speaks* (New York: Pathfinder Press, 1970), 215–225. On American socialist thought at this time, see James Weinstein, *The Decline of Socialism in America, 1912–1925* (New York: Monthly Review Press, 1967), chapters 1 and 2.

13. Theodore Roosevelt, "Message Communicated to the Two Houses of Congress at the Beginning of the Second Session of the Fifty-Seventh Congress," and "At the Banquet of the Chamber of Commerce in New York, at New York, November 11, 1902," reprinted in Theodore Roosevelt, *Addresses and Presidential Messages of Theodore Roosevelt, 1902–1904* (New York: Knickerbocker Press, 1904), 82–87, 346–376.

14. See, for example, Woodrow Wilson, "Address at Kansas City, Missouri, May 5, 1911," reprinted in *The Politics of Woodrow Wilson: Selections from His Speeches and Writings,* ed. August Heckscher, 166–170 (New York: Harper and Brothers, 1956).

15. Strike statistics for this period are available in Montgomery, *Workers' Control in America,* 97.

16. Commons quoted in Bruno Ramirez, *When Workers Fight: The Politics of Industrial Relations in the Progressive Era, 1898–1916* (Westport, Conn.: Greenwood Press, 1978), 176.

17. Clarence E. Wunderlin, *Visions of a New Industrial Order: Social Science and Labor Theory in America's Progressive Era* (New York: Columbia University Press, 1992), chapter 8.

18. John R. Commons et al., *History of Labour in the United States,* vol. 2 (New York: Macmillan, 1918), 528–529. On Commons's ideas about trade agreements, see John Commons and John Andrews, *Principles of Labor Legislation* (New York: Harper and Brothers, 1936). Also see Wunderlin, *Visions of a New Industrial Order,* 108, 116; John A. DeBrizzi, *Ideology and the Rise of Labor Theory in America* (Westport, Conn.: Greenwood Press, 1983); Bari Jane Watkins, "The Professors and the Unions: American Academic Social Theory and Labor Reform, 1883–1915" (Ph.D. diss., Yale University, 1976).

19. Francis E. Rourke, "The Department of Labor and the Trade Unions," *Western Political Quarterly* 7, no. 4 (December 1954): 659, 660, 667; O. L. Harvey et al., *The Anvil and the Plow: U.S. Department of Labor 1913–1963* (Washington: U.S. Department of Labor Office of Information, Publications, and Reports, 1963).

20. Quoted in Joseph A. McCartin, *Labor's Great War: The Struggle for Industrial Democracy and the Origins of Modern American Industrial Relations, 1912–1921* (Chapel Hill: University of North Carolina Press, 1997), 19.

21. From *Congressional Record*, LI (1914), Part 12, 11677–11701, quoted in Graham Adams Jr., *Age of Industrial Violence, 1910–1915: The Activities and Findings of the United States Commission on Industrial Relations* (New York: Columbia University Press, 1966), 40.

22. On the U.S. Commission on Industrial Relations, see Adams, *Age of Industrial Violence;* James Weinstein, *The Corporate Ideal in the Liberal State, 1900–1918* (Boston: Beacon Press, 1968), chapter 7; Melvyn Dubofsky, *The State and Labor in Modern America* (Chapel Hill: University of North Carolina Press, 1994), 54–56; McCartin, *Labor's Great War,* chapter 1.

23. Adams, *Age of Industrial Violence,* 73–74.

24. Ibid., 218.

25. Quoted in David M. Kennedy, *Over Here: The First World War and American Society* (Oxford: Oxford University Press, 1980), 62–63.

26. Ibid., 39.

27. McCartin, *Labor's Great War,* 58.

28. Ibid., 90–93.

29. Other federal departments of similar function included the War Industries Board, the War Trade Board, and the War Finance Corporation.

30. McCairn, *Labor's Great War,* 104.

31. Quoted in Elliot J. Gorn, *Mother Jones: The Most Dangerous Woman in America* (New York: Hill and Wang, 2001), 247.

32. Quoted in Dubofsky, *The State and Labor in Modern America,* 39. Since 1906, the AFL had allied itself increasingly with the Democratic Party and had worked to elect pro-labor politicians especially at the local level. With the Clayton Act, the Adamson Act, and the establishment of the federal Labor Department during the Wilson administration, the state appeared to have welcomed organized labor.

33. Gary to Senate Investigation of the steel strike of 1919, in "Gary Testifies to Senate Committee," *New York Times,* October 3, 1919.

34. John Nerone, *Violence against the Press: Policing the Public Sphere in U.S. History* (New York: Oxford University Press, 1994), 181. In addition, direct violence also affected the radical press, as exemplified by the January 5, 1918, attack on the Pigott Printing Concern, which published the *Daily Call* and the *Industrial Worker.* See Nerone, *Violence against the Press,* 183.

35. Judge Gary quoted in David Brody, *Labor in Crisis: The Steel Strike of 1919* (Philadelphia: Lippincott, 1965), 98.

36. "Steel Mills Ready to Fight Strikers," *Washington Post,* September 21, 1919.

37. Charles W. Eliot, "Road toward Industrial Peace," *New York Times,* September 21, 1919.

38. "Industrial War," *New York Times,* September 24, 1919.

39. The *New York Times* explained on September 21, 1919, that "Americans are fearful that a series of strikes might result in well-nigh universal disorders and possibly a revolution."

40. "Police Disperse Steel Strikers," *Washington Post,* September 22, 1919; "Steel Workers and State Police Clash near Pittsburgh," *New York Times,* September 22, 1919.

41. Brody, *Labor in Crisis,* 112; "Steel Strike Analysis," *Pittsburgh Leader,* September 22, 1919; "Fighting Partners," *Washington Post,* September 22, 1919. Periodicals reviewed for September 1919–January 1920 include the *New York Times, New York World,*

Washington Post, Chicago Tribune, Chicago Herald and Examiner, Pittsburgh Leader, Pittsburgh Post, The Iron Age, American Federationist, United Mine Workers' Journal, Socialist Review, Nation, New Republic, Survey, Outlook, and assorted IWW periodicals and pamphlets. A helpful summary and analysis of Pennsylvania newspapers and journals is in the Interchurch World Movement's *Public Opinion and the Steel Strike, Supplementary Reports of the Investigators to the Commission of Inquiry* (New York: Harcourt, Brace, 1921). Also see Byung Soo Lee, "Power and Knowledge: Newspapers' Coverage of the Steel Strike of 1919–1920" (Ph.D. diss., University of Missouri–Columbia, 1993).

42. *Pittsburgh Leader,* September 22, 1919; "The Steel War," *Chicago Tribune,* October 6, 1919; *Washington Post,* September 25, 30, 1919.

43. "The Steel War," *Chicago Tribune,* October 6, 1919; "Both Works Crippled," *Washington Post,* September 30, 1919; "Gains Claimed by Both Sides in Steel Strike," *Pittsburgh Leader,* September 28, 1919.

44. "Mother Jones Urges Strikers to Violence," *New York Times,* October 24, 1919.

45. The radical press is discussed in Robert K. Murray, *Red Scare: A Study in National Hysteria, 1919–1920* (New York: McGraw-Hill, 1955), 142. Jacob Margolis, "The Present Crisis in the Steel Industry," *Socialist Review* 8, no. 1 (1919): 32.

46. Sidney Lens, *The Labor Wars: From the Molly Maguires to the Sitdowns* (New York: Doubleday, 1973), 238–241; "Syndicalism" quoted in "Do You Know What a 'Syndicalist' Is? It's What W. Z. Foster Says That He Is," *Pittsburgh Leader,* September 23, 1919.

47. Cobb's 1907 editorial reprinted in John L. Heaton, *Cobb of the "World"—A Leader in Liberalism, Compiled from His Editorial Articles and Public Addresses* (Freetown, N.Y.: Books for Libraries Press, 1924), 71.

48. Ambrose Bierce quoted in David Nasaw, *The Chief: The Life of William Randolph Hearst* (Boston: Houghton Mifflin, 2000), 173. Later, having successfully run for Congress, Hearst editorialized in his paper that the Democratic Party must do all in its power to "give justice and victory to union efforts" (quoted in ibid., 163). Editorial differences between several major papers are also discussed in Lee, "Power and Knowledge."

49. "Steel Strike Backers," *New York Times,* October 22, 1919.

50. "The Industrial Outlook," *Washington Post,* September 21, 1919.

51. "Labor Day Thoughts," *New York Times,* September 15, 1919; "Managers of Mills to Combat Strike," *New York Times,* September 21, 1919; G. R. Brown, "Fear of Reprisals Prolonging Strike," *Washington Post,* October 1, 1919; *Pittsburgh Leader,* October 2, 6, 8, 1919.

52. Though the expression "un-American" undoubtedly hurt labor far more than it did capital.

53. Brody, *Labor in Crisis,* 134–135; "Sovietized Mill Aim of Strikers," *Chicago Tribune,* October 5, 1919; "Reds Call Gary Strikers to Rise," *New York Times,* October 14, 1919. The slavery idea, maintained typically by radicals at this point, seemed a bit out of touch with the main of striker rhetoric.

54. "Right of Hearing Is Strike Demand Asserts Gompers," *Pittsburgh Leader,* September 26, 1919.

55. "The Strike and the Conference," *Washington Post,* September 23, 1919.

56. Reprinted in "Labor and the Public," *Pittsburgh Leader,* September 26, 1919.

57. "The Steel Strike," *Chicago Tribune,* October 2, 1919; "The Steel Strike," *Chicago Herald and Examiner,* September 23, 1919; *New York Times,* August 29, 1919.

58. *Wall Street Journal,* October 9, 1919.

59. *Chicago Tribune,* September 28, 1919.

60. "Strike Quiz by Senate Tomorrow," *Chicago Herald and Examiner,* September 24, 1919; "Senate Hunts Radicalism in Steel Strike," *Chicago Herald and Examiner,* September 25, 1919.

61. "Private War at Public Cost," *New York World,* October 6, 1919.

62. Wilson quoted in Brody, *Labor in Crisis,* 122.

63. "That Conference," *United Mine Workers' Journal,* October 1, 1919.

64. "Three Groups Prepare Labor Programs," *New York Times,* October 9, 1919.

65. "Has Wilson Something to Offer?" *Pittsburgh Leader,* October 21, 1919; Even the *Wall Street Journal* chastised the capital group for its obstinacy. See "Strikes Now Danger to Nation's Advance," *Wall Street Journal,* October 24, 1919.

66. Gregory Mason, "The Labor Crisis and the People—What Does the Present Industrial Crisis Mean? III. The Industrial Deadlock," *Outlook* (October 29, 1919): 226.

67. Ibid., 226, 228.

68. The expression "lean" is taken from Irving Bernstein's seminal work on labor in the 1920s, *The Lean Years: A History of the American Worker, 1920–1933* (Boston: Houghton Mifflin, 1960).

69. Dubofsky, *The State and Labor in Modern America,* 97.

70. On the long-term implications of federal intervention in World War I, see Jeffrey Haydu, *Making American Industry Safe for Democracy: Comparative Perspectives on the State and Employee Representation in the Era of World War I* (Urbana: University of Illinois Press, 1997); McCartin, *Labor's Great War,* 199–227, quote on page 209.

71. Dubofsky, *The State and Labor in Modern America,* 84, 92.

72. Craig Phelan, *William Green: Biography of a Labor Leader* (Albany: State University of New York Press, 1989), 45; David Montgomery, "Thinking about American Workers in the 1920s," *International Labor and Working-Class History* 32 (fall 1987): 15.

73. According to Bruce Kaufman, "The term *industrial relations* entered the American lexicon in 1912 when President William Howard Taft proposed and Congress approved the creation of a nine-person investigative committee called the Commission on Industrial Relations" (Bruce E. Kaufman, *The Origins and Evolution of the Field of Industrial Relations in the United States* [Ithaca, N.Y.: ILR Press, 1993], 3).

74. According to one insider, there was "a peculiar congeniality between the war and these men. It is as if the war and they had been waiting for each other" (quoted in William Leuchtenburg, "The New Deal and the Analogue of War," in *Change and Continuity in Twentieth-Century America,* ed. John Braeman, Robert H. Bremner, and Everett Walters [Columbus: Ohio State University Press, 1964], 88). On interwar labor relations experts, see Ronald W. Schatz, "From Commons to Dunlop: Rethinking the Field and Theory of Industrial Relations," in *Industrial Democracy in America: The Ambiguous Promise,* ed. Nelson Lichtenstein and Howell John Harris, 89–92 (Cambridge: Cambridge University Press, 1996).

75. On the idea of "industrial democracy" in the 1920s, see Steven Fraser, "The Labor Question," in *The Rise and Fall of the New Deal Order, 1930–1980,* ed. Steven Fraser and Gary Gerstle, 55–84 (Princeton, N.J.: Princeton University Press, 1989).

76. Morris Llewellyn Cooke, "An All-American Basis for Industry" (Philadelphia: s.n., 1919), 1, 6, 2.

77. Robert Julius Anderson, "Capital, Labor, and the Public: Nine Great Questions Before Us Today," *Industrial Management* 59, no. 2 (February 1920): 117–119; Eugene E. Prussing, "Labor, Preferred," *The World's Work* 45, no. 4 (February 1923): 417–421.

78. On the abundant use of Americanisms by labor at this time, see Gary Gerstle, *Working-Class Americanism: The Politics of Labor in a Textile City, 1914–1960* (Cambridge: Cambridge University Press, 1989). The UTW example is taken from Gerstle, *Working-Class Americanism*, 79.

79. Robert Shogun, *The Battle of Blair Mountain: The Story of America's Largest Labor Uprising* (Oxford: Westview Press, 2004), 50, 122, 82.

80. On the 1922 shopmen's strike, see Colin J. Davis, *Power at Odds: The 1922 National Railroad Shopmen's Strike* (Urbana: University of Illinois Press, 1997); Dubofsky, *The State and Labor*.

81. Steve Fraser, "Dress Rehearsal for the New Deal: Shop-Floor Insurgents, Political Elites, and Industrial Democracy in the Amalgamated Clothing Workers," in *Working Class America: Essays on Labor, Community, and American Society,* ed. Michael H. Frisch and Daniel J. Walkowitz, 222, 240 (Urbana: University of Illinois Press, 1983). See also Steve Fraser, "The Labor Question," in Fraser and Gerstle, eds., *The Rise and Fall of the New Deal Order*, 62–63. My reading of "industrial democracy" does not refute Fraser's reading of the 1920s; rather, I add new context in terms of the widening scope of the "public" in the lead-up to the New Deal.

CHAPTER 6   CO-OPTING THE COMBATANTS

1. Joseph A. McCartin, *Labor's Great War: The Struggle for Industrial Democracy and the Origins of Modern American Industrial Relations, 1912–1921* (Chapel Hill: University of North Carolina Press, 1997).

2. The chairman of the Republican Convention of 1932, Bertrand Snell, added that Hoover had "solidified labor and capital against the enemy" of Depression. Comparisons to World War I by contemporaries are excellently documented in William Leuchtenburg, "The New Deal and the Analogue of War," in *Change and Continuity in Twentieth-Century America,* ed. John Braeman, Robert H. Bremner, and Everett Walters (Columbus: Ohio State University Press, 1964). Snell is quoted on page 100, Hoover on page 83, Meyer on page 99.

3. Ibid., 101.

4. On Roosevelt's rhetoric, see David Green, *The Language of Politics in America: Shaping Political Consciousness from McKinley to Reagan* (Ithaca, N.Y.: Cornell University Press, 1992), chapter 5. On workers' perceptions of FDR, see Lizabeth Cohen, *Making a New Deal: Industrial Workers in Chicago, 1919–1939* (Cambridge: Cambridge University Press, 1990), 283–289.

5. Elizabeth Faue, *Community of Suffering and Struggle: Women, Men, and the Labor Movement in Minneapolis, 1915–1945* (Chapel Hill: University of North Carolina Press, 1991), 20; Melvyn Dubofsky, *The State and Labor in Modern America* (Chapel Hill: University of North Carolina Press, 1994), 108. For a contemporary, optimistic account of women workers in the 1930s, see Mary Heaton Vorse, *Labor's New Millions* (New York: Modern Age Books, 1938). On the gendered nature of labor discourse, see Alice Kessler Harris, *Gendering Labor History* (Urbana: University of Illinois Press, 2007), Ileen DeVault, *United Apart: Gender and the Rise of Craft Unionism* (Ithaca:

Cornell University Press, 2004). Robert H. Zieger, *American Workers, American Unions*, 2nd ed. (Baltimore: Johns Hopkins University Press, 1994), 24.

6. And, as Melvyn Dubofsky points out, direct links between the Wilson and Roosevelt administrations are numerous and concrete, beginning with the fact that Roosevelt himself served in the Wilson administration. See Melvyn Dubofsky, *The State and Labor in Modern America* (Chapel Hill: University of North Carolina Press, 1994), 108–110.

7. Rhonda F. Levine, *Class Struggle and the New Deal: Industrial Labor, Industrial Capital, and the State* (Lawrence: University Press of Kansas, 1988), 72–73.

8. Leuchtenburg, "The New Deal and the Analogue of War," 101.

9. David M. Kennedy, *Freedom from Fear: The American People in Depression and War, 1929–1945* (New York: Oxford University Press, 1999), 245; Cohen, *Making a New Deal*, 285. On the 1930s' "security consciousness," see Nelson Lichtenstein, *State of the Union: A Century of American Labor* (Princeton, N.J.: Princeton University Press, 2002), 25–30. Analysis of working-class sentiment in the 1930s has yielded a raft of scholarly work. Liz Cohen's study of Chicago's industrial workers, for example, finds that workers connected political activism in the Democratic Party with a broader sense of class interest. Similarly, in his *Working-Class Americanism: The Politics of Labor in a Textile City, 1914–1960* (Cambridge: Cambridge University Press, 1989), Gary Gerstle shows that working-class and American identity were fused together in the writings and speeches of unionists in Rhode Island. While the degree to which workers saw themselves as members of a discrete "class" is debatable, these studies reveal the extent to which revitalized worker militancy was accompanied by a sharpened sense of public rights. For contrary evidence that class thinking was not a priority, see James R. McGovern, *And a Time for Hope: Americans in the Great Depression* (Westport, Conn.: Praeger, 2000), chapter 11; Gerald W. Johnson, "The Average American and the Depression," *Current History* (February 1932): 671–675; Melvyn Dubofsky, "Not So 'Turbulent Years': Another Look at America in the 1930s," in *Hard Work: The Making of Labor History* (Urbana: University of Illinois Press, 2000), 130–150.

10. Dubofsky, *The State and Labor in Modern America*, 116.

11. On the failure of the General Textile Strike of 1934, see Janet Irons, *Testing the New Deal: The General Textile Strike of 1934 in the American South* (Urbana: University of Illinois Press, 2000), and John A. Salmond, *The General Textile Strike of 1934: From Maine to Alabama* (Columbia: University of Missouri Press, 2002).

12. Priscilla Murolo and A. B. Chitty, *From the Folks Who Brought You the Weekend: A Short, Illustrated History of Labor in the United States* (New York: New Press, 2001), 201–202.

13. National Labor Relations Board, *Legislative History of the National Labor Relations Act, 1935*, vol. 2 (Washington, D.C.: Government Printing Office, 1949), 3278.

14. Len De Caux, "Looking Ahead," *Union News Service*, December 10, 1945.

15. Michael Kazin, *The Populist Persuasion* (New York: Basic Books 1995), 139.

16. Thomas Gobel, "Becoming American: Ethnic Workers and the Rise of the CIO," *Labor History* 29, no. 2 (spring 1988): 173–198.

17. Eric Foner, *The Story of American Freedom* (New York: Norton, 1998), 211; "A Labor Army That Has Learned Strategy," *Union News Service*, November 16, 1936; "General Motors versus America," *Union News Service*, February 1, 1937.

18. On "industrial democracy," see Nelson Lichtenstein and Howell John Harris, eds., *Industrial Democracy in America: The Ambiguous Promise* (Cambridge: Cambridge University Press, 1996).

19. Ton Morrow, "Song of the CIO," *United Auto Worker,* August 21, 1937; "Strikes and the Free Flow of Commerce," *United Auto Worker,* June 26, 1937.

20. Christopher Tomlins, "AFL Unions in the 1930s: Their Performance in Historical Perspective," *Journal of American History* 65 (1979): 1021–1042.

21. Kazin, *Populist Persuasion,* 146; Elizabeth Faue, *Community of Suffering and Struggle: Women, Men, and the Labor Movement in Minneapolis, 1915–1945* (Chapel Hill: University of North Carolina Press, 1991); John L. Lewis, "The Battle for Industrial Democracy," broadcast over National Broadcast Corporation radio on July 6, 1936, speech reprinted in *Vital Speeches of the Day* 2, no. 22 (August 1, 1936): 675–678.

22. On the Roosevelt voter realignment, see Kristi Anderson, *The Creation of a Democratic Majority, 1928–1936* (Chicago: University of Chicago Press, 1979). On workers and national politics, see Bruce Nelson, "Give Us Roosevelt: Workers and the New Deal Coalition," *History Today* 40 (January 1990): 40–48.

23. Christopher L. Tomlins, *The State and the Unions: Labor Relations, Law, and the Organized Labor Movement in America, 1880–1960* (Cambridge: Cambridge University Press, 1985), 106; Sumner Slichter, "The Changing Character of American Industrial Relations," *American Economic Review* 29 (March 1939): 122, 136.

24. Jerold S. Auerbach, *Labor and Liberty: The La Follette Committee and the New Deal* (Indianapolis: Bobbs-Merrill, 1966), 105, 218. On the nature and extent of employer repression, see Stephen H. Norwood, *Strikebreaking and Intimidation: Mercenaries and Masculinity in Twentieth-Century America* (Chapel Hill: University of North Carolina Press, 2002).

25. On this concept generally, see Howell John Harris, *The Right to Manage: Industrial Relations Policies of American Business in the 1940s* (Madison: University of Wisconsin Press, 1982).

26. Eugene G. Grace, "Industry and Public," speech presented at the 54th General Meeting of the American Iron and Steel Institute, New York, May 28, 1936, reprinted in *Vital Speeches of the Day* 2, no. 22 (August 1, 1936): 678–682.

27. Calculated from "Historical Statistics" in David M. Gordon, Richard Edwards, and Michael Reich, *Segmented Work, Divided Workers: The Historical Transformation of Labor in the United States* (Cambridge: Cambridge University Press, 1982), 177; Murolo and Chitty, *From the Folks Who Brought You the Weekend,* 193.

28. Each of these strikes has received excellent scholarly treatment. On the General Textile Strike of 1934, see Irons, *Testing the New Deal,* and Salmond, *The General Textile Strike of 1934;* on the Minneapolis Teamsters' Strike, see Faue, *Community of Suffering and Struggle;* on the General Motors sit-down strike, see Sidney Fine, *Sit-Down: The General Motors Strike of 1936–1937* (Ann Arbor: University of Michigan Press, 1969). All are placed nicely in context in Irving Bernstein's classic *The Turbulent Years: A History of the American Worker, 1933–1941* (Boston: Houghton Mifflin, 1969).

29. My analysis is taken from a survey of the *New York Times,* December 1936–February 1937.

30. "The State of the Union Today," *United States News,* August 14, 1933; Hugh S. Johnson, "Warning to Labor of Peril in Tolerating Strikes," *United States News,* October 16, 1933.

31. David Lawrence, "Blue Eagles for Labor Unions?" *United States News,* July 23, 1934; "Labor Troubles: Obstacle to Recovery," *United States News,* August 6, 1934.

32. "The Industrial War," *Fortune* 16, no. 5 (November 1937): 105.

33. Edward Levinson, "Labor on the March," *Harper's Magazine* 174 (May 1937), 642–650.

34. George E. Sokolsky, "The Split in Labor," *Atlantic Monthly* 158 (October 1936), 465.

35. "The Week," *New Republic* 92 (August 18, 1937), 30.

36. "Cause of Strikes? An Even Division of Press Opinion," *United States News,* June 11, 1934.

37. Levinson, "Labor on the March," *Harper's Magazine* 174 (May 1937), 645.

38. *Time* surveyed between December 28, 1936, and February 22, 1937; "On the March," *Time* (February 1, 1937), 11.

39. "Labor: The Battle in the Automobile Industry," *United States News,* January 4, 1937; "On the March," *Time* (February 1, 1937); *New York Times,* January 5, 1937.

40. "Public opinion" as such began to be systematically studied by theorists in the late nineteenth century. See Carroll J. Glynn, Susan Herbst, Garrett J. O'Keefe, and Robert Y. Shapiro, *Public Opinion* (Boulder, Colo.: Westview Press, 1999), chapter 2.

41. Fine, *Sit-Down,* 230.

42. "Editorial Comment—Pro and Con on the 'Sit Down' Strikes," *United States News,* January 11, 1937; "Strikers and the Law: Viewpoint of Editors," *United States News,* February 8, 1937.

43. "Strikes and Their Relation to the Cycles of Business," *United States News,* June 11, 1934. For an earlier "cyclical" analysis of strikes, see Alvin H. Hansen, "Cycles of Strikes," *American Economic Review* 11 (1921): 616–621. Hansen argued that "strikes correlate inversely with the business cycle in periods of long-run falling prices, while they correlate directly with the business cycle in periods of long-run rising prices."

44. Edwin Emery and Michael Emery, *The Press and America: An Interpretive History of Mass Media,* 4th ed. (Englewood Cliffs, N.J.: Prentice Hall, 1978), 369.

45. Linda Gordon, "Dorothea Lange: The Photographer as Agricultural Sociologist," *Journal of American History* 93, no. 3 (2006): 726.

46. In Webb's words, *Life* was a "middle-class primer." Sheila M. Webb, "'America Is a Middle-Class Nation': The Presentation of Class in the Pages of *Life,*" in *Class and News,* ed. Don Heider, 169, 170 (Lanham, Md.: Rowman and Littlefield, 2004).

47. Richard H. Pells, *Radical Visions and American Dreams: Culture and Social Thought in the Depression Years* (Middletown, Conn.: Wesleyan University Press, 1973), chapter 6.

48. According to the *Oxford English Dictionary,* usage of "management" dates as early as the eighteenth century, though not until the nineteenth century would anything like the modern term be employed. See "management" in the *Oxford English Dictionary,* 2nd ed., vol. 9 (Oxford: Clarendon Press, 1989), 294.

49. Labor management societies started in 1912 with the Society to Promote the Science of Management, followed in 1917 by the Society of Industrial Engineers, in 1922 with the American Management Association, and in 1934 with the Society for the Advancement of Management. See George Filipetti, *Industrial Management in Transition,* rev. ed. (Homewood, Ill.: Irwin, 1953), 1.

50. Frederick Winslow Taylor, *The Principles of Scientific Management* (New York: Harper and Brothers, 1919).

51. The "specifically American" comment is from Peter F. Drucker, *Management: Tasks, Responsibilities, Practices* (New York: Harper and Row, 1974), 5. According to Drucker, the idea of "management" is as old as the writings of Adam Smith (21–23). Here I am concerned with the use of the term as a signifier of a specific unit of social relations.

52. This phrase, coined by Herbert Hoover in his 1909 book *Principles of Mining* (New York: McGraw-Hill, 1909), was popularly quoted by managerial proponents in the 1930s.

53. The origins of the process of increased managerial control are articulated in Daniel Nelson, *Managers and Workers: Origins of the Twentieth-Century Factory System in the United States, 1880–1920*, 2nd ed. (Madison: University of Wisconsin Press, 1995). Gordon, Edwards, and Reich, *Segmented Work, Divided Workers*, 176.

54. Quoted in Andrea Gabor, *The Capitalist Philosophers: The Geniuses of Modern Business—Their Lives, Times, and Ideas* (New York: Crown Business, 2000), 82.

55. Wier quote and commentary in George E. Sokolsky, "The Industrial Front," *Atlantic Monthly* 159 (March 1937), 260–261.

56. Adolf A. Berle Jr., and Gardiner C. Means, *The Modern Corporation and Private Property* (New York: Macmillan, 1933); quoted in Gabor, *The Capitalist Philosophers*, 75.

57. Harry W. Laidler, "More Government in Business," *Annals of the American Academy of Political and Social Science* 178 (March 1935): 148–154.

58. Edwin E. Witte, *The Government in Labor Disputes* (New York: McGraw-Hill, 1932), 10, 6, 236, 290. Also see Alfred L. Bernheim and Dorothy Van Doren, eds., *Labor and the Government: An Investigation of the Role of the Government in Labor Relations* (New York: McGraw-Hill, 1935).

59. William M. Leiserson, *Right and Wrong in Labor Relations* (Berkeley: University of California Press, 1938), 10, 73, 74, 86.

60. Harris, *The Right to Manage*, 181–182.

61. In their seminal 1939 study *Management and the Worker* (Cambridge, Mass.: Harvard University Press, 1967), management specialists Fritz Roethlisberger and William J. Dickson developed the theme of the importance of managers in satisfying employees.

62. See Frank T. Carlton, "On Union-Management Co-operation," *American Journal of Economics and Sociology* 2, no. 2 (January 1943): 262–263.

63. Harris, *The Right to Manage*, 74.

64. Importantly, this did not mean a "rolling over" for big business. They resisted organized labor's inroads and remained more influential in war planning even as they supposedly worked side-by-side with them. As one liberal War Production Board member reported, the interests of labor were typically regarded as "undigested lumps in the stomachs of management people." See Nelson Lichtenstein, *The Most Dangerous Man in Detroit: Walter Reuther and the Fate of American Labor* (New York: Basic Books, 1995), 173.

CHAPTER 7   A KIND OF PEACE

1. Walter P. Reuther, "We Shall March Together," in *Selected Papers of Walter P. Reuther*, ed. Henry M. Christman, 56, 57 (New York: Macmillan, 1961).

2. See Nelson Lichtenstein, *Labor's War at Home: The CIO in World War II* (Cambridge: Cambridge University Press, 1982); James B. Atleson, *Labor and the Wartime State:*

Labor Relations and Law during World War II (Urbana: University of Illinois Press, 1998).

3. Walter Reuther, "500 Planes a Day—A Program for the Utilization of the Automobile Industry for Mass Production of Defense Planes," in Reuther, *Selected Papers of Walter P. Reuther*, 1–12. CIO wartime membership totals appear in Lichtenstein, *Labor's War at Home*, 80. Importantly, the Ford Motor Company did construct Willow Run during the war and built military aircraft at the facility.

4. Patricia Bronte, "Detroit Sees UAW Victory Coming," *Union News Service*, December 10, 1945; Barton J. Bernstein, "Walter Reuther and the General Motors Strike of 1945–1946," *Michigan History* 49, no. 3 (September 1965): 263; Irving Howe and B. J. Widick, *The UAW and Walter Reuther* (New York: Da Capo, 1973), chapter 6. On organized labor's efforts to maintain government interference in the economy, see Julie Meyer, "Trade Union Plans for Post-War Reconstruction in the United States," *Social Research* 11 (1944): 491–505.

5. "UAW Fights for the People," *Union News Service*, November 26, 1945.

6. Nelson Lichtenstein, *The Most Dangerous Man in Detroit: Walter Reuther and the Fate of American Labor* (New York: Basic Books, 1995), 234; "'Terrible Strike' Being Forced on Us, Thomas Tells," *New York Times*, November 18, 1945; Bernstein, "Walter Reuther and the General Motors Strike," 264; Walter W. Ruch, "Reuther Asserts GM Strives to Be Economic Dictator," *New York Times*, November 25, 1945.

7. Lichtenstein, *The Most Dangerous Man in Detroit*, 223.

8. "G.M. Strike, '46 Model," *Nation*, December 1, 1945, 567–568; Walter Reuther, "This Is Your Fight!" *Nation*, January 12, 1946, 35–36.

9. *The Daily Worker*, November 27, 1945, quoted in Howe and Widick, *The UAW and Walter Reuther*, 145.

10. "Nation-Wide Strike Shuts GM Plants," *New York Times*, November 22, 1945.

11. Nelson Lichtenstein, *State of the Union: A Century of American Labor* (Princeton, N.J.: Princeton University Press, 2002), 110.

12. Walter W. Ruch, "Rising Threat of Auto Strike Casts Pall over All Detroit," *New York Times*, November 19, 1945; *New York Times*, December 30, 1945.

13. "G.M. Striker Has a Very Busy Life," *Life*, January 21, 1946, 28–29.

14. "G.M. Wants a Strike," *Nation*, November 3, 1945, 448–449; "Truman and Labor," *Nation*, December 29, 1945, 724–725; Alfred Friendly, "American Industry's Grand Strategy," *Nation*, January 19, 1946, 62–63.

15. "Plotting a New Depression," *New Republic*, December 17, 1945.

16. Quoted in Lichtenstein, *The Most Dangerous Man in Detroit*, 235.

17. "D-Day in Detroit," *Time*, November 26, 1945, 21; *CIO News Service*, January 7, 1946; "Union Demands GM Arbitrate," *New York Times*, November 20, 1945; "GM Asks Court Ban," *New York Times*, December 14, 1945; *Detroit Free Press*, December 11, 1945.

18. For the period of November 1945–March 1946, I looked at the *New York Times*, *Washington Post*, *Detroit News*, *Detroit Free Press*, *Wall Street Journal*, *US News*, *Life*, *Time*, *Fortune*, *Nation*, *Atlantic Monthly*, *New Republic*, *Union News Service*, *American Federationist*, and *United Auto Worker*.

19. "C.I.O. Forces Shutdown with Industry," *Life*, January 21, 1946, 24–27; "Nation-Wide Strike Shuts GM Plants," *New York Times*, November 22, 1945; *Detroit News*, November 20, 1945.

20. Steve Babson, *The Unfinished Struggle: Turning Points in American Labor, 1877–Present* (Lanham, Md.: Rowman and Littlefield, 1999), 56; Michael Kazin, *The Populist Persuasion* (New York: Basic Books 1995), 146.

21. "G.M. Striker Has a Very Busy Life," *Life,* January 21, 1946, 28–29.

22. Importantly, this did not mean that America had become color blind. Rather, as David Roediger suggests, by this point former "new immigrants" had largely escaped racial "in-between" designations and had become white ethnics. A white/nonwhite racial regime remained firmly entrenched. See David Roediger, *Working toward Whiteness: How America's Immigrants Became White—The Strange Journey from Ellis Island to the Suburbs* (New York: Basic Books, 2005).

23. "GM Raise of 15 Pct. Is Favored by Public," *Detroit News,* December 30, 1945.

24. Lawrence Resner, "Many Specialists on Reuther Staff," *New York Times,* November 23, 1945. On the new use of "capital" see, for example, Samuel A. Tower, "Capital Is Shaping Wage-Price Policy to End Big Strikes," *New York Times,* February 4, 1946.

25. "Texts of the UAW and Romney Statements," *New York Times,* November 20, 1945; Walter W. Ruch, "Reuther Asserts GM Strives to Be Economic Dictator," *New York Times,* November 25, 1945; *New York Times,* December 30, 1945.

26. Bernstein, "Walter Reuther and the General Motors Strike," 265; "Dangerous Mixture," *New York Times,* December 12, 1945.

27. David Lawrence, "Labor-Management Parley Sees Economic War Brew," *Detroit News,* November 20, 1945.

28. "GM, Packard, Nash Victories," *Union News Service,* March 18, 1946; Lichtenstein, *The Most Dangerous Man in Detroit,* 246; Kazin, *Populist Persuasion,* 161; "Whose 'Victory'?" *New York Times,* March 14, 1946.

29. "Should We Be Optimistic?" *Life,* January 21, 1946, 30.

30. "Strikes," *Detroit News,* January 11, 1946; "An Old Time Umpire Might Settle Strikes," *Detroit News,* November 14, 1945. On sports allusion and metaphor in the 1930s, see Elizabeth Faue, *Community of Suffering and Struggle: Women, Men, and the Labor Movement in Minneapolis, 1915–1945* (Chapel Hill: University of North Carolina Press, 1991), 74, 77.

31. *Wall Street Journal,* November 5, 1945. Also see "Can Strikes Be Stopped? The Search for a Formula," *United States News,* November 2, 1945.

32. On industrial pluralism, see Katherine Van Wezel Stone, "The Post-War Paradigm in American Labor Law," *Yale Law Review* 90, no. 7 (June 1981): 1509–1580; Daniel R. Ernst, "Common Laborers? Industrial Pluralists, Legal Realists, and the Law of Industrial Disputes, 1915–1943," *Law and History Review* 11, no. 1 (spring 1993): 59–100; Reuel E. Schiller, "From Group Rights to Individual Liberties: Post-War Labor Law, Liberalism, and the Waning of Union Strength," *Berkeley Journal of Employment and Labor Law* 20, no. 1 (1999): 1–73; Christopher Tomlins, "The New Deal, Collective Bargaining, and the Triumph of Industrial Pluralism," *Industrial and Labor Relations Review* 39, no. 1 (October 1985): 19–34.

33. Wayne Leslie McNaughton, *The Development of Labor Relations Law* (Washington, D.C.: American Council on Public Affairs, 1941), 5–6.

34. "Seeds of Civil War Seen in Labor Rows," *New York Times,* January 16, 1946.

35. Sumner Slichter, *The Challenge of Industrial Relations: Trade Unions, Management, and the Public Interest* (Ithaca, N.Y.: Cornell University Press, 1947), 15–16, 122, 172.

36. Irving G. McCann, *Why the Taft-Hartley Law?* (New York: Committee for Constitutional Government, 1950), 2, 125.

37. While the passage of the Taft-Hartley Act confirmed for labor the sense that interventionary federal policies could still hurt union interests in favor of big business, the groundwork for a permanent federal presence in labor relations had already been established. Taft-Hartley merely illustrated the tack that it would take.

38. "Double Assault," *Time*, July 7, 1947, 7.

39. Edwin E. Witte, "An Appraisal of the Taft-Hartley Act," *American Economic Review* 38 (1948): 370; George Meany, "The Taft-Hartley Act," *American Federationist* 54, no. 12 (December 1947): 9; Robert Dallek, *Harry S. Truman: The American Presidents Series* (New York: Holt, 2008), 56. On inconsistencies within labor opinion on Taft-Hartley, see A. H. Raskin, "Taft-Hartley and Labor's Perspective," *Commentary* 4, no. 5 (November 1947): 435–440. For a contemporary perspective on Taft-Hartley and minority rights, see Clarence Mitchell, "Notes on the Taft-Hartley Act," *The Crisis* 55, no. 10 (October 1948): 300–301.

40. *Organizer*, February 14, 1950, quoted in Elizabeth A. Fones-Wolf, *Selling Free Enterprise: The Business Assault on Labor and Liberalism, 1945–1960* (Urbana: University of Illinois Press, 1994), 50.

41. Witte, "An Appraisal of the Taft-Hartley Act," 382.

42. Arthur M. Schlesinger Jr., *The Vital Center: The Politics of Freedom* (Boston: Houghton Mifflin, 1949), 253; John Kenneth Galbraith, *American Capitalism: The Concept of Countervailing Power* (Boston: Houghton Mifflin, 1956), 133; C. Wright Mills, *White Collar: The American Middle Classes* (New York: Oxford University Press, 1951). It also should be noted that Mills's concept of the power elite challenged the view of a true democratically pluralist society. His book *The Power Elite* also provides us with evidence of the influence of this model in the 1950s. See C. Wright Mills, *The Power Elite* (New York: Oxford University Press, 1956). Importantly, Schlesinger recognized that "class conflict" still had an enduring, even necessary role to play in America.

CONCLUSION   THE END OF CLASS CONFLICT?

1. "New Affluence, Unity for Labor," *Life* (December 12, 1955), 26–35.

2. Dublin quoted in Nelson Lichtenstein, *State of the Union: A Century of American Labor* (Princeton, N.J.: Princeton University Press, 2002), 149.

3. Daniel Bell, *The End of Ideology: On the Exhaustion of Political Ideas in the Fifties* (Glencoe, Ill.: Free Press, 1960). The inherent stability of equally powerful social groups was an idea seconded by economist John Kenneth Galbraith in his 1952 book, *American Capitalism: The Concept of Countervailing Power* (Boston: Houghton Mifflin, 1956). It should be noted that there was considerable debate over Bell's arguments. See Chaim I. Waxman, ed., *The End of Ideology Debate* (New York: Simon and Schuster, 1968).

4. Harold L. Wilensky, "Class, Class Consciousness, and American Workers," in *Labor in a Changing America*, ed. William Haber, 12–44 (New York: Basic Books, 1966).

5. Ibid., 27, 18. Wilensky also used a 1958 study of Paterson, New Jersey, textile workers regarding a survey that asked them whether or not "classes get along." According to this study, only 21 percent felt they were "enemies." However, Wilensky did not dismiss social conflict as such, writing: "The 'end of ideology,' the end of class war, is not the end of conflict."

6. *Chicago News,* April 10, 1899, quoted in Jean Bethke Elshtain, *Jane Addams and the Dream of American Democracy: A Life* (New York: Basic Books, 2002), 124.

7. Jane Addams, "The Settlement as a Factor in the Labor Movement," in *The Jane Addams Reader,* ed. Jean Bethke Elshtain, 52–54 (New York: Basic Books, 2002); Jane Addams, *Twenty Years at Hull-House* (New York: Signet, 1960), 158. A useful brief overview of Addams's take on class conflict is in Shelton Stromquist, *Reinventing "The People": The Progressive Movement, the Class Problem, and the Origins of Modern Liberalism* (Urbana: University of Illinois Press, 2006), 25–28.

8. Martin J. Burke, *The Conundrum of Class: Public Discourse on the Social Order in America* (Chicago: University of Chicago Press, 1995); James L. Huston, *Securing the Fruits of Labor: The American Concept of Wealth Distribution, 1765–1900* (Baton Rouge: Louisiana State University Press, 1998).

9. See Roger Keeran, *The Communist Party and the Auto Workers Union* (Bloomington: Indiana University Press, 1980), for a detailed examination of the impact of the self-purging on industrial unionism.

10. Louis Adamic, *Dynamite: The Story of Class Violence in America,* rev. ed. (New York: Viking, 1934); Samuel Yellen, *American Labor Struggles* (New York: Russell, 1936). Emblematic of New Left labor history are works by writers such as Herbert Gutman and David Montgomery. A recent work on the subject is Sharon Smith, *Subterranean Fire: A History of Working-Class Radicalism in the United States* (Chicago: Haymarket Books, 2006). On the dissonance between divisive reality and pluralist optimism, see Lichtenstein, *State of the Union,* chapter 3, and James B. Atleson, *Labor and the Wartime State: Labor Relations and Law during World War II* (Urbana: University of Illinois Press, 1998), chapter 12.

11. Elizabeth A. Fones-Wolf, *Selling Free Enterprise: The Business Assault on Labor and Liberalism, 1945–1960* (Urbana: University of Illinois Press, 1994).

12. Ibid., 70, 46–47.

13. Robert Lynd, "Labor-Management Cooperation: How Far, to What End?" *Labor and Nation* (January–February 1948), quoted in Fones-Wolf, *Selling Free Enterprise,* 32.

14. Eric N. Waltenburg, *Choosing Where to Fight: Organized Labor and the Modern Regulatory State, 1948–1987* (Albany: State University of New York Press, 2002), 9.

15. David Brody, "Workplace Contractualism: A Historical/Comparative Analysis," in *In Labor's Cause: Main Themes on the History of the American Worker* (New York: Oxford University Press, 1993), 241.

16. Section 1(b), Short Title and Declaration of Policy, *Labor-Management Relations Act of 1947,* U.S. Code, vol. 29, section 141 (1947).

17. And as George Lipsitz pointed out, despite his official protest, "President Truman had previously endorsed most of the main provisions of Taft-Hartley" (quoted in his *Rainbow at Midnight: Labor and Culture in the 1940s* (Urbana: University of Illinois Press, 1994), 169.

18. Jon Bekken, "The Working-Class Press at the Turn of the Century," in *Ruthless Criticism: New Perspectives in U.S. Communication History,* ed. William S. Solomon and Robert W. McChesney, 155 (Minneapolis: University of Minnesota Press, 1993).

19. Alan Brinkley, "The New Deal and the Idea of the State," in *The Rise and Fall of the New Deal Order, 1930–1980,* ed. Steven Fraser and Gary Gerstle, 109 (Princeton, N.J.: Princeton University Press, 1989).

20. Howard Brick, "The Postcapitalist Vision in Twentieth-Century American Thought," in *American Capitalism: Social Thought and Political Economy in the Twentieth Century,* ed. Nelson Lichtenstein, 21–46 (Philadelphia: University of Pennsylvania Press, 2006).

21. David T. Z. Mindich, *Tuned Out: Why Americans Under 40 Don't Follow the News* (New York: Oxford University Press, 2005), 28–29; Christopher R. Martin, "'Upscale' News Audiences and the Transformation of Labour News," *Journalism Studies* 9, no. 2 (2008): 178–194.

22. For a recent example of popular working-class study, see Barbara Ehrenreich, *Nickel and Dimed: On (Not) Getting By in America* (New York: Henry Holt, 2002). Furthermore, class as a category of analysis has never been proven irrelevant.

23. Cited in Christopher R. Martin, *Framed!: Labor and the Corporate Media* (Ithaca, N.Y.: Cornell University Press, 2004), 12.

24. Michael Parenti, *Inventing Reality: The Politics of the Mass Media* (New York: St. Martin's Press, 1986), 84–85, 81. Writes Deepa Kumar: for the media, "there is no such thing as public interest. Rather, the public is divided into the tiny elite that benefits from globalization policies and the vast majority of workers who do not" (quoted in Deepa Kumar, *Outside the Box: Corporate Media, Globalization, and the UPS Strike* [Urbana: University of Illinois Press, 1997], ix).

25. Antonio Gramsci, *Selections from the Prison Notebooks,* ed. and trans. by Quintin Hoare and Geoffrey Nowell Smith (New York: International Publishers, 1971), 80.

26. For an example from the left, see Paul Krugman, "Bush's Class War Budget," *New York Times,* February 11, 2005. From the right, see "Class War Revelation," *Wall Street Journal,* April 15, 2005.

27. Lou Dobbs, *The War on the Middle Class: How the Government, Big Business, and Special Interest Groups Are Waging War on the American Dream and How to Fight Back* (New York: Penguin, 2005).

BIBLIOGRAPHY

PRIMARY SOURCES

Research Databases

American Periodicals Series Microfilm
    Collection
Historical Index to the *New York Times*

Historical Newspapers Online
Periodicals Contents Index

Daily Newspapers

Baltimore Sun (1877, 1894)
Boston Evening Transcript (1877)
Boston Globe (1860)
Chicago Herald and Examiner (1919)
Chicago Times (1877, 1894)
Chicago Tribune (1877, 1894, 1919)
Cincinnati Commercial Tribune (1788)
Cleveland Plain Dealer (1886)
Detroit Free Press (1945–1946)
Detroit News (1945–1946)
Harrisburg Independent (1877)
Los Angeles Times (1886)
Martinsburg Statesman (1902)
Mauch Chunk Coal Gazette (1902)
Miners' Journal (1902)
New Orleans Daily Picayune (1886)
New Orleans Times (1877)

New York Herald (1850)
New York Sun (1877)
New York Times (1877, 1886, 1894, 1902,
    1919, 1945–1946)
New York Tribune (1850, 1853–1854)
New York World (1894, 1919)
Pittsburgh Commercial Gazette (1919)
Pittsburgh Leader (1919)
Pittsburgh Post (1919)
St. Louis Globe-Democrat (1886)
St. Louis Post-Dispatch (1886)
San Antonio Daily Light (1886)
San Francisco Chronicle (1877, 1886, 1894)
San Francisco Examiner (1894)
Waco Daily Examiner (1886)
Wall Street Journal (1936–1937, 1945–1946)
Washington Post (1894, 1919, 1945–1946)

Magazines and Journals

The Alarm
American Federationist (AFL)
American Workman (Boston, July 1869)
Andover Review
The Arena
Atlantic Monthly

Baptist Quarterly Review
The Century Magazine
The Chautauquan.
CIO News
Contemporary Review
The Crisis

Current Opinion
Frank Leslie's Illustrated Newspaper
Fortune
The Forum
Galaxy
Harper's New Monthly Magazine
Harper's Weekly
Harvard Business Review
Hunt's Merchant Magazine and Commercial Review
International Review
The Iron Age
John Swinton's Paper
Journal of the Brotherhood of Locomotive Engineers
Journal of United Labor (Knights of Labor)
Labor Standard
Life
Locomotive Firemen's Magazine
Mechanic's Advocate
Nation
National Labor Tribune
New Republic
Niles' Weekly Register
North American Review
Our Continent

Outlook
Overland Review
Public Opinion
Puck
Quarterly Journal of Economics
Radical Review
Railroad Gazette
Railroad Trainmen's Journal
Railway Age
The Railway Times
Scientific American
Scribner's
The Socialist
Socialist Review
Survey
Time
Union News Service (CIO)
Unitarian Review
United Auto Worker (UAW)
United Mine Workers' Journal (UMWA)
United States News
Weekly Miners' Journal
Woodhull and Claflin's Weekly
The Workingman (Philadelphia, 1870)
Workingman's Advocate

Primary Source Articles, Books, and Government Documents

Abbot, Lyman. "Danger Ahead." *Century Magazine* 31 (1885–1886): 51–59.

Adams, Charles Francis, Jr. "The Brotherhood of Locomotive Engineers." *The Nation* 24 (March 22, 1877): 173.

———. *Railroads: Their Origin and Problems*. New York: G. P. Putnam's Sons, 1878.

Adams, Henry Carter. "Economics and Jurisprudence." *Economic Studies* 2 (February 1897): 24–33.

———. "An Interpretation of the Social Movements of Our Time." *International Journal of Ethics* 2 (October 1891): 32–50.

Addams, Jane. "A Modern Lear." In Graham R. Taylor, *Satellite Cities*, 68–90. New York: Appleton, 1915.

Alexander, Winthrop. "Ten Years of Riot Duty." *Journal of the Military Service Institution of the United States* 19 (July 1896): 1–62.

Anderson, Robert Julius. "Capital, Labor, and the Public: Nine Great Questions Before Us Today." *Industrial Management* 59, no. 2 (February 1920): 117–119.

Basler, Roy P., ed. *The Collected Works of Abraham Lincoln,* vol. 4. New Brunswick, N.J.: Rutgers University Press, 1953–1954.

Bell, Daniel. *The End of Ideology: On the Exhaustion of Political Ideas in the Fifties*. Glencoe, Ill.: Free Press, 1960.

Bernheim, Alfred L., and Dorothy Van Doren, eds., *Labor and the Government: An Investigation of the Role of the Government in Labor Relations*. New York: McGraw-Hill, 1935.

Bolles, Albert S. *The Conflict between Labor and Capital*. Philadelphia: Lippincott, 1876.

Brownson, Orestes. *The Laboring Classes,* 3rd ed. Boston: Greene, 1840.

Burns, James D. *Three Years among the Working-Classes in the United States during the War.* London: Smith, Elder, 1865.

Burns, W. *The Pullman Boycott, A Complete History of the Great R.R. Strike.* St. Paul: McGill Printing Company, 1894.

Carey, Henry C. *Capital and Labor.* Philadelphia: Collins, 1873.

———. *Principles of Social Science.* Philadelphia: Lippincott, 1858–1859.

Carlton, Frank T. "On Union-Management Co-operation." *American Journal of Economics and Sociology* 2, no. 2 (January 1943): 262–263.

Carnegie, Andrew. *Triumphant Democracy; or, Fifty Years' March of the Republic.* New York: Charles Scribner's Sons, 1888.

Carwardine, Reverend William. *The Pullman Strike.* Chicago: Illinois Labor History Society, 1973. Originally published 1894.

Chamberlain, Neil W., and Jane Metzger Schilling. *The Impact of Strikes: Their Social and Economic Costs.* Westport, Conn.: Greenwood Press, 1954.

Clark, John Bates. *The Philosophy of Wealth: Economic Principles Newly Formulated.* New York: Kelley, 1967.

Clark, John Bates, and Franklin S. Giddings. *The Distributive Process.* Boston: Ginn, 1888.

Clews, Henry. "Shall Capital or Labor Rule?" *North American Review* 142 (1886): 598–602.

Commons, John R., et al., eds., *A Documentary History of American Industrial Society,* vols. 1–6, 9, 10. New York: Russell and Russell, 1958.

———. "Is Class Conflict in America Growing and Is It Inevitable?" *American Journal of Sociology* 13 (1908): 756–783.

———. *Labor and Administration.* New York: Macmillan, 1913.

———. *Myself: The Autobiography of John R. Commons.* Madison: University of Wisconsin Press, 1964.

Commons, John R., and John Andrews. *Principles of Labor Legislation.* New York: Harper and Brothers, 1936.

Cooke, Morris Llewellyn. "An All-American Basis for Industry." Philadelphia: s.n., 1919.

Dacus, J. A. *Annals of the Great Strikes in the United States.* St. Louis: Scammel, 1877.

D'Arusmont, Frances Wright. "The People at War." *Free Equirer,* November 27, 1830.

Debs, Eugene. "Homestead and Ludlow." *International Socialist Review,* August 1914.

De Caux, Len. "Looking Ahead." *Union News Service,* December 10, 1945.

Dubofsky, Melvyn, and Joseph A. McCartin, eds. *American Labor: A Documentary Collection.* New York: Palgrave Macmillan, 2004.

Dunn, R. W. *The Americanization of Labor: The Employers' Offense against the Trade Unions.* New York: International Publishers, 1927.

Elwyn, Alfred L. *Glossary of Supposed Americanisms.* Philadelphia: Lippincott, 1859.

Ely, Richard T. *The Labor Movement in America.* 1886. Reprint, New York: Arno, 1969.

———. *Recent American Socialism.* Baltimore: Johns Hopkins University, 1885.

Filipetti, George. *Industrial Management in Transition,* rev. ed. Homewood, Ill.: Irwin, 1953.

Fitch, J. A. "A Strike for Freedom." *The Survey* 42, no. 26 (September 27, 1919): 891–892.

———. "The Closed Shop." *The Survey* 43, no. 3 (November 8, 1919): 53–56.

Foster, William Z. *The Great Steel Strike and Its Lessons.* New York: Huebsch, 1920.

Friendly, Alfred. "American Industry's Grand Strategy." *Nation* (January 19, 1946): 62–63.

Galbraith, John Kenneth. *American Capitalism: The Concept of Countervailing Power.* Boston: Houghton Mifflin, 1956.

Garfield, James A. "The Army of the United States." *North American Review* 126 (April 1878): 193–216.

Garraty, John Arthur, ed. *Labor and Capital in the Gilded Age: Testimony Taken by the Senate Committee upon the Relations between Labor and Capital, 1883* (Boston: Little, Brown, 1968.

George, Henry. *Progress and Poverty: An Inquiry into the Cause of Industrial Depressions and of Increase of Want with Increase of Wealth.* New York: Doubleday and McClure, 1900.

Gompers, Samuel. "Hold Yourselves Well in Hand." *American Federationist* 23, no. 11 (November 1916): 1074–1075.

———. "The I.W.W. Strikes." *American Federationist* 20, no. 8 (August 1913): 622–624.

———. *Seventy Years of Life and Labor: An Autobiography,* edited by Nick Salvatore. Ithaca, N.Y.: ILR Press, 1984.

Grace, Eugene G. "Industry and Public." Speech presented at the 54th General Meeting of the American Iron and Steel Institute, New York, May 28, 1936. Reprinted in *Vital Speeches of the Day* 2, no. 22 (August 1, 1936): 678–682.

Grant, T. B. "Pullman and Its Lessons." *American Journal of Politics* (August 1894): 190–205.

Green, Ben. E. *The Irrepressible Conflict between Labor and Capital.* Philadelphia: Claxton, Remsen, and Haffelfinger, 1872.

Grosvener, W. M. "The Communist and the Railway." *International Review* 4 (September 1877): 585–586.

Hansen, Alvin H. "Cycles of Strikes." *American Economic Review* 11 (1921): 616–621.

Harte, Walter Blackburn. "A Review of the Chicago Strike of 1894." *Arena,* 58 (September 1894): 497–532.

Harvey, O. L., et al. *The Anvil and the Plow: U.S. Department of Labor 1913–1963.* Washington, D.C.: U.S. Department of Labor Office of Information, Publications, and Reports, 1963.

Heaton, John L. *Cobb of the "World"—A Leader in Liberalism, Compiled from His Editorial Articles and Public Addresses.* Freetown, N.Y.: Books for Libraries Press, 1924.

Heckscher, August, ed. *The Politics of Woodrow Wilson: Selections from His Speeches and Writings.* New York: Harper and Brothers, 1956.

Heywood, F. H. "The Great Strike." *Radical Review* 1 (November 1877): 1–25.

Hoover, Herbert. *Principles of Mining.* New York: McGraw-Hill, 1909.

Industrial Workers of the World Pamphlets. Chicago: Industrial Workers of the World, n.d.

Interchurch World Movement. *Public Opinion and the Steel Strike, Supplementary Reports of the Investigators to the Commission of Inquiry.* New York: Harcourt, Brace, 1921.

———. *Report on the Steel Strike of 1919 by the Commission of Inquiry.* New York: Harcourt, Brace, and Howe, 1920.

Jervis, John B. *The Question of Labor and Capital.* New York: G. P. Putnam's Sons, 1877.

Johnson, Gerald W. "The Average American and the Depression." *Current History* (February 1932): 671–675.

Johnson, Hugh S. "Warning to Labor of Peril in Tolerating Strikes." *United States News,* October 16, 1933.

Jones, Jesse H. "The Labor Problem. A Statement of the Question from the Labor Reform Side." *International Review* 9 (1880): 51–68.

Keller, Albert Galloway, ed. *William Graham Sumner: The Forgotten Man and Other Essays.* New Haven, Conn.: Yale University Press, 1918.

Knights of Labor, comp. *Labor: Its Rights and Wrongs.* Washington, D.C.: Labor Publishing Co., 1886.

———. *Preamble and Declaration of Principles.* N.p., n.d.

Lawrence, David. "Blue Eagles for Labor Unions?" *United States News,* July 23, 1934.

Leggett, William. *Democratick Editorials: Essays in Jacksonian Political Economy.* Edited by Lawrence White. Indianapolis: Liberty Press, 1984.

Leiserson, William M. *Right and Wrong in Labor Relations.* Berkeley: University of California Press, 1938.

Lewis, John L. "The Battle for Industrial Democracy." Broadcast over National Broadcast Corporation radio on July 6, 1936. Speech reprinted in *Vital Speeches of the Day* 2, no. 22 (August 1, 1936): 675–678.

Manning, William. *The Key of Liberty: Showing the Causes Why a Free Government Has Always Failed and a Remedy Against It.* In *The Key of Liberty: The Life and Democratic Writings of William Manning, a Laborer, 1747–1814,* edited by Michael Merrill and Sean Wilentz. Cambridge, Mass: Harvard University Press, 1993.

Martin, Edward Winslow [James Dabney McCabe]. *The History of the Great Riots.* New York: Kelley, 1971.

Marx, Karl, and Frederick Engels. *Marx and Engels on the United States.* Compiled by Nelly Rumyansteva. Moscow: Progress, 1979.

Mason, J. W. "Pullman and Its Real Lessons." *American Journal of Politics* (September 1894): 392–398.

McCann, Irving G. *Why the Taft-Hartley Law?* New York: Committee for Constitutional Government, 1950.

McChesney, Robert W., and Ben Scott, eds. *Our Unfree Press: 100 Years of Radical Media Criticism.* New York: New Press, 2004.

McNaughton, Wayne Leslie. *The Development of Labor Relations Law.* Washington, D.C.: American Council on Public Affairs, 1941.

McNeill, George, ed. *The Labor Movement: The Problem of Today.* New York: Bridgman, 1887.

Meany, George. "The Taft-Hartley Act." *American Federationist* 54, no. 12 (December 1947): 8–9.

Merz, C. "The A.F. of L. Moves Forward." *New Republic,* June 7, 1919, 181–183.

Meyer, Julie. "Trade Union Plans for Post-War Reconstruction in the United States." *Social Research* 11 (1944): 491–505.

Miles, Nelson A. "The Lessons of the Recent Strikes." *North American Review* 159 (1984): 186–187.

Mills, C. Wright. *The Power Elite.* New York: Oxford University Press, 1956.

———. *White Collar: The American Middle Classes.* New York: Oxford University Press, 1951.

Mitchell, Clarence. "Notes on the Taft-Hartley Act." *The Crisis* 55, no. 10 (October 1948): 300–301.

Mitchell, John. *Organized Labor: Its Problems, Purposes and Ideals and the Present and Future of American Wage Earners.* Philadelphia: American Book and Bible House, 1903.

Molineux, E. L. "Riots in Cities and Their Suppression." *Journal of the Military Service Institution of the United States* 4 (1883): 337.

Mussey, H. R. "The Steel-Makers." *The Nation,* May 1, 1920, 580–582.

National Labor Relations Board. *Legislative History of the Labor-Management Relations Act, 1947.* 2 vols. Washington, D.C.: Government Printing Office, 1949.

———. *Legislative History of the National Labor Relations Act, 1935.* 2 vols. Washington, D.C.: Government Printing Office, 1949.

Newton, R. Heber. "Communism." *Unitarian Review* (December 1881): 505.

Otis, Colonel Ewell S. "The Army in Connection with the Labor Riots of 1877." *Journal of the Military Service Institution of the United States* 5 (September 1884): 292–325; 6 (June 1885): 117–139.

Porter, Fitz John. "How to Quell Mobs." *North American Review* 141 (1885): 358–359.

Porter, Robert B. "The Truth about the Strike." *Galaxy* 24 (December 1877): 725–732.

Prussing, Eugene E. "Labor, Preferred." *The World's Work* 45, no. 4 (February 1923): 417–421.

Raskin, A. H. "Taft-Hartley and Labor's Perspective." *Commentary* 4, no. 5 (November 1947): 435–440.

Reeve, C. H. "The Ethics of Strikes and Lockouts." *American Journal of Politics* 2 (January 1893): 75–85.

Remington, Frederick. "Chicago Under the Mob." *Harper's Weekly*, July 21 1894, 680–681.

Reuther, Walter. "This Is Your Fight!" *Nation*, January 12, 1946, 35–36.

Roethlisberger, Fritz, and William J. Dickson. *Management and the Worker.* Cambridge, Mass.: Harvard University Press, 1967.

Roosevelt, Theodore. *Addresses and Presidential Messages of Theodore Roosevelt, 1902–1904.* New York: Knickerbocker Press, 1904.

———. *Theodore Roosevelt: An Autobiography.* New York: Macmillan, 1913.

Schlesinger, Arthur M., Jr. *The Vital Center: The Politics of Freedom.* Boston: Houghton Mifflin, 1949.

———, ed. *Writings and Speeches of Eugene V. Debs.* New York: Hermitage Press, 1949.

Scott, Thomas A. "The Recent Strikes." *North American Review* 125 (1877): 357.

Sinclair, Upton. *The Brass Check: A Study of American Journalism.* Pasadena: Upton Sinclair, 1920.

———. *The Flivver King.* 1937. Reprint, Illinois: Illinois Labor History Society, 1988.

Slichter, Sumner. *The Challenge of Industrial Relations: Trade Unions, Management, and the Public Interest.* Ithaca, N.Y.: Cornell University Press, 1947.

———. "The Changing Character of American Industrial Relations." *American Economic Review* 29 (March 1939): 121–137.

Smith, Goldwin. "The Labour War in the United States." *Contemporary Review* 30 (September 1877): 529–541.

Socialistic Labor Party. *Platform, Constitution, and Resolutions.* Detroit: National Executive Committee of the Socialistic Labor Party, 1880.

Sombart, Werner. *Why Is There No Socialism in the United States?* Translated by Patricia M. Hocking and C. T. Husbands. White Plains, N.Y.: International Arts and Sciences Press, 1976.

Steward, Ira. *The Eight Hour Movement.* Boston: Labor Reform Association, 1865.

Stone, Lucy. "The Strikers and the Mob." *Woman's Journal,* July 28, 1877, 236.

Strong, Josiah. *Our Country: Its Possible Future and Its Present Crisis.* New York: Baker and Taylor, 1885.

Sumner, William Graham. "Industrial War." *Forum* 2 (1886): 1–6.

———. *What Social Classes Owe to Each Other.* 1883. Reprint, Caldwell, Idaho: Caxton, 1954.

Sylvis, James C. *The Life, Speeches, Labors, and Essays of William H. Sylvis.* Philadelphia: Claxton, Remsen, and Haffelfinger, 1872.

Taussig, F. W. "The Southwest Strike of 1886." *Quarterly Journal of Economics* 1 (January 1887): 185–216.

Taylor, Frederick Winslow. *The Principles of Scientific Management.* New York: Harper and Brothers, 1919

Taylor, G. "At Gary." *Survey,* November 8, 1919, 65–66.

Tocqueville, Alexis de. *Democracy in America,* vol. 2. New York: Vintage Books, 1945.

Tussey, Jean Y., ed. *Eugene V. Debs Speaks.* New York: Pathfinder Press, 1970.

United States Congress. House of Representatives. "Investigation by a Select Committee of the House of Representatives relative to the Causes of the General Depression in Labor and Business." In Miscellaneous Documents of the House of Representatives for the Third Session, Forty-fifth Congress, 1878–1879. Vol. 3, doc. 29. Washington, D.C.: Government Printing Office, 1879.

United States Senate. *Report Investigating Strike in Steel Industries.* 66th Congress, 1st Session, Senate Reports, vol. A, no. 289. Washington, D.C.: Government Printing Office, 1919.

United States Strike Commission. *Report on the Chicago Strike of June–July, 1894.* Washington, D.C.: Government Printing Office, 1895.

Von Holst, H. "Are We Awakened." *Journal of Political Economy* (September 1894): 485–516.

Vorse, Mary Heaton. "Aliens." *Outlook,* May 5, 1920, 24–26.

———. "Civil Liberty in the Steel Strike." *The Nation,* November 15, 1919, 633–635.

———. "Derelicts of the Steel Strike." *The Survey,* December 4, 1920, 355–358.

———. *Labor's New Millions.* New York: Modern Age Books, 1938.

———. "The Steel Strike." *The Liberator,* January 1920, 16.

Walker, Amasa. *The Science of Wealth: A Manual of Political Economy.* Boston: Little, Brown, 1866.

Wilensky, Harold L. "Class, Class Consciousness, and American Workers." In *Labor in a Changing America,* edited by William Haber. New York: Basic Books, 1966.

Witte, Edwin E. "An Appraisal of the Taft-Hartley Act." *American Economic Review* 38 (1948): 368–382.

———. *The Government in Labor Disputes.* New York: McGraw-Hill, 1932.

Woodhull, Victoria C. *A Lecture on the Great Social Problem of Labor and Capital.* New York: Journeymen Printers' Co-operative Association, 1871.

SECONDARY SOURCES

Books

Aaron, Daniel. *The Unwritten War: American Writers and the Civil War.* New York: Knopf, 1973.

Adamic, Louis. *Dynamite: The Story of Class Violence in America,* rev. ed. New York: Viking, 1934.

Adams, Graham, Jr. *Age of Industrial Violence, 1910–1915: The Activities and Findings of the United States Commission on Industrial Relations.* New York: Columbia University Press, 1966.

Albarran, Alan B. *Media Economics: Understanding Markets, Industries and Concepts.* Ames: Iowa State University Press, 1996.

Allen, Ruth A. *The Great Southwest Strike.* Austin: University of Texas Press, 1942.

Anderson, Kristi. *The Creation of a Democratic Majority, 1928–1936.* Chicago: University of Chicago Press, 1979.

Appleby, Joyce *Inheriting the Revolution: The First Generation of Americans.* Cambridge, Mass.: Belknap Press, 2000.

Atack, Jeremy, and Peter Passell. *A New Economic View of American History from Colonial Times to 1940,* 2nd ed. New York: Norton, 1994.

Atleson, James B. *Labor and the Wartime State: Labor Relations and Law during World War II.* Urbana: University of Illinois Press, 1998.

Auerbach, Jerold S. *Labor and Liberty: The La Follette Committee and the New Deal.* Indianapolis: Bobbs-Merrill, 1966.

Avrich, Paul. *The Haymarket Tragedy.* Princeton, N.J.: Princeton University Press, 1984.

Babson, Steve. *The Unfinished Struggle: Turning Points in American Labor, 1877–Present.* Lanham, Md.: Rowman and Littlefield, 1999.

Baldasty, Gerald J. *The Commercialization of News in the Nineteenth Century.* Madison: University of Wisconsin Press, 1992.

Bernstein, Irving. *The Lean Years: A History of the American Worker, 1920–1933.* Boston: Houghton Mifflin, 1960.

———. *The Turbulent Years: A History of the American Worker, 1933–1941.* Boston: Houghton Mifflin, 1969.

Bernstein, Iver. *The New York City Draft Riots: Their Significance for American Society and Politics in the Age of the Civil War.* New York: Oxford University Press, 1990.

Bourdieu, Pierre. *Language and Symbolic Power.* Edited and introduced by John B. Thompson. Translated by Gino Raymond and Matthew Adamson. Cambridge, Mass.: Harvard University Press, 1991.

Brecher, Jeremy. *Strike!* San Francisco: Straight Arrow Books, 1972.

Brian, Denis. *Pulitzer: A Life.* New York: Wiley and Sons, 2001.

Boyer, Richard O., and Herbert M. Morais. *Labor's Untold Story.* New York: United Electrical, Radio and Machine Workers of America, 1970.

Brody, David. *In Labor's Cause: Main Themes on the History of the American Worker.* New York: Oxford University Press, 1993.

———. *Labor in Crisis: The Steel Strike of 1919.* Philadelphia: Lippincott, 1965.

———. *Steelworkers in America: The Nonunion Era.* Cambridge, Mass.: Harvard University Press, 1960.

———. *Workers in Industrial America: Essays on the Twentieth Century Struggle.* New York: Oxford University Press, 1980.

Bruce, Robert V. *1877: Year of Violence.* Chicago: Dee, 1989.

Buder, Stanley. *Pullman: An Experiment in Industrial Order and Community Planning, 1880–1930.* New York: Oxford University Press, 1967.

Burbank, David T. *Reign of the Rabble: The St. Louis General Strike of 1877.* New York: Kelley, 1966.

Burke, Martin J. *The Conundrum of Class: Public Discourse on the Social Order in America.* Chicago: University of Chicago Press, 1995.

Cahn, William. *A Pictorial History of American Labor.* New York: Crown, 1972.

Chandler, Alfred D., Jr. *The Railroads: The Nation's First Big Business.* New York: Harcourt, Brace and World, 1965.

———. *The Visible Hand: The Managerial Revolution in American Business.* Cambridge, Mass.: Harvard University Press, 1977.

Cleveland, Grover. *The Government in the Chicago Strike of 1894.* Princeton, N.J.: Princeton University Press, 1913.

Cmiel, Kenneth. *Democratic Eloquence: The Fight over Public Speech in Nineteenth-Century America.* New York: Morrow, 1990.

Cohen, Lizabeth. *Making a New Deal: Industrial Workers in Chicago, 1919–1939.* Cambridge: Cambridge University Press, 1990.

Cohen, Nancy. *The Reconstruction of American Liberalism, 1865–1914.* Chapel Hill: University of North Carolina Press, 2002.

Commons, John R., D. J. Saposs, H. L. Sumner, E. B. Mittelman, H. E. Hoagland, J. B. Andrews, and S. Perlman, eds. *History of Labour in the United States*. 4 vols. New York: Macmillan, 1918–1935.

Conkin, Paul K. *Prophets of Prosperity: America's First Political Economists*. Bloomington: Indiana University Press, 1980.

Cornell, Robert J. *The Anthracite Coal Strike of 1902*. New York: Russell and Russell, 1971.

Cunliffe, Marcus. *Chattel Slavery and Wage Slavery: The Anglo-American Context, 1830–1860*. Athens: University of Georgia Press, 1979.

Dallek, Robert. *Harry S. Truman: The American Presidents Series*. New York: Holt, 2008.

David, Henry. *The History of the Haymarket Affair: A Study in the American Social- Revolutionary Movements*. New York: Farrar and Rinehart, 1936.

Davis, Colin J. *Power at Odds: The 1922 National Railroad Shopmen's Strike*. Urbana: University of Illinois Press, 1997.

Davis, Mike. *Prisoners of the American Dream: Politics and Economy in the History of the U.S. Working Class*. New York: Verso, 1986.

Davis, Susan G. *Parades and Power: Street Theater in Nineteenth-Century Philadelphia*. Philadelphia: Temple University Press, 1986.

Dawley, Alan. *Class and Community: The Industrial Revolution in Lynn*. Cambridge, Mass.: Harvard University Press, 1976.

DeBrizzi, John A. *Ideology and the Rise of Labor Theory in America*. Westport, Conn.: Greenwood Press, 1983.

Denning, Michael. *Mechanic Accents: Dime Novels and Working Class Culture in America*. London: Verso, 1987.

DeVault, Ileen. *United Apart: Gender and the Rise of Craft Unionism*. Ithaca: Cornell University Press, 2004.

Deverell, William. *Railroad Crossing: Californians and the Railroad, 1850–1910*. Berkeley: University of California Press, 1994.

Dijk, Teun A. van., editor. *Discourse as Structure and Process*. London: Sage, 1997.

Dobbs, Lou. *The War on the Middle Class: How the Government, Big Business, and Special Interest Groups Are Waging War on the American Dream and How to Fight Back*. New York: Penguin, 2005.

Dobson, C. R. *Masters and Journeymen: A Prehistory of Industrial Relations, 1717–1800*. London: Helm, 1980.

Drucker, Peter F. *Management: Tasks, Responsibilities, Practices*. New York: Harper and Row, 1974.

Dubofsky, Melvyn. *Industrialism and the American Worker, 1865–1920*, 2nd ed. Arlington Heights, Ill.: Harlan Davidson, 1985.

———. *The State and Labor in Modern America*. Chapel Hill: University of North Carolina Press, 1994.

———. *We Shall Be All: A History of the Industrial Workers of the World*. Chicago: Quadrangle Books, 1969.

Duranti, Alessandro. *Linguistic Anthropology*. Cambridge: Cambridge University Press, 2000.

Edwards, Richard. *Contested Terrain: The Transformation of the Workplace in the Twentieth Century*. New York: Basic Books, 1979.

Eggert, Gerald G. *Railroad Labor Disputes: The Beginnings of Federal Strike Policy*. Ann Arbor: University of Michigan Press, 1967.

Emery, Edwin, and Michael Emery. *The Press and America: An Interpretive History of Mass Media*, 4th ed. Englewood Cliffs, N.J.: Prentice Hall, 1978.

Faue, Elizabeth. *Community of Suffering and Struggle: Women, Men, and the Labor Movement in Minneapolis, 1915–1945*. Chapel Hill: University of North Carolina Press, 1991.

Faust, Drew Gilpin. *This Republic of Suffering: Death and the American Civil War*. New York: Knopf, 2008.

Feldberg, Michael. *The Turbulent Era: Riot and Disorder in Jacksonian America*. New York: Oxford University Press, 1980.

Filippelli, Ronald, ed. *Labor Conflict in the United States: An Encyclopedia*. New York: Garland, 1990.

Fine, Sidney. *Laissez Faire and the General Welfare State: A Study of Conflict in American Thought, 1865–1901*. Ann Arbor: University of Michigan Press, 1956.

———. *Sit-Down: The General Motors Strike of 1936–1937*. Ann Arbor: University of Michigan Press, 1969.

Fink, Leon. *Workingmen's Democracy: The Knights of Labor and American Politics*. Urbana: University of Illinois Press, 1985.

Foner, Eric. *Free Soil, Free Labor, Free Men*. Oxford: Oxford University Press, 1995.

———. *Politics and Ideology in the Age of the Civil War*. New York: Oxford University Press, 1980.

———. *The Story of American Freedom*. New York: Norton, 1998.

Foner, Philip S. *The Great Labor Uprising of 1877*. New York: Monad Press, 1977.

———. *History of the Labor Movement in the United States*, vol. 1: *From Colonial Times to the Founding of the American Federation of Labor*. New York: International Publishers, 1962.

———. *History of the Labor Movement in the United States*, vol. 2: *From the Founding of the A.F. of L. to the Emergence of American Imperialism*, 2nd ed. .New York: International Publishers, 1975.

———. *History of the Labor Movement in the United States*, vol. 3: *The Policies and Practices of the American Federation of Labor, 1900–1909*. New York: International Publishers, 1973.

Forbath, William E. *Law and the Shaping of the American Labor Movement*. Cambridge, Mass.: Harvard University Press, 1991.

Foucault, Michel. *The Archaeology of Knowledge and the Discourse on Language*. Translated by A. M. Sheridan Smith. New York: Pantheon, 1972.

———. *The History of Sexuality*, vol. 1: *An Introduction*. Translated by Robert Hurley. New York: Vintage Books, 1990.

Fraser, Steven. *Labor Will Rule: Sidney Hillman and the Rise of American Labor*. New York: Free Press, 1991.

Fraser, Steven, and Gary Gerstle, eds. *The Rise and Fall of the New Deal Order, 1930–1980*. Princeton, N.J.: Princeton University Press, 1989.

Fredrickson, George M. *The Inner Civil War: Northern Intellectuals and the Crisis of the Union*. New York: Harper and Row, 1965.

Frisch, Michael H., and Daniel J. Walkowitz, eds. *Working-Class America: Essays on Labor, Community, and American Society*. Urbana: University of Illinois Press, 1983.

Gabor, Andrea. *The Capitalist Philosophers: The Geniuses of Modern Business—Their Lives, Times, and Ideas*. New York: Crown Business, 2000.

Gerstle, Gary. *Working-Class Americanism: The Politics of Labor in a Textile City, 1914–1960*. Cambridge: Cambridge University Press, 1989.

Giddens, Anthony. *The Class Structure of the Advanced Societies*. New York: Harper and Row, 1975.

Gilhooley, Leonard. *No Divided Allegiance: Essays in Brownson's Thought.* New York: Fordham University Press, 1980.

Gilje, Paul A. *Rioting in America.* Bloomington: Indiana University Press, 1996.

———. *The Road to Mobocracy: Popular Disorder in New York City, 1763–1834.* Chapel Hill: University of North Carolina Press, 1987.

Ginger, Ray. *The Bending Cross: A Biography of Eugene Victor Debs.* New Brunswick, N.J.: Rutgers University Press, 1949.

Glaberman, Martin. *Wartime Strikes: The Struggle against the No-Strike Pledge in the U.A.W. during World War II.* Detroit: Bewick, 1980.

Glickstein, Jonathan A. *Concepts of Free Labor in Antebellum America.* New Haven, Conn.: Yale University Press, 1991.

Glynn, Carroll J., Susan Herbst, Garrett J. O'Keefe, and Robert Y. Shapiro. *Public Opinion.* Boulder, Colo.: Westview Press, 1999.

Goodwyn, Lawrence. *The Populist Moment: A Short History of the Agrarian Revolt in America.* New York: Oxford University Press, 1978.

Gordon, David M., Richard Edwards, and Michael Reich. *Segmented Work, Divided Workers: The Historical Transformation of Labor in the United States.* Cambridge: Cambridge University Press, 1982

Gorn, Elliot J. *Mother Jones: The Most Dangerous Woman in America.* New York: Hill and Wang, 2001.

Grace, George W. *The Linguistic Construction of Reality.* London: Helm, 1987.

Gramsci, Antonio. *Further Selections from the Prison Notebooks.* Edited and translated by Derek Boothman. London: Lawrence and Wishart, 1995.

———. *Selections from the Prison Notebooks.* Edited and translated by Quintin Hoare and Geoffrey Nowell Smith. New York: International Publishers, 1971.

Green, David. *The Language of Politics in America: Shaping Political Consciousness from McKinley to Reagan.* Ithaca, N.Y.: Cornell University Press, 1992.

Green, Marguerite. *The National Civic Federation and the American Labor Movement, 1900–1925.* Washington, D.C.: Catholic University of America Press, 1956.

Greene, Jack P. *Intellectual Construction of America: Exceptionalism and Identity from 1492 to 1800.* Chapel Hill: University of North Carolina Press, 1993.

Grob, Gerald N. *Workers and Utopia: A Study of Ideological Conflict in the American Labor Movement, 1865–1900.* Chicago: Quadrangle Books, 1969.

Grossman, Jonathan P. *William Sylvis: Pioneer of American Labor.* New York: Columbia University Press, 1945.

Gutman, Herbert G. *Work, Culture, and Society in Industrializing America: Essays in American Working-Class and Social History.* New York: Knopf, 1976.

Halker, Clark D. *For Democracy, Workers, and God: Labor Song-Poems and Labor Protest, 1865–1895.* Urbana: University of Illinois Press, 1991.

Harris, Alice Kessler. *Gendering Labor History.* Urbana: University of Illinois Press, 2007.

Harris, Howell John. *The Right to Manage: Industrial Relations Policies of American Business in the 1940s.* Madison: University of Wisconsin Press, 1982.

Haskell, Thomas. *The Emergence of Professional Social Science: The American Social Science Association and the Nineteenth-Century Crisis of Authority.* Urbana: University of Illinois Press, 1977.

Hatch, Nathan O. *The Democratization of American Christianity.* New Haven, Conn.: Yale University Press, 1989.

Hattam, Victoria. *Labor Visions and State Power: The Origins of Business Unionism in the United States.* Princeton, N.J.: Princeton University Press, 1993.

Haydu, Jeffrey. *Making American Industry Safe for Democracy: Comparative Perspectives on the State and Employee Representation in the Era of World War I.* Urbana: University of Illinois Press, 1997.

Heider, Don, ed. *Class and News.* Lanham, Md.: Rowman and Littlefield, 2004.

Higham, John. *Strangers in the Land: Patterns of American Nativism, 1860–1925,* 2nd ed. New York: Atheneum, 1973.

Hirsch, Susan E. *Roots of the American Working Class: The Industrialization of the Crafts in Newark, 1800–1860.* Philadelphia: University of Pennsylvania Press, 1978.

Hoornstra, Jean, and Trudy Heath, eds. *American Periodicals, 1741–1900.* Ann Arbor, Mich.: UMI Research Press, 1979.

Howe, Irving, and B. J. Widick. *The UAW and Walter Reuther.* New York: Da Capo, 1973.

Hugins, Walter. *Jacksonian Democracy and the Working Class: A Study of the New York Workingmen's Movement, 1829–1837.* Stanford, Calif.: Stanford University Press, 1960.

Huston, James L. *Securing the Fruits of Labor: The American Concept of Wealth Distribution, 1765–1900.* Baton Rouge: Louisiana State University Press, 1998.

Irons, Janet. *Testing the New Deal: The General Textile Strike of 1934 in the American South.* Urbana: University of Illinois Press, 2000.

Jacoby, Daniel. *Laboring for Freedom: A New Look at the History of Labor in America.* Armonk, N.Y.: Sharp, 1998.

Jimerson, Randall. *The Private Civil War: Popular Thought during the Sectional Conflict.* Baton Rouge: Louisiana State University Press, 1988.

John, Richard R. *Spreading the News: The American Postal System from Franklin to Morse.* Cambridge, Mass.: Harvard University Press, 1995.

Johnson, Paul. *A Shopkeeper's Millennium: Society and Revivals in Rochester, New York, 1815–1837.* New York: Hill and Wang, 1978.

Johnson, Russell L. *Warriors into Workers: The Civil War and the Formation of Urban-Industrial Society in a Northern City.* New York: Fordham University Press, 2003.

Johnson-Cartee, Karen S. *News Narratives and News Framing: Constructing Political Reality.* Lanham, Md.: Rowman and Littlefield, 2004.

Jones, Gareth Stedman. *Languages of Class: Studies in English Working Class History, 1832–1982.* Cambridge: Cambridge University Press, 1983.

Josephson, Matthew. *The Robber Barons: The Great American Capitalists, 1861–1901.* New York: Harcourt Brace Jovanovich, 1962.

Kammen, Michael. *A Season of Youth: The American Revolution and the Historical Imagination.* Ithaca, N.Y.: Cornell University Press, 1988.

Katz, Mark Philip. *From Appomattox to Montmartre: Americans and the Paris Commune.* Cambridge, Mass.: Harvard University Press, 1998.

Katznelson, Ira, and Aristide Zolberg, eds. *Working-Class Formation: Nineteenth-Century Patterns in Western Europe and the United States.* Princeton, N.J.: Princeton University Press, 1986.

Kaufman, Bruce E. *The Origins and Evolution of the Field of Industrial Relations in the United States.* Ithaca, N.Y.: ILR Press, 1993.

Kaufman, Stuart Bruce. *Samuel Gompers and the Origins of the American Federation of Labor, 1848–1896.* Westport, Conn.: Greenwood Press, 1973.

Kazin, Michael. *The Populist Persuasion.* New York: Basic Books, 1995.

Keeran, Roger. *The Communist Party and the Auto Workers Union.* Bloomington: Indiana University Press, 1980.

Kennedy, David M. *Freedom from Fear: The American People in Depression and War, 1929–1945.* New York: Oxford University Press, 1999.

———. *Over Here: The First World War and American Society*. Oxford: Oxford University Press, 1980.

Kimeldorf, Howard. *Battling for American Labor: Wobblies, Craft Workers, and the Making of the Union Movement*. Berkeley: University of California Press, 1999.

Knowles, K.G.J.C. *Strikes—A Study in Industrial Conflict*. Oxford: Blackwell, 1952.

Kulikoff, Allan. *The Agrarian Origins of Capitalism*. Charlottesville: University Press of Virginia, 1992.

Kumar, Deepa. *Outside the Box: Corporate Media, Globalization, and the UPS Strike*. Urbana: University of Illinois Press, 1997.

La Capra, Dominick. *Rethinking Intellectual History: Texts, Contexts, Language*. Ithaca, N.Y.: Cornell University Press, 1983.

Lakoff, George, and Mark Johnson. *Metaphors We Live By*. Chicago: University of Chicago Press, 1980.

Larson, John Lauritz. *Bonds of Enterprise: John Murray Forbes and Western Development in America's Railway Age*. Cambridge, Mass.: Harvard University Press, 1984.

Laslett, John H. M. *Reluctant Proletarians: A Comparative History of American Socialism*. Westport, Conn.: Greenwood Press, 1984.

———, ed. *The United Mine Workers of America: A Model of Industrial Solidarity?* University Park: Pennsylvania State University Press, 1996.

Laslett, John H. M., and Seymour M. Lipset, eds. *Failure of a Dream? Essays in the History of American Socialism*. Berkeley and Los Angeles: University of California Press, 1984.

Laurie, Bruce. *Artisans into Workers: Labor in Nineteenth-Century America*. Urbana: University of Illinois Press, 1997.

———. *Working People of Philadelphia, 1800–1850*. Philadelphia: Temple University Press, 1980.

Lazerow, Jama. *Religion and the Working Class in Antebellum America*. Washington, D.C.: Smithsonian Institution Press, 1995.

Lears, T. J. Jackson. *No Place of Grace: Antimodernism and the Transformation of American Culture, 1880–1920*. Chicago: University of Chicago Press, 1994.

Lee, Alfred McClung. *The Daily Newspaper in America: The Evolution of a Social Instrument*. New York: Octagon, 1937.

Lens, Sidney. *The Labor Wars: From the Molly Maguires to the Sitdowns*. New York: Doubleday, 1973.

Leonard, Thomas C. *Above the Battle: War-Making in America from Appomattox to Versailles*. New York: Oxford University Press, 1978.

Levine, Bruce. *The Spirit of 1848: German Immigrants, Labor Conflict, and the Coming of the Civil War*. Urbana: University of Illinois Press, 1992.

Levine, Rhonda F. *Class Struggle and the New Deal: Industrial Labor, Industrial Capital, and the State*. Lawrence: University Press of Kansas, 1988.

Licht, Walter. *Industrializing America: The Nineteenth Century*. Baltimore: Johns Hopkins University Press, 1995.

———. *Working for the Railroad: The Organization of Work in the Nineteenth Century*. Princeton, N.J.: Princeton University Press, 1983.

Lichtenstein, Nelson. *Labor's War at Home: The CIO in World War II*. Cambridge: Cambridge University Press, 1982.

———. *The Most Dangerous Man in Detroit: Walter Reuther and the Fate of American Labor*. New York: Basic Books, 1995.

———. *State of the Union: A Century of American Labor*. Princeton, N.J.: Princeton University Press, 2002.

Lichtenstein, Nelson, and Howell John Harris, eds., *Industrial Democracy in America: The Ambiguous Promise.* Cambridge: Cambridge University Press, 1996.

Lichtenstein, Nelson, and Stephen Meyer, eds. *On the Line: Essays in the History of Auto Work.* Urbana: University of Illinois Press, 1989.

Lindsey, Almont. *The Pullman Strike: The Story of a Unique Experiment and a Great Labor Upheaval.* Chicago: University of Chicago Press, 1971.

Lipsitz, George. *Rainbow at Midnight: Labor and Culture in the 1940s.* Urbana: University of Illinois Press, 1994.

Luxon, Norval Neil. *Niles' Weekly Register: News Magazine of the Nineteenth Century.* Baton Rouge: Louisiana State University Press, 1947.

Martin, Christopher R. *Framed!: Labor and the Corporate Media.* Ithaca, N.Y.: Cornell University Press, 2004.

Marx, Karl. *Capital,* vol. 1. London: Penguin Group, 1976.

Marx, Leo. *The Machine in the Garden: Technology and the Pastoral Ideal in America.* New York: Oxford University Press, 1964.

McCartin, Joseph A. *Labor's Great War: The Struggle for Industrial Democracy and the Origins of Modern American Industrial Relations, 1912–1921.* Chapel Hill: University of North Carolina Press, 1997.

McGovern, James R. *And a Time for Hope: Americans in the Great Depression.* Westport, Conn.: Praeger, 2000.

Meier, August, and Elliot Rudwick. *Black Detroit and the Rise of the UAW.* New York: Oxford University Press, 1979.

Meltzer, Milton. *Bread and Roses: The Struggle for American Labor, 1865–1915.* New York: Vintage Sundial Books, 1967.

Mindich, David T. Z. *Tuned Out: Why Americans Under 40 Don't Follow the News.* New York: Oxford University Press, 2005.

Montgomery, David. *Beyond Equality: Labor and the Radical Republicans, 1862–1872.* New York: Knopf, 1967.

———. *The Fall of the House of Labor: The Workplace, the State, and American Labor Activism, 1865–1925.* New York: Cambridge University Press, 1987.

———. *Workers' Control in America: Studies in the History of Work, Technology, and Labor Struggles.* Cambridge: Cambridge University Press, 1979.

Moody, J. Carroll, and Alice Kessler-Harris, eds. *Perspectives on American Labor History: The Problems of Synthesis.* De Kalb: Northern Illinois University Press, 1989.

Moorhead, James H. *American Apocalypse: Yankee Protestants and the Civil War, 1860–1869.* New Haven, Conn.: Yale University Press, 1978.

Mott, Frank Luther. *American Journalism, A History: 1690–1960,* 3rd ed. New York: Macmillan, 1969.

Murolo, Priscilla, and A. B. Chitty. *From the Folks Who Brought You the Weekend: A Short, Illustrated History of Labor in the United States.* New York: New Press, 2001.

Murray, Robert K. *Red Scare: A Study in National Hysteria, 1919–1920.* New York: McGraw-Hill, 1955.

Nasaw, David. *The Chief: The Life of William Randolph Hearst.* Boston: Houghton Mifflin, 2000.

Nelson, Daniel. *Managers and Workers: Origins of the Twentieth-Century Factory System in the United States, 1880–1920,* 2nd ed. Madison: University of Wisconsin Press, 1995.

Nerone, John. *Violence against the Press: Policing the Public Sphere in U.S. History.* New York: Oxford University Press, 1994.

Nicholson, Philip Yale. *Labor's Story in the United States.* Philadelphia: Temple University Press, 2004.

Norwood, Stephen H. *Strikebreaking and Intimidation: Mercenaries and Masculinity in Twentieth-Century America.* Chapel Hill: University of North Carolina Press, 2002.

Olds, M. *Analysis of the Interchurch World Movement Report on the Steel Strike.* New York: G. P. Putnam's Sons, 1923.

Page, Charles H. *Class and American Sociology: From Ward to Ross.* New York: Schocken Books, 1969

Palladino, Grace. *Another Civil War: Labor, Capital, and the State in the Anthracite Regions of Pennsylvania, 1840–68.* Urbana: University of Illinois Press, 1990

Palmer, Bryan. *Descent into Discourse.* Philadelphia: Temple University Press, 1990.

Paludin, Phillip Shaw. *A People's Contest: The Union and Civil War, 1861–1865.* Lawrence: University Press of Kansas, 1996.

Papke, David Ray. *The Pullman Case: The Clash of Labor and Capital in Industrial America.* Lawrence: University Press of Kansas, 1999.

Parenti, Michael. *Inventing Reality: The Politics of the Mass Media.* New York: St. Martin's Press, 1986.

Phelan, Craig. *Divided Loyalties: The Public and Private Life of Labor Leader John Mitchell.* Albany: State University of New York Press, 1994.

———. *William Green: Biography of a Labor Leader.* Albany: State University of New York Press, 1989.

Pocock, J.G.A. *Politics, Language, and Time: Essays on Political Thought and History.* London: Methuen, 1972.

Pollack, Norman, ed. *The Populist Mind.* Indianapolis: Bobbs-Merrill, 1967.

Pringle, Henry. *Theodore Roosevelt: A Biography.* New York: Cornwall Press, 1931.

Rachlin, Allan. *News as Hegemonic Reality: American Political Culture and the Framing of News Accounts.* New York: Praeger, 1988.

Rader, Benjamin G. *The Academic Mind and Reform: The Influence of Richard T. Ely in American Life.* Lexington: University of Kentucky Press, 1966.

Ramirez, Bruno. *When Workers Fight: The Politics of Industrial Relations in the Progressive Era, 1898–1916.* Westport, Conn.: Greenwood Press, 1978.

Reddy, William. *Money and Liberty in Modern Europe: A Critique of Historical Understanding.* Cambridge: Cambridge University Press, 1987.

Rice, Stephen P. *Minding the Machine: Languages of Class in Early Industrial America.* Berkeley: University of California Press, 2004.

Robbins, William G. *Colony and Empire: The Capitalist Transformation of the American West.* Lawrence: University Press of Kansas, 1994.

Robertson, Andrew W. *The Language of Democracy: Political Rhetoric in the United States and Britain, 1790–1900.* Ithaca, N.Y.: Cornell University Press, 1995.

Rock, Howard B. *Artisans of the New Republic: The Tradesmen of New York City in the Age of Jefferson.* New York: New York University Press, 1979.

Rodgers, Daniel. *Contested Truths: Keywords in American Politics since Independence.* New York: Basic Books, 1987.

Roediger, David. *The Wages of Whiteness: Race and the Making of the American Working Class,* rev. ed. London: Verso, 1999.

———. *Working toward Whiteness: How America's Immigrants Became White—The Strange Journey from Ellis Island to the Suburbs.* New York: Basic Books, 2005.

Rose, Anne C. *Victorian America and the Civil War.* New York: Cambridge University Press, 1992.

Ross, Dorothy. *The Emergence of Social Science.* Cambridge: Cambridge University Press, 1990.

Ross, Steven J. *Workers on the Edge: Work, Leisure, and Politics in Industrializing Cincinnati, 1788–1890.* New York: Columbia University Press, 1985.

Roy, William G. *Socializing Capital: The Rise of the Large Industrial Corporation in America.* Princeton, N.J.: Princeton University Press, 1997.

Ryan, Mary P. *Civic Wars: Democracy and Public Life in the American City during the Nineteenth Century.* Berkeley: University of California Press, 1997.

Salmond, John A. *The General Textile Strike of 1934: From Maine to Alabama.* Columbia: University of Missouri Press, 2002.

Salvatore, Nick. *Eugene V. Debs: Citizen and Socialist.* Urbana: University of Illinois Press, 1982.

Saxton, Alexander. *The Rise and Fall of the White Republic: Class Politics and Mass Culture in Nineteenth-Century America.* New York: Verso, 1990.

Schiller, Dan. *Objectivity and the News.* Philadelphia: University of Pennsylvania Press, 1981.

Schneirov, Richard, Shelton Stromquist, and Nick Salvatore, eds. *The Pullman Strike and the Crisis of the 1890s: Essays on Labor and Politics.* Urbana: University of Illinois Press, 1999.

Schudson, Michael. *Discovering the News: A Social History of American Newspapers.* New York: Basic Books, 1978.

———. *Origins of the Ideal of Objectivity in the Professions: Studies in the History of American Journalism and American Law, 1830–1940.* New York: Garland, 1990.

———. *The Power of News.* Cambridge, Mass.: Harvard University Press, 1995.

Sellers, Charles. *The Market Revolution: Jacksonian America, 1815–1846.* New York: Oxford University Press, 1991.

Sewell, William. *Work and Revolution in France: The Language of Labor from the Old Regime to 1848.* New York: Cambridge University Press, 1980.

Shogun, Robert. *The Battle of Blair Mountain: The Story of America's Largest Labor Uprising.* Oxford: Westview Press, 2004.

Skowronek, Stephen. *Building a New American State: The Expansion of National Administrative Capacities, 1877–1920.* Cambridge: Cambridge University Press, 1982.

Smith, Carl S. *Urban Disorder and the Shape of Belief: The Great Chicago Fire, the Haymarket Bomb, and the Model Town of Pullman.* Chicago: University of Chicago Press, 1995.

Smith, Page. *The Rise of Industrial America: A People's History of the Post-Reconstruction Era.* New York: Penguin Books, 1984.

Smith, Sharon. *Subterranean Fire: A History of Working-Class Radicalism in the United States.* Chicago: Haymarket Books, 2006.

Soltow, Lee, and Edward Stevens, *The Rise of Literacy and the Common School in the United States: A Socio-Economic Analysis to 1870.* Chicago: University of Chicago Press, 1981.

Stott, Richard B. *Workers in the Metropolis: Class, Ethnicity, and Youth in Antebellum New York City.* Ithaca, N.Y.: Cornell University Press, 1990.

Stowell, David O. *Streets, Railroads, and the Great Strike of 1877.* Chicago: University of Chicago Press, 1999.

Stromquist, Shelton. *A Generation of Boomers: The Pattern of Railroad Labor Conflict in Nineteenth-Century America.* Chicago: University of Illinois Press, 1987.

Thompson, E. P. *The Making of the English Working Class.* New York: Knopf, 1966.

Thorne, Florence Calvert. *Samuel Gompers—American Statesman.* New York: Philosophical Library, 1957.

Tomlins, Christopher L. *The State and the Unions: Labor Relations, Law, and the Organized Labor Movement in America, 1880–1960.* Cambridge: Cambridge University Press, 1985.

Trachtenberg, Alan. *The Incorporation of America: Culture and Society in the Gilded Age.* New York: Hill and Wang, 1982.

Tuchman, Gaye. *Making News: A Study in the Construction of Reality.* New York: Free Press, 1978.

Vinovskis, Maris A., ed. *Toward a Social History of the American Civil War: Exploratory Essays.* Cambridge: Cambridge University Press, 1990.

Voss, Kim. *The Making of American Exceptionalism: The Knights of Labor and Class Formation in the Nineteenth Century.* Ithaca, N.Y.: Cornell University Press, 1993.

Walkowitz, Daniel, ed. *The Working Class in America.* Urbana: University of Illinois Press, 1981.

Waltenburg, Eric N. *Choosing Where to Fight: Organized Labor and the Modern Regulatory State, 1948–1987.* Albany: State University of New York Press, 2002.

Ward, James A. *Railroads and the Character of America, 1820–1887.* Knoxville: University of Tennessee Press, 1986.

Ware, Norman. *The Industrial Worker, 1840–1860: The Reaction of American Industrial Society to the Advance of the Industrial Revolution.* Chicago: Quadrangle Books, 1964.

———. *The Labor Movement in the United States, 1860–1895: A Study in Democracy.* Gloucester, Mass.: Smith, 1959.

Weinstein, James. *The Corporate Ideal in the Liberal State, 1900–1918.* Boston: Beacon Press, 1968.

———. *The Decline of Socialism in America, 1912–1925.* New York: Monthly Review Press, 1967.

Weir, Robert E. *Beyond Labor's Veil: The Culture of the Knights of Labor.* University Park: Pennsylvania State University Press, 1996.

White, Hayden. *Tropics of Discourse: Essays in Cultural Criticism.* Baltimore: Johns Hopkins University Press, 1985.

Wilentz, Sean. *Chants Democratic: New York City and the Rise of the American Working Class, 1788–1850.* New York: Oxford University Press, 1984.

Williams, Raymond. *Keywords: A Vocabulary of Culture and Society.* New York: Oxford University Press, 1976.

Wilson, Christopher P. *The Labor of Words: Literary Professionalism in the Progressive Era.* Athens: University of Georgia Press, 1985.

Winters, Donald E., Jr. *The Soul of the Wobblies: The I.W.W., Religion, and American Culture in the Progressive Era, 1905–1917.* Westport, Conn.: Greenwood Press, 1985.

Wunderlin, Clarence E. *Visions of a New Industrial Order: Social Science and Labor Theory in America's Progressive Era.* New York: Columbia University Press, 1992.

Yellen, Samuel. *American Labor Struggles.* New York: Russell, 1936.

Zboray, Ronald J. *A Fictive People: Antebellum Reading Development and the American Reading Public.* New York: Oxford University Press, 1993.

Zieger, Robert H. *American Workers, American Unions,* 2nd ed. Baltimore: Johns Hopkins University Press, 1994.

Essays, Articles, and Dissertations

Anderson, Margo J. "The Language of Class in Twentieth-Century America." *Social Science History* 12 (1988): 349–375.

Babcock, Havilah. "The Press and the Civil War." *Journalism Quarterly* 6 (March 1929): 1–5.

Bekken, Jon. "The Working Class Press at the Turn of the Century." In *Ruthless Criticism: New Perspectives in U.S. Communication History,* edited by William S. Solomon and Robert W. McChesney, 151–175. Minneapolis: University of Minnesota Press, 1993.

Berggren, Douglas. "The Use and Abuse of Metaphor I." *Review of Metaphysics* 16, no. 2 (December 1962): 237–258.

Bernstein, Barton J. "Walter Reuther and the General Motors Strike of 1945–46." *Michigan History* 49, no. 3 (September 1965): 260–277.

Bernstein, Irving. "The Growth of American Unions." *American Economic Review* 44 (June 1954): 301–318.

Bestor, Arthur. "The Evolution of the Socialist Vocabulary." *Journal of the History of Ideas* 9 (1948): 259–302.

Breed, Warren. "Social Control in the Newsroom: A Functional Analysis." *Social Forces* 33, no. 4 (1955): 326–335.

Briggs, Asa. "The Language of 'Class' in Early Nineteenth-Century England." In *Essays in Labour History,* edited by Asa Briggs and John Saville, 47–73. London: Macmillan, 1960.

Case, Theresa Ann. "Free Labor on the Southwestern Railroads: The 1885–1886 Gould System Strikes." Ph.D. diss., University of Texas at Austin, 2002.

———. "The Radical Potential of the Knights' Biracialism: The 1885–1886 Gould System Strikes and Their Aftermath." *Labor: Studies in Working-Class History of the Americas* 4, no. 4 (winter 2007): 83–107.

Debouzy, Marianne. "Workers' Self-Organization and Resistance in the 1877 Strikes." In *American Labor and Immigration History, 1877–1920s: Recent European Research,* edited by Dirk Hoerder, 61–77. Urbana: University of Illinois Press, 1983.

Dubofsky, Melvyn. "Not So 'Turbulent Years': Another Look at America in the 1930s." In *Hard Work: The Making of Labor History,* 130–150. Urbana: University of Illinois Press, 2000.

Elder, Glen H., Jr. "Military Times and Turning Points in Men's Lives." *Developmental Psychology* 22, no. 2 (1986): 233–245.

Ernst, Daniel R. "Common Laborers? Industrial Pluralists, Legal Realists, and the Law of Industrial Disputes, 1915–1943." *Law and History Review* 11, no. 1 (spring 1993): 59–100.

Franzosi, Roberto. "The Press as a Socio-Historical Data: Issues in the Methodology of Data Collection from Newspapers." *Historical Methods* 20, no. 1 (winter 1987): 5–16.

Friedman, Gerald. "Strike Success and Union Ideology: The United States and France, 1880–1914." *Journal of Economic History* 48 (March 1988): 1–26.

———. "Worker Militancy and Its Consequences: Political Responses to Labor Unrest in the United States, 1877–1914." *International Labor and Working-Class History* 40 (fall 1991): 5–17.

Furner, Mary O. "Knowing Capitalism: Public Investigation and the Labor Question in the Long Progressive Era." In *The State and Economic Knowledge: The American and British Experiences,* edited by Mary O. Furner and Barry Supple, 241–286. New York: Cambridge University Press, 1990.

Gobel, Thomas. "Becoming American: Ethnic Workers and the Rise of the CIO." *Labor History* 29, no. 2 (spring 1988): 173–198.

Golding, Peter, and Graham Murdock. "Culture, Communications, and Political Economy." In *Mass Media and Society,* edited by James Curran and Michael Gurevitch, 15–32. London: Arnold, 1991.

Gonce, Richard A. "John R. Commons's 'Five Big Years,' 1899–1904." *American Journal of Economics and Sociology* 61, no. 4 (2002): 755–777.

Gordon, Linda. "Dorothea Lange: The Photographer as Agricultural Sociologist." *Journal of American History* 93, no. 3 (2006): 698–727.

Grimsted, David. "Ante-Bellum Labor: Violence, Strike, and Communal Arbitration." *Journal of Social History* 19 (1985): 5–28.

———. "Rioting in Its Jacksonian Setting." *American Historical Review* 77 (April 1972): 361–397.

Issac, Rhys. "Preachers and Patriots: Popular Culture and the Revolution in Virginia." In *The American Revolution: Explorations in the History of American Radicalism,* edited by Alfred Young, 125–156. DeKalb: Northern Illinois University Press, 1976.

Hartog, James K., and Douglas M. McLeod. "A Multipersectival Approach to Framing Analysis: A Field Guide." In *Framing Public Life: Perspectives on Media and Our Understanding of the Social World,* edited by Stephen Reese et al. Mahwah, N.J.: Lawrence Erlbaum Associates, 2001.

Hattam, Victoria. "Economic Visions and Political Strategies: American Labor and the State, 1865–1896." *Studies in American Political Development* 4 (1990): 82–129.

Hudson, Peter. "Proletarian Experience, Class Interest, and Discourse: How Far Can Classical Marxism Still Be Defended?" *Politikon* 14 (1987): 16–35.

Huston, James L. "Facing an Angry Labor: The American Public Interprets the Shoemakers' Strike of 1860." *Civil War History* 28, no. 3 (1982): 197–212.

Jeffrys, Zonita. "The Attitude of the Chicago Press toward the Labor Movement, 1873 to 1879." Master's thesis, University of Chicago, 1936.

Kaster, Gregory. "We Will Not Be Slaves to Avarice: The American Labor Jeremiad, 1827–1877." Ph.D. diss., Boston University, 1990.

Katz, Mark Philip "Americanizing the Paris Commune, 1861–1877." Ph.D. diss., Princeton University, 1994.

Katz, Michael. "Social Class in North American Urban History." *Journal of Interdisclipinary History* 11 (1981): 579–606.

Ketchum, Alton. "The Search for Uncle Sam." *History Today,* April 1990: 20–26.

Lause, Mark. "The American Radicals and Organized Marxism: The Initial Experience." *Labor History* 33 (1992): 55–80.

Leach, Eugene E. "Chaining the Tiger: The Mob Stigma and the Working Class, 1863–1894." *Labor History* 35, no. 2 (spring 1994): 187–215.

Lears, T. J. Jackson. "The Concept of Cultural Hegemony: Problems and Possibilities." *American Historical Review* 90, no. 3 (June 1985): 567–593.

Lee, Byung Soo. "Power and Knowledge: Newspapers' Coverage of the Steel Strike of 1919–1920." Ph.D. diss., University of Missouri–Columbia, 1993.

Lemisch, Jesse. "Jack Tar in the Streets: Merchant Seamen in the Politics of Revolutionary America." *William and Mary Quarterly* 25, no. 3 (1968): 371–407.

Leuchtenburg, William. "The New Deal and the Analogue of War." In *Change and Continuity in Twentieth-Century America,* edited by John Braeman, Robert H. Bremner, and Everett Walters, 81–143. Columbus: Ohio State University Press, 1964.

Lips, Roger. "Orestes Brownson." In *American Literary Critics and Scholars, 1800–1850,* edited by John W. Rathbun and Monica M. Grecu, 35–43. Detroit: Gale, 1987.

MacIntyre, Alasdair. "The Essential Contestability of Some Social Concepts." *Ethics* 84 (1973): 1–9.

Mackey, Philip English. "Law and Order, 1877: Philadelphia's Response to the Railroad Riots." *Pennsylvania Magazine of History and Biography* 96, no. 2 (April 1972): 183–202.

———. "Not Only the Ruling Class to Overcome, but Also the So-Called Mob: Class, Skill, and Community in the St. Louis General Strike of 1877." *Journal of Social History* 19 (1985): 213–239.

Magee, Bryan. "The Language of Politics." *Encounter* 66 (1986): 20–26.

Martin, Christopher R. "'Upscale' News Audiences and the Transformation of Labour News." *Journalism Studies* 9, no. 2 (2008): 178–194.

McFarland, C. K., and Robert L. Thistlewaite. "20 Years of a Successful Labor Paper: *The Working Man's Advocate*, 1829–1849." *Journalism Quarterly* 60, no. 1 (1983): 35–40.

Montgomery, David. "Strikes in Nineteenth-Century America." *Social Science Quarterly* 4 (February 1980): 81–103.

———. "Thinking about American Workers in the 1920s." *International Labor and Working- Class History* 32 (fall 1987): 4–30.

Nelson, Bruce. "Give Us Roosevelt: Workers and the New Deal Coalition." *History Today* 40 (January 1990): 40–48.

Noakes, John A. "Official Frames in Social Movement Theory: The FBI, HUAC, and the Communist Threat in Hollywood." *Sociological Quarterly* 41, no. 4 (autumn 2000): 657–680.

Nord, David Paul. "The Business Values of American Newspapers: The 19th Century Watershed in Chicago." *Journalism Quarterly* 61 (1984): 265–273.

———. "The Evangelical Origins of Mass Media in America, 1815–1835." *Journalism Monographs* 88 (1984): 1–30.

Olsen, Mark, and Louis George Harvey. "Contested Methods: Daniel T. Rodgers's *Contested Truths*." *Journal of the History of Ideas* 49 (1989): 653–668.

Price, Vincent, and David Tewksbury. "Switching Trains of Thought: The Impact of News Frames on Readers' Cognitive Responses." *Communication Research* 24 (1997): 481–506.

Richter, Melvin. "Reconstructing the History of Political Languages: Pocock, Skinner, and the *Geschichtliche Grundbegriffe*." *History and Theory* 39 (1990): 38–70.

Rock, Howard B. "The Perils of Laissez-Faire: The Aftermath of the New York Bakers' Strike of 1801." *Labor History* 17, no. 3 (1976): 372–387.

Rodgers, Daniel T. "In Search of Progressivism." *Reviews in American History* (December 1982): 113–131.

Ross, Dorothy. "Socialism and American Liberalism: Academic Social Thought in the 1880s." *Perspectives in American History* 11 (1977–1978): 7–79.

Ross, Steven J. "The Culture of Political Economy: Henry George and the American Working Class." *South California Quarterly* 65 (1983): 148–155.

Rourke, Francis E. "The Department of Labor and the Trade Unions." *Western Political Quarterly* 7, no. 4 (December 1954): 656–672.

Salvatore, Nick. "Railroad Workers and the Great Strike of 1877: The View from a Small Midwest City." *Labor History* 21, no. 4 (fall 1980): 522–545.

Saxton, Alexander. "Problems of Class and Race in the Origins of the Mass Circulation Press." *American Quarterly* 36 (1984): 211–234.

Schiller, Reuel E. "From Group Rights to Individual Liberties: Post-War Labor Law, Liberalism, and the Waning of Union Strength." *Berkeley Journal of Employment and Labor Law* 20, no. 1 (1999): 1–73.

Schneriov, Richard. "Chicago's Great Upheaval of 1877." *Chicago History* (1980): 3–17.

Skinner, Quentin. "Language and Social Change." In *The State of the Language,* edited by Leonard Michaels and Christopher Ricks, 562–578. Berkeley and Los Angeles: University of California Press, 1980.

Slaner, Philip A. "The Railroad Strikes of 1877." *Marxist Quarterly* 1, no. 2 (April–June 1937): 214–236.

Stone, Katherine Van Wezel. "The Post-War Paradigm in American Labor Law." *Yale Law Review* 90, no. 7 (June 1981): 1509–1580.

Stowell, David O. "Albany's Great Strike of 1877." *New York History* 76, no. 1 (January 1995): 31–55.

———. "'Small Property Holders' and the Great Strike of 1877: Railroads, City Streets, and the Middle Classes." *Journal of Urban History* 21, no. 6 (September 1995): 741–763.

Thompson, E. P. "Eighteenth-Century English Society: Class Struggle without Class?" *Social History* 3 (1978): 133–166.

Tomlins, Christopher L. "The New Deal, Collective Bargaining, and the Triumph of Industrial Pluralism." *Industrial and Labor Relations Review* 39, no. 1 (October 1985): 19–34.

Vinovskis, Maris A. "Searching for Classes in Urban North America." *Journal of Urban History* 11 (1985): 353–360.

Watkins, Bari Jane. "The Professors and the Unions: American Academic Social Theory and Labor Reform, 1883–1915." Ph.D. diss., Yale University, 1976.

Wilentz, Sean. "Against Exceptionalism: Class Consciousness and the American Labor Movement." *International Labor and Working Class History* 26 (fall 1984): 1–24.

———. "Artisan Republican Festivals and the Rise of Class Conflict in New York City, 1788–1837." In *Working-Class America: Essays on Labor Community and American Society,* edited by Michael H. Frisch and Daniel J. Walkowitz, 37–77. Urbana: University of Illinois Press, 1983.

———. "The Rise of the American Working Class, 1776–1877: A Survey." In *Perspectives on American Labor History: The Problems of Synthesis,* edited by J. Carroll Moody and Alice Kessler-Harris, 83–151. De Kalb: Northern Illinois University Press, 1989.

Wilson, Susan E. "Theodore Roosevelt's Role in the Anthracite Coal Strike of 1902." *Labor's Heritage* 3, no. 1 (1991): 4–23.

Yearley, Clifton K., Jr. "The Baltimore and Ohio Railroad Strike of 1877." *Maryland Historical Magazine* 51, no. 3 (September 1956): 188–211.

INDEX

Ford Motor Company, 208n3
foreigners, fear of, 22, 54, 88, 101, 123, 187n65
Fortune, 141, 155, 208n18
Fort Worth, Texas, 73
Fort Worth Gazette, 75
Foster, Charles, 103
Foster, William Z., 118, 120, 122; "Syndicalism" [pamphlet], 122
"four minute men," 113
framing theories, 4–5, 174n20
Frank Leslie's Illustrated Newspaper (a k a *Leslie's Illustrated Weekly*), 33, 34, 35, 49, 50
Fraser, Steven, 131, 202n75, 203n81
Free Enquirer, 24
free enterprise, 169
free labor ideology, 22
French Revolution references, 101
front-page stories, 11, 47, 82, 100, 123, 125, 157

Galambos, Louis, 94
Galaxy, 55
Galbraith, John Kenneth, *American Capitalism*, 164, 210n3
Gallup, George, 144
Gallup Poll, 144–145
Gary, Judge Elbert H., 116, 118, 122
Gary, Indiana, 123
General Managers' Association, 79, 80
General Motors, 153–161
General Motors sit-down strike (1936–1937), 137, 140, 142–144, 145, 156
General Motors strike (1945), 153–161; federal intervention, 159; media coverage, 155, 156, 158
general strikes, 18, 24, 119, 153
General Textile Strike (1934), 135, 140, 205n28
George, Henry, 187n71, 193n91; *Progress and Poverty*, 43
Germans, 175n26, 181n89
Gerstle, Gary, 173n4, 203n78, 204n9
Glickstein, Jonathan A., 181n81
"Golden Rod" (pseud.), "After the Strike" [poem], 88
Gompers, Samuel, 96, 97, 109, 111, 115, 123–124, 198n50, 199n10
Gordon, Linda, 146
Gould, Jay, 71, 77
government: agencies, 117, 133, 152; commissions, 159, 195n12; interference in economy, 208n4; intervention, 105, 139, 140–141, 148; as "public" representative, 110, 112, 115; as "referee," 161; role of, 110, 112, 115, 133–136, 140–142, 148–149; as social guardian, 149. *See also* federal government; state governments
"government by injunction," 105
Gramsci, Antonio, 2–3, 77; *The Prison Notebooks*, 3, 171
Grand Army of the Republic, 84, 187n60
Great Awakening, Second, 20

Great Depression, 136, 139; effects, 157; and the Great War, 134
Great Northern Railroad, 80
Great Railroad Strike (1877), 46–56; causes, 51, 55; and the Civil War, 56; foreign threat, 54; impact of, 50–55; "instant histories," 55, 56; press coverage, 47–50
Great Shoemakers' Strike (1860), 33–36, 34, 35
Great Southwest Strike (1886), 70–77, 74; as battle, 73; causes, 70; impact, 72; media coverage, 72–77, 91–92; as "rebellion," 73
"great third class," 90, 101, 133
Great Upheaval, 69
Great War: experience, 120, 127, 133; references, 116, 130, 133–134
Greeley, Horace, 31
Green, William, 128, 135
Gutman, Herbert G., 185n31, 211n10

Hall, Charles A., 72
handbills, 25
Hanna, Mark, 96, 99
"harmony of interests," 30, 60, 68, 69, 184n15; in media, 181n80
Harper's Magazine, 141, 142
Harper's Monthly, 33
Harper's Weekly, 74, 76, 88, 92, 129, 189n16, 191n54, 193n88
Harriman, Mrs. J. Borden, 111, 112
Harris, Alice Kessler, 203n5
Harrisburg Independent, 185n34
Harrison, Carter, II, 81
hatters, 21
Hayes, Rutherford B., 50
Haywood, William, 112
Hazard's Register of Pennsylvania, 181n87
headlines, 33, 47, 73
Hearst, William Randolph, 4, 61, 122, 201n48
hegemony, 4; of capital, 3, 77
Herbst, Susan, 206n40
hierarchy, challenged, 19
Hillman, Sidney, 131, 135, 152
historical materialism, 66
Hoover, Herbert, 133–134, 203n2; *Principles of Mining*, 207n52
hours, 18, 24
Hunt's Merchant Magazine and Commercial Review, 31
Huston, James L., 182n92, 185n25, 197n38

ideology, 167
illustrations, 33, 34, 34, 55, 72, 74, 76, 85–87, 85, 86, 120, 145. *See also* cartoons
Immigrant Restriction Acts (1921 and 1924), 128
immigrants, 87–88, 100–101, 123, 157; fear of, 118–119
Independent, 54
Indianapolis Daily Sentinel, 45
industrial commissions, 133; government-mediated, 112–113
industrial committees, 139
Industrial Conference (1919), 125–126

Wilentz, Sean, 176n9, 177nn18,23
Wilkes-Barre, Pennsylvania, 100
Wilkes-Barre Times, 103, 197n36
Wilson, C. E., 154
Wilson, William, 114
Wilson, Woodrow, 110, 125–126, 199n14
Wisconsin Idea, 112
Witte, Edwin E., *The Government in Labor Disputes*, 149
Wobblies. *See* Industrial Workers of the World (IWW)
women in the labor movement, 52, 134
women workers, 20, 24, 203n5
workday, 18
worker activism, 43
workers, changing roles, 177n18. *See also* Chinese workers; women workers; *and by industry*

working class: as guardian of public interest, 151; origins, 21; public image, 43
Working Man's Advocate, 20, 23, 28, 186n53
Workingmen's Party, 23, 53
Workman. See American Workman
work stoppages. *See* strikes
World War I, 113–117, 203n2; references, *121. See also* Great War
World War II, 152, 157
Wright, Carroll D., 67, 104, 111
Wright, Frances, 24, 25

xenophobia, 22. *See also* foreigners, fear of; nativism

Yellen, Samuel, 168

Zieger, Robert H., 204n5

ABOUT THE AUTHOR

TROY RONDINONE is an associate professor of history at Southern Connecticut State University. He is also on the editorial board of Connecticut History and the executive board of the Greater New Haven Labor History Association.